The Individual, the Family, and Social Good: Personal Fulfillment in Times of Change

Volume 42 of
the Nebraska Symposium
on Motivation

University of Nebraska Press
Lincoln and London 1995

Volume 42 of the Nebraska Symposium on Motivation

The Individual, the Family, and Social Good: Personal Fulfillment in Times of Change

Richard A. Dienstbier   *Series Editor*
Gary B. Melton   *Volume Editor*

Presenters

James Garbarino   *Professor of Human Development and Family Studies and Director of the Family Life Development Center, Cornell University*

Allen M. Parkman   *Regents Professor of Management, University of New Mexico*

Tom R. Tyler   *Professor of Psychology, University of California, Berkeley*

Peter Degoey   *Graduate Student in Psychology, University of California, Berkeley*

Mati Heidmets

Dean of Social Sciences and Professor of Social and Environmental Psychology, Tallinn (Estonia) Pedagogical University

Jill E. Korbin

Professor of Anthropology, Case Western Reserve University

Eleanor E. Maccoby

Professor Emerita of Psychology, Stanford University

Ronald Roesch

Professor of Psychology and Director, Mental Health, Law, and Policy Institute, Simon Fraser University

The Individual, the Family, and Social Good: Personal Fulfillment in Times of Change is
Volume 42 in the series
CURRENT THEORY AND RESEARCH
IN MOTIVATION

"The Library of Congress has cataloged
this serial publication as follows:"
Nebraska Symposium on Motivation.
Nebraska Symposium on Motivation.
[Papers] v. [1]–1953–
Lincoln, University of Nebraska Press.
v. illus., diagrs. 22cm. annual.
Vol. 1 issued by the symposium under
its earlier name: Current Theory and
Research in Motivation.
Symposia sponsored by the Dept. of
Psychology of the University of Nebraska.
1. Motivation (Psychology)
BF683.N4   159.4082   53-11655
Library of Congress

Preface

The volume editor for this 42nd edition of the Nebraska Symposium on Motivation is Professor Gary Melton. Gary planned this volume, selected and invited the contributors, and coordinated all aspects of the editing. My thanks to our contributors for excellent chapters developed and delivered in timely fashion, and to Gary for his editorial excellence in seeing the volume through to its completion. Shortly after the symposium session that led to this volume, Gary departed the University of Nebraska. Fortunately for us, while he was still at Nebraska he accomplished and built so much that it will take him years to completely disengage from those endeavors. Even long past that future date I know we will continue to be influenced by his stellar work, for his impact is of international proportions. We will miss Gary Melton.

This volume continues the changes in our procedures begun a few years ago. I mention them now as I have in several preceding volumes to alert you, our readers and our future symposium participants and attenders, since the changes are designed to facilitate your attending the symposium. To make your presence at the symposium more rewarding, we have consolidated all symposium activities into one session spanning several days. And to allow you the possibility of traveling to the symposium as a participant, we have begun an annual tradition of inviting posters on topics relevant to the main theme of each volume.

This symposium series is supported largely by funds donated in the memory of Professor Harry K. Wolfe to the University of Nebraska Foundation by the late Professor Cora L. Friedline. This symposium volume, like those of the recent past, is dedicated to the memory of Professor Wolfe, who brought psychology to the University of Nebraska. After studying with Professor Wilhelm Wundt, Professor Wolfe returned to his native Nebraska to establish the first undergraduate laboratory of psychology in the nation. As a student at Nebraska, Professor Friedline studied psychology under Professor Wolfe.

We are grateful to the late Professor Friedline for this bequest, and to the University of Nebraska Foundation for continued financial support for the series.

RICHARD A. DIENSTBIER
Series Editor

Contents

Introduction: Personal Satisfaction and the Welfare of Families, Communities, and Society

Gary B. Melton
University of South Carolina

This volume of the Nebraska Symposium on Motivation is unusual. The backgrounds of the authors are more diverse than ever before—approached only by the symposium I organized about a decade ago in observance of the 10th anniversary of the Law/Psychology Program (Melton, 1985). The authors are drawn from anthropology, economics, law, and several subdisciplines of psychology.

More important, though, than the interdisciplinary approach in this year's symposium is its tone. The most notable innovation in this year's symposium is *affect*! Although the central question of the link between personal gratification and social welfare is a classic one in theories of motivation, the level of emotional charge in some chapters has no precedent in the Nebraska symposium's illustrious history, as far as I am aware. Other chapters will engender a visceral response in some readers that may be without parallel in the symposium's 42 years.

Whether expressly or implicitly, most of the chapters in this year's symposium are tinged with prophetic concern—anxiety about the state of contemporary family life and the (un)likelihood of reconciling individual family members' interests with those of the family as a whole. Even some of the ostensibly neutral, traditionally "rational" academic discussions will probably arouse that concern in some readers, especially those chapters that touch on gender and generational relations.

In that regard, I doubt that the current symposium could have occurred early in its history. As illustrated by the creation and evolution of the University of Nebraska–Lincoln (UNL) Law/Psychology Program (Melton, 1990), whose 20th anniversary—along with the International Year of the Family—is marked with this volume, the academy has changed. Initially prodded by Bronfenbrenner's (1974, 1977) observations about the sterility and questionable verisimilitude of much research on child development and family life, researchers have been pulled from the ivory tower by the demand of those in the trenches for help in dealing with the seemingly ever more complex and ever less tractable problems of families and communities. The result has been the growth of many problem-focused (rather than discipline-focused) centers, institutes, and other interdisciplinary programs (Gallagher, 1990; McCall, 1990), such as UNL's own Center on Children, Families, and the Law. Although that form of organization is still somewhat anomalous in the broader sociology of the academy, it is leading, I believe, to more thoughtful policy analyses and more useful and careful research about problems of great importance to individual families and the society as a whole.

The Dramatic Change in Families

CHANGES IN FAMILY STRUCTURE

More than a reflection of a particular academic style, however, the topic for this symposium is a product of the times. The scope of this change in university structure and study appears trivial in comparison with the sea change that has occurred in family life. As Popenoe (1990, 1993) has chronicled (see also Garbarino, this volume; Parkman, this volume), families look dramatically different than they did a generation ago. The litany of changes in family structure that occurred in the United States after 1960 is stunning:

- The fertility rate declined by nearly one half.
- The proportion of families with a sole male breadwinner fell by about two thirds; the proportion of married mothers of young children in the paid work force tripled.

- The proportion of children living with a single parent nearly tripled; the majority of African-American children now live with a single parent.
- The number of births outside marriage rose fivefold (now nearly two thirds of African-American births and one fourth overall).
- The ratio of divorced to married people quadrupled, and divorce is now substantially more likely than death to be the means of marriage dissolution.
- The median age of marriage increased by four years, and the proportion of adults never marrying increased substantially from a nearly nonexistent point in the 1950s. (Only 3% of American women born in the late 1930s and early 1940s and thus reaching marital age around 1960 did not marry.)
- The proportion of nonfamily households doubled; most of them consist of just one person.
- The proportion of marriages preceded by cohabitation increased by a factor of six, as did the proportion of cohabiting unmarried couples in the population.

These facts are stunning in themselves, but they are made even more powerful by the dramatic change that has occurred not only in family structure per se but also in the nature of the relations between the family and the community and of the disparities between the "haves" and the "have nots." Regardless of social class, parents today rarely believe that they can count on neighbors and other "natural" helpers (e.g., clergy and family physicians) for help with the everyday problems of child rearing and family life (Melton, 1992a). That isolation is especially "toxic" (to use Garbarino's term, this volume) for families without the resources to buy help from professionals:

With the continuing shifts of population from inner cities and many small towns and rural communities, traditional sources of informal help have become increasingly unavailable. Although this decline in neighborliness is part of broader changes in family and community life, it has been hastened by increases in migration rates and the proportion of families living in poverty. Far too many urban, rural, and small-town neighborhoods have been drained. Families faced with a struggle merely to survive not only have few material resources to share, but they also may have exhausted their emotional resources. When people feel that they have minimal control over their lives, they are likely to have little motivation to sustain their community. Fear also can push people away from each other, and the search for a safe haven can deplete the remaining energy of people facing nearly continuous grave challenges. In neighborhoods that provide a dangerous physical environment and that have high rates of crime, parents face an exceptionally difficult task to keep their children safe. Too often they do so virtually alone. (U.S. Advisory Board on Child Abuse and Neglect, 1993, p. 18)

CHANGES IN FAMILY ATTITUDES

These changes in family structure and social networks have been accompanied by equally dramatic shifts in attitudes and beliefs about family life (Popenoe, 1993; see also Posner, 1992). The proportion of people agreeing that "all couples should have children" is much smaller than it was a generation ago; so is the proportion of women identifying child rearing as "one of the most enjoyable things about being a woman today." In 1962, one half of survey respondents agreed that, even if a couple does not get along, they should remain together when there are children in the family; by 1985, only about one in six concurred. The percentage expressing a belief that a woman who never marries "must be sick, neurotic, or immoral" fell from 80% in 1957 to 25% in 1985; it would probably be substantially smaller today. Marriage is no longer perceived as necessary for sexual expression; the proportion of American adults condemning premarital intercourse as "morally wrong" dropped from 85% in 1967 to 37% in 1979.

As a whole, these attitudinal changes illustrate a societal shift from a concept of the family as a set of relationships based on economic and social obligations to one as a means of achieving personal fulfillment. There is intense disagreement about the cause and consequences of this ideological shift (cf. Cowan, 1993, and Stacey, 1993, with Popenoe, 1993; for a similar range of views, see Glenn, 1987), but it is undeniable that the shift has occurred.

Whitehead's summary of the phenomenon is succinct: "Quite simply, many Americans have changed their minds. They changed their minds about staying together for the children; about the necessity of putting children's needs before their own; about marriage as a lifelong commitment; and about what it means to be unmarried and pregnant. And many American men changed their minds about the obligations of a father and husband" (Whitehead, 1992, p. 5).

Whitehead (1992) framed the ideological shift as one affecting *Americans* in particular. Some of the trends that Popenoe (1993) noted have been especially acute in the United States (e.g., the number of unplanned pregnancies), and others (e.g., the economic support available to children in single-mother households) are particularly significant in this country because of a national reluctance to build generous public entitlement programs. Otherwise, though, Whitehead's description could apply to most of the industrialized world.

CHANGE IN FAMILY LAW

These global changes in family structure and related attitudes have been paralleled by nearly universal shifts in family law in industrialized countries. An area of law that only recently was typified by conflicts among jurisdictions is now remarkable for the commonality of its basic elements.

As Glendon (1989) has shown in her important comparative work: "Despite contrasts in the legal and political contexts of law reform, the national differences among Western family law systems have diminished steadily over the past two decades. Indeed, in countries that are culturally quite diverse, there has been a remarkable coincidence of similar legal developments produced at about the same time, in apparent independence from one another" (Glendon, 1989, p. 1).

These legal changes have signaled and perhaps to some degree stimulated social and economic changes in family roles and relationships. Consistent with the general emphasis on fulfillment in family relationships, the law has taken an increasingly psychologically minded approach, with no-fault divorce and presumptions in favor of shared parenting after divorce. Reflecting the view of families as consensual and egalitarian (rather than authoritarian and hierarchical), legal authorities around the world have adopted facial equality between husbands and wives (in regard, e.g., to property settlements after divorce), eliminated disadvantaged statuses within families (e.g., as regards illegitimacy), and deregulated marriage itself (through elimination of requirements for parental permission, waiting periods, and use of particular surnames and through de facto recognition of nonmarital cohabitation).

Legislatures and courts may have gone further in this respect than have many of the citizens subject to their edicts (see, e.g., Maccoby, this volume; Maccoby & Mnookin, 1992). As Glendon (1989) has aptly summarized: "In spite of the fact that the notion of equality (variously understood) has been one of the most powerful transforming influences in modern family law, the principal unresolved problems for family law and policy remain those relating to the situation of women who are raising children, performing the bulk of other homemaking and caretaking roles, and working at jobs where their pay, status, and security are inferior to those of most male workers" (p. 307).

Even if transformations in the legal status of women and children have not necessarily been accompanied by comparable changes in social reality, such legal reforms have occurred with such force and uniformity that they have been given constitutional status in the United States and risen to the level of international law in the global context. Indeed, the United States stands nearly alone among the world's democracies in having failed to ratify either the Convention on the Rights of the Child or the Convention to End All Forms of Discrimination Against Women.

Change in Everyday Life

CHANGES A GENERATION AGO

In considering the meaning of these changes, it may be useful to reminisce about the 1960s, a time early in the symposium's history and a time when many of the students reading this book had not yet been born. Such time travel is instructive, I think, in considering why discussion of family issues—or, to use the political buzzword, *family values*—arouses such passion almost everywhere in the industrialized world today.

No doubt most readers joining me on this historical trek remember Bob Dylan's "The Times They Are A-Changin'," which served as an anthem for some of us who were adolescents in the 1960s. The lyrics (at least as I remember them) now seem almost quaint—embarrassing relics of a romantic, albeit emotionally and politically charged idealism that was prevalent at the time. It is hard to imagine an MTV video built around the plea:

Come, Senators, Congressmen, please heed the call.
Don't bolt up your windows;
Don't block up the hall. . . .
For the times they are a-changin'.

Whatever the realism of that particular expectation, it reflected an accurate perception that Western society and, to nearly as large an extent, Eastern Europe were beginning a period of dramatic macrolevel change—change that manifested itself in extraordinary shifts in both social structure and conventional ideology. Although the contours of change may not have always been accurately perceived, no one doubted that dramatic change was occurring. People were *involved*; I intend all the surplus meanings of that word.

When I visited the John F. Kennedy Museum in Boston a few years ago, I was reminded of the sense of emotional investment in social change that many of us experienced in the 1960s, particularly in the later part of the decade during the zenith of Robert Kennedy's political influence. As I watched films and observed artifacts of the social upheaval that occurred during the era, I was surprised by the intensity of emotional response and the flood of memories that I experienced. The comments that I overheard and the expressions of emotion I observed suggested that my reaction was typical.

Nonetheless, much of the change that occurred in the 1960s seemed removed from everyday life. At least metaphorically, Dylan was right; the principal players seemed indeed to be senators and congressmen and others in power. *Involvement* meant *persuasion*—shouting or encouraging others to shout until those in authority heard that a new social order was emerging. Regardless of the level of involvement by individual citizens in such political action, the ultimate decision makers were judges, legislators, and political leaders.

Even the day-to-day changes were framed in terms of personal expression of new *social* norms, and those normative shifts were viewed as responsive to social risks. Change was perceived as *institutional*, whether it involved desegregation of lunch counters and schools or modernization of the language and rituals of the wedding ceremony. Even if the focus of change was deeply personal (e.g., the content of one's wedding vows), the act of change was categorized as political.

CHANGE TODAY

Today, by contrast, the change that is on the minds of many people is *personal*, and the risks that worry not only the contributors to this volume but also the public at large are threats to *personal* security. Bronfenbrenner's (1990) depiction of contemporary society and of family life in particular—"increasing instability, inconsistency, and hectic character" (p. 35, emphasis in the original)—comports with common experience. Whether on the left or the right, commentators worry that "stamped on the reverse side of the coinage of individual liberty, family privacy, and sex equality are alienation, powerlessness, and dependency" (Glendon, 1989, p. 147). This sense of anomie is multiplied at a societal level: the normally staid National Research Council (1993) undoubtedly echoed the fears of millions of parents when it titled one of its recent reports *Losing Generations*.

The Policy Dilemma

Despite this widespread angst, I suspect that the changes in family law that swept the nation—indeed most of the industrialized world—in the 1960s and early 1970s remain ambivalently popular. The abortion debate is analogous. Although people who have strong views on the issue (whether "pro-life" or "pro-choice") dominate the public discussion, the more common stance of the average person is ambivalent: moral qualms about abortion in tandem with pragmatic concerns about the desirability of tight restrictions on availability of abortion (Rodman et al., 1987). In other words, the modal sentiment is that abortion is unfortunate and that completely unrestricted access to abortion would send the wrong message, but also that erection of insurmountable obstacles to abortion would lead to enormous social costs. Relatively few people want to return to the time before *Roe*—mainly, though, because they believe that in some situations abortion avoids even more negative outcomes for the pregnant woman, her family, and society.

Although I am unaware of public-opinion polls directly on point, I suspect that the modal view of reforms in divorce laws, for example, is similar. Many adults may have moral qualms about the ease with which divorce can be obtained and a sense of anxiety about the social consequences that may result from such a policy. At the same time, though, I am confident that few would advocate a return to a situation in which spouses were unable to acknowledge honestly that they found their relationship unfulfilling or even painful (cf. Korbin, this volume) and in which they lacked the legal capacity to dissolve their marriage without recriminations.

The shifts that have occurred in the sense of obligation and commitment in family life are the product to a large extent of changes that almost everyone regards as positive. People of goodwill everywhere applaud the expansion of opportunities that has followed the decline of family-based subsistence labor and, especially in the developed world, the corollary decline in the full-time occupation of women in domestic chores. These economic changes have been accompanied or perhaps even caused by expansion in communication and information technology and, therefore, the marketplace of ideas. The widespread and sometimes dramatic political reform that has typified the late 20th century—including the shift in the status of women and children—is a direct result (cf. Heidmets, this volume). Although many may find the related shake-up in family life to be unsettling, most people also welcome the opportunities to adopt roles and to join relationships on the basis of their personal meaning and to avoid those that are based on power and fear.

As Henryk Sokalski, the United Nations's coordinator of the observance of the International Year of the Family, has summarized, such changes "provide evidence that individuals are exerting more and more control over their own destinies and are enjoying additional opportunities for more diversified lives" (Sokalski, 1993, p. 7). Seen in such a light, the shift in family attitudes is just one manifestation—although undoubtedly a particularly critical aspect—of a much broader modern phenomenon in which personal expression defines the self.

Describing contemporary America as the "republic of choice," law-and-society scholar Lawrence Friedman (1990) has argued persuasively that the expansive view of personal autonomy that dominates 20th-century jurisprudence is not only unprecedented but also applicable in almost every domain of life that people regard as personally significant. For example, people today generally eschew religion grounded in duty ("thou shalt . . .") and faith and instead typically define religion in terms of its personal satisfaction and its potential role in personal growth. Religious authorities thus find themselves struggling to promote and preserve religious commitment as they seek to offer spiritual meaning.

The central problem of family policy is the need to avoid the analogous "rather than": How do we promote family life that brings personal fulfillment, permits absorption in activities outside the family, *and* features noncontingent perpetual responsibility of family members to care for each other for richer or poorer, in sickness and health?

At one level, this question is based on the practical problems of societal survival. In particular, as Bronfenbrenner (1990) has summarized, healthy child development appears to be based on the child's "strong, mutual, irrational, emotional attachment" to an adult "who is committed to the child's well-being and development, preferably for life" (p. 29). The emphasis in this context should be placed on *irrational*. Stated colloquially, the most important elements in healthy child development are two people who are absolutely crazy about each other—a relationship that is greatly strengthened by the support and perhaps equally irrational involvement of a third party, preferably of the opposite sex, and indeed fourth, fifth, and sixth parties. Accordingly, to maintain a strong society across generations, we need adults who not only *enjoy* children but who also *commit* themselves to support and guide their own and their neighbors' children.

At another level, the central problem can be expressed as a paradox: Is it possible to achieve personal fulfillment within the family without mutual commitment? Although his proposition is difficult to prove, I suspect that Popenoe (1993) is correct: "People today, most of all children, dearly want families in their lives. They long for that special, and hopefully life-long, social and emotional bond that family relationship brings" (p. 540).

Not only do people commonly say that family relationships are the most important aspects of their lives (Mellman et al., 1990), but their actions correspond to this belief. The divorce rate is paralleled by the remarriage rate (Shiono & Quinn, 1994), as even those people who have found particular marriages unsatisfying appear typically to have an unshaken faith in the institution. The very vehemence of the public debates about family values and privacy also suggests the fundamental significance of the family. Indeed, as life becomes ever more hectic, neighborhoods become even less cohesive, and work consumes increasingly more time, people may expect more and more from their "personal [family] relationships at the very time that social conditions have rendered them increasingly fragile" (Glendon, 1989, p. 147).

The flip side of the paradox is the question of whether personal fulfillment can be obtained in the face of competing family demands and even of violence and exploitation within the family (see Korbin, this volume). Family stability and gender equality may not be fully compatible. Parkman (this volume) argues that marriage and the family benefit from specialization of function between spouses. Maccoby (this volume) notes that the de facto division of labor within married couples is substantially more traditional than the law expects, and she comes close to asserting that such a division is the natural social order.

Even if, as I will argue, family demands and personal fulfillment are not inevitably in conflict, the achievement of a balance is undeniably a continuing issue for many individuals and the community as a whole. Clearly, policymakers face a daunting challenge in any attempt to foster or facilitate the commitment, intimacy, and respect that most people seek in family relationships. Describing the ideology underlying the International Year of the Family, Sokalski (1993) concluded that the family "should . . . be conceived as a very special relationship: one of equity and reciprocity between genders and generations, based on biology, law, custom or choice, and often upon economics" (p. 7). How can a relationship based on reciprocity— a relationship that may be the fundamental building block of society—sustain itself in a social order in which personal autonomy is emphasized, authority and obligation are disdained, and specialized roles and the inequality in relationships that may result are discouraged? This question is especially poignant and profound in the context of shrinking social and economic relationships for families.

What Can Be Done?

Popenoe (1993) has framed the current situation as " 'end-of-the-line' family decline" (p. 540). I do not believe, however, that the situation is apocalyptic, although I do think that we have reached a crossroads. We need to weave a new social fabric that is matched to modern realities.

The contributors to this volume provide clues about the material that is needed to weave the fabric. Society should be reordered (see Heidmets, this volume) so that the critical nexus is between the state and the neighborhood, not the state and the family, that is, so that a supportive *family environment* (an idea about which more will be said later) is present. We must strengthen neighborhoods so that families enjoy a decent standard of living and share an ethic of neighborliness (see Garbarino, this volume; Korbin, this volume). At the same time, care must be taken to order incentives (see Parkman, this volume) and foster participation (see Tyler, this volume) in order to build personal commitment to family life.

We also need to consider the possibility of new family forms that blend respect for individual family members with both family and community responsibility to ensure their welfare (cf. Heidmets, this volume). The recommendations of the U.S. Advisory Board on Child Abuse and Neglect (1993) provide some useful directions in that regard.

In general, the way out of the paradoxes I have discussed may be to recognize that there is no contradiction in both protecting personal privacy (individual rights within the family) and building a societal context supportive of family life—or, in the felicitous wording of the Convention on the Rights of the Child, a *family environment*. Evolving international law on family life supports such an approach. International human-rights treaties provide for special protection for the family "as the natural and fundamental group unit of society" (e.g., International Covenant on Civil and Political Rights, article 23; International Covenant on Economic, Social and Cultural Rights, article 10) and "the natural environment for the growth and well-being of all its members and particularly children" (Convention on the Rights of the Child, Preamble).

Such an approach is based on recognition of the centrality of family life in the promotion of human dignity:

However frail and faltering they may currently seem to be, families remain, for most of us, the only theater in which we can realize our full capacity for good or evil, joy or suffering. By attaching us to beings and feelings that are perishable, families expose us to conflict, pain, and loss. They give rise to tension between love and duty, reason and passion, immediate and long-range objectives, egoism and altruism. But relationships between husbands and wives, parents and children, can also provide frameworks for resolving such tensions. Even though . . . the principal bonds which remain to unite the family [after the loosening of legal and economic ties] may be the ties of human affection, we can perhaps—if we are hopeful—recognize in those fragile connections analogies for the Love that invites a response from all men and women of good will. (Glendon, 1989, p. 31)

Precisely because those experiences are so basic to human dignity—to meaning in life—and indeed to relatedness in the broader community, they should be taken seriously enough by society to elicit legal and political structures supportive of family life: "The effective functioning of child-rearing processes in the family and other child settings requires public policies and practices that provide place, time, stability, status, recognition, belief systems, customs, and actions in support of child-rearing activities not only on the part of parents, friends, neighbors, co-workers, communities, and the major economic, social, and political institutions of the entire society" (Bronfenbrenner, 1990, p. 37).

In short, respect for personal dignity implies social responsibility to safeguard intimacy. Individual rights lack meaning without social relatedness; relationships are unsatisfying without mutual respect. Accordingly, personal autonomy is maximized in the context of community; social cohesion is most likely when rights talk is taken seriously.

The Broader Picture: Why Do People Behave as They Do?

Although the questions raised in this volume about the future of the family are critically important in themselves, the issues raised are illustrative of broader problems in psycholegal studies and psychology. Debate about personal fulfillment in family life can illuminate broader questions about the role of law and other social institutions in shaping human behavior.

PSYCHOLEGAL STUDIES

In the past decade, I have been working to develop a jurisprudential framework, which I call *psychological jurisprudence* (see, e.g., Melton, 1990, 1992b). This approach is intended not only to guide psychologists of law in their choice of topics for research but also to assist legal authorities (judges and legislators) in the development and application of legal rules.

Most fundamentally, I have posited that law is a good thing. Law promotes fundamental values; by doing so, it confirms the worth of humanity—indeed each citizen's unique personality—and promotes community identity through announcement and reification of community norms and values (cf. Tyler, this volume). Law also provides a forum for ordered, fair resolution of disputes that threaten the social fabric, including the most intimate relationships, and it establishes structures that create or sustain behavior consistent with those values (a system of behavioral cues).

To fulfill its purposes, the law must take people seriously. Accordingly, legal authorities should pay close attention to everyday experience. They must avoid falsification or mystification of experience, and they must protect those aspects of life that are most important to human dignity. By undertaking systematic examinations of social reality, psychologists of law thus can assist the legal system in fulfilling its mission and heightening its legitimacy and acceptance (see Tyler, this volume). Justice requires psychological-mindedness.

The distinguishing feature of psychological jurisprudence is its reliance on *subjective experience* as the primary unit of analysis, especially in the determination of the meaning of core legal constructs. I have identified several general benefits that should arise from the application of a psychological-jurisprudential approach:

- It should illuminate ways that legal principles should be formulated and applied if they are to match social reality. In particular, it should identify those aspects of life that are most fundamental to sense of dignity.

- It should enhance a sense of community through explication of the values of the community and provision of cues for behavior consistent with those values.
- It should clarify the variables affecting legal socialization, so that settings and policies can be designed in a manner that will enhance the development of democratic values.
- It should enable legal policymakers to develop and refine rules and establish structures consistent with the promotion of human welfare.
- Through apparent concern for citizens' interests and reduction of discrepancies between legal realities and social expectations, it should increase the perceived legitimacy of the legal system and enhance citizens' respect for the law. (Melton, 1992, pp. 387–388)

Few can doubt the personal, social, and legal significance of the issues considered in this symposium, so a psychological jurisprudence—for that matter, any jurisprudential approach—should provide some illumination of such questions. The most basic is the scope of family behavior that is deserving of special legal protection (see, e.g., Justice Harry Blackmun's dissent in *Bowers v. Hardwick*, 1986, in the appendix to this chapter).

THE PSYCHOLOGY OF MOTIVATION

Similarly, this symposium addresses fundamental questions about the psychology of motivation as expressed in intimate relationships. Perhaps the most basic issue in personality theory has been the question of the compatibility between individual gratification and social good, a problem that attracted the interest of philosophers, theologians, and creative writers long before psychology became a distinct discipline. Although debates about the intrinsic goodness or

Excerpt from *Bowers v. Hardwick* (1986, pp. 204–205, 214, citations omitted). Justice Blackmun wrote a dissent on behalf of four justices from the Supreme Court's ruling that the constitutional right to privacy does not bar states from prohibiting homosexual behavior.

evil of humanity are no longer central to the field, they do continue to arise as policy analysts consider whether social behavior can be motivated by altruistic as well as avaricious concerns (a discussion joined in this volume by Parkman, in contrast with Tyler and Degoey).

Whatever the general answers to these questions, issues remain about how they can be generalized to family life. Consideration of rational choice in family relationships leaves scholars open to the charge that they are ignoring the emotional aspects of family life. Such dimensions are so intrinsic to contemporary views of the family that there only may be some measure of blasphemy in even suggesting that the "glue" that cements family relationships may be essentially the same force that motivates individual behavior in other contexts.

Regardless of the nature of the motivation, however, there is good reason to wonder whether it can be harnessed to strengthen family life. The authors consider the ways in which political (Heidmets), cultural (Korbin), and legal (Maccoby) structures shape family relationships and affect personal satisfaction within them. Like Garbarino (this volume), they all wonder, at least implicitly, whether deference to individual rights is compatible with objective social good and subjective sense of community, especially when family relationships are typified by power imbalances (cf. Korbin, this volume; Maccoby, this volume).

These are difficult problems that will not be resolved by a single volume. Nonetheless, the opening sections of this chapter provide a stark reminder of their critical importance. In the postmodern era, the safety net has holes in it. To fill in those gaps, careful interdisciplinary scholarship is needed to provide the knowledge that may serve as the foundation for a new social order. We must create a society in which respect is mutual and in which personal gratification and social commitment are intertwined. Nothing less than a social transformation should be the goal.

APPENDIX

A PSYCHOLOGICAL-JURISPRUDENTIAL APPROACH: AN EXCERPT FROM AN OPINION BY JUSTICE HARRY BLACKMUN

The Court concludes . . . that none of our prior cases dealing with various decisions that individuals are entitled to make free of governmental interference "bears any resemblance to the claimed constitutional right of homosexuals to engage in acts of sodomy that is asserted in this case." While it is true that these cases may be characterized by their connection to protection of the family, the Court's conclusion that they extend no further than this boundary ignores . . . [our] warning against "clos[ing] our eyes to the basic reasons why certain rights associated with the family have been accorded shelter under the Fourteenth Amendment's Due Process Clause." We protect those rights not because they contribute, in some direct and material way, to the general public welfare, but because they form so central a part of an individual's life. . . . And so we protect the decision whether to marry precisely because marriage "is an association that promotes a way of life, not causes; a harmony in living, not faiths; a bilateral loyalty, not commercial or social projects." We protect the decision whether to have a child because parenthood alters so dramatically an individual's self-definition, not because of demographic considerations or the Bible's command to be fruitful and multiply. And we protect the family because it contributes so powerfully to the happiness of individuals, not because of a preference for stereotypical household. The Court [has] recognized . . . that the "ability independently to define one's identity that is central to any concept of liberty" cannot truly be exercised in a vacuum; we all depend on the "emotional enrichment from close ties with others."

Only the most willful blindness could obscure the fact that sexual intimacy is "a sensitive, key relationship of human existence, central to family life, community welfare, and the development of human personality." The fact that individuals define themselves in a significant way through their intimate sexual relationships with others suggests, in a Nation as diverse as ours, that there may be many "right" ways of conducting those relationships, and that much of the richness of a relationship will come from the freedom an individual has to *choose* the form and nature of these intensely personal bonds.

. . . I can only hope that . . . the Court soon will reconsider its analysis and conclude that depriving individuals of the right to choose for themselves how to conduct their Nation's history [could do more harm] than tolerance of nonconformity could ever do. Because I think the Court today betrays those values, I dissent.

REFERENCES

Bowers v. Hardwick, 478 U.S. 186 (1986).
Bronfenbrenner, U. (1974). Developmental research, public policy, and the ecology of childhood. *Child Development, 45,* 1–5.
Bronfenbrenner, U. (1977). Toward an experimental ecology of human development. *American Psychologist, 32,* 513–531.
Bronfenbrenner, U. (1990). Discovering what families do. In D. Blankenhorn, S. Bayme, & J. B. Elshtain (Eds.), *Rebuilding the nest: A new commitment to the American family* (pp. 27–51). Milwaukee: Family Service America.
Cowan, P. A. (1993). The sky *is* falling, but Popenoe's analysis won't help us do anything about it. *Journal of Marriage and the Family, 55,* 548–553.
Friedman, L. M. (1990). *The republic of choice: Law, authority, and culture.* Cambridge MA: Harvard University Press.
Gallagher, J. J. (1990). Emergence of policy studies and policy institutes. *American Psychologist, 45,* 1316–1318.
Glendon, M. A. (1989). *The transformation of family law: State, law, and family in the United States and Western Europe.* Chicago: University of Chicago Press.
Glenn, N. (Ed.). (1987). The state of the American family [Special issue]. *Journal of Family Issues, 8*(4).
Maccoby, E. E., & Mnookin, R. H. (1992). *Dividing the child: Social and legal dilemmas of custody.* Cambridge MA: Harvard University Press.
McCall, R. B. (1990). Promoting interdisciplinary and faculty-service-provider relations. *American Psychologist, 12,* 1319–1324.
Mellman, M., Lazarus, E., & Rivlin, A. (1990). Family time, family values. In D. Blankenhorn, S. Bayme, & J. B. Elshtain (Eds.), *Rebuilding the nest: A new commitment to the American family* (pp. 73–92). Milwaukee: Family Service America.
Melton, G. B. (Ed.) (1985). *The law as a behavioral instrument.* Nebraska Symposium on Motivation. Lincoln: University of Nebraska Press.
Melton, G. B. (1990). Realism in psychology and humanism in law: Psycholegal studies at Nebraska. *Nebraska Law Review, 69,* 251–277.
Melton, G. B. (1992a). It's time for neighborhood research and action. *Child Abuse and Neglect, 16,* 909–913.
Melton, G. B. (1992b). The law is a good thing (psychology is, too): Human rights in psychological jurisprudence. *Law and Human Behavior, 16,* 381–398.
National Research Council, Panel on High-Risk Youth. (1993). *Losing generations: Adolescents in high-risk settings.* Washington DC: National Academy Press.
Popenoe, D. (1990). Family decline in America. In D. Blankenhorn, S. Bayme, & J. B. Elshtain (Eds.), *Rebuilding the nest: A new commitment to the American family* (pp. 39–51). Milwaukee: Family Service America.
Popenoe, D. (1993). American family decline, 1960–1990: A review and appraisal. *Journal of Marriage and the Family, 55,* 527–555.

Posner, R. A. (1992). *Sex and reason.* Cambridge MA: Harvard University Press.

Rodman, H., Sarvis, B., & Bonar, J. (1987). *The abortion question.* New York: Columbia University Press.

Shiono, P. H., & Quinn, L. S. (1994). Epidemiology of divorce. *Future of Children,* 4(1), 15–28.

Sokalski, H. J. (1993). Aims of the International Year of the Family. *Development, 1993*(4), 6–10.

Stacey, J. (1993). Good riddance to "the family": A response to David Popenoe. *Journal of Marriage and the Family, 55,* 545–547.

U.S. Advisory Board on Child Abuse and Neglect. (1992). *Neighbors helping neighbors: A new national strategy for the protection of children.* Washington DC: U.S. Government Printing Office.

Whitehead, B. D. (1992, Spring/Summer). A new familism. *Family Affairs.*

Growing Up in a Socially Toxic Environment: Life for Children and Families in the 1990s

James Garbarino
Cornell University

When I was a high school student, I used to write a column for the school newspaper, one of those columns that make fun of everything and are an enduring feature of life in adolescent journalism. One month a piece I wrote making fun of the fraternities in my high school made a lot of my peers angry at me. As a result, late one night I was the victim of a drive-by littering—a car pulled up and dumped garbage on the lawn of my house.

When I visit schools and communities I often think about that incident and wonder what would happen if I were an adolescent today. In fact, what might well happen is that I would be the victim of a drive-by shooting. Times have indeed changed.

There is a story going around that, in 1940, American teachers asked to identify the major discipline problems in their schools listed gum chewing, talking out of turn, running in the halls, cutting in lines, violating dress code, littering, and making noise. When surveyed in 1990, so the story goes, teachers listed drug abuse, alcohol abuse, pregnancy, suicide, rape, robbery, and assault (*Current Events*, 1993). Whether the story is apocryphal or not, it resonates with an emerging sense of unease about the quality of the social environment in which American children are growing up.

Of course, when I was in high school, there were certainly students who used drugs and alcohol, girls who got pregnant, and child abuse. But for the most part we did not know about it. With the benefit of hindsight, these problems are now evident. Some of the change is simply one of awareness on the part of adults of the problems that children and youth encounter. This awareness is demonstrated in areas like child abuse, where increased professional and public awareness in the 1970s and 1980s led to skyrocketing rates of reported child maltreatment.

But I do not think the current situation is simply a matter of greater awareness and better reporting to the authorities. Children today are in trouble. Evidence of this is found, for example, in Thomas Achenbach's Child Behavior Checklist, a survey used to identify a wide range of emotional and behavioral problems from a list of 118 specific items. Parents or other adults who know the child indicate the presence and intensity of the 118 behaviors or feelings, such as "can't sit still, restless, or hyperactive," "lying or cheating," "feels worthless or inferior," "cruelty, bullying or meanness to others," and "nervous, high-strung, or tense."

Since 1974, there has been a significant increase in 45 of the problems and a decrease in only one (the amount of time children spend with friends) (Achenbach & Howell, 1993). Negative feelings like apathy and sadness as well as feelings of distress all increased. Moreover, children reported disliking school more. To some extent, parents and teachers, the ones likely to fill out the survey, may be more sensitive to children than they were in 1974, but the difference is not totally explicable in these terms.

In 1976, 10% of the children in the survey were judged to be doing poorly enough to be candidates for therapy—that is, they were in the "clinical range" (even though only 3% were seing therapists). By 1989, 18% were doing badly enough to warrant therapy (and 8% were receiving it). Achenbach's data certainly conform to my own observations: more children are in trouble today than before.

But before I analyze the socially toxic nature of the environment for children today, I must defuse one potential criticism in advance. I am not saying that everything is worse now than it was in earlier decades, and certainly not that things were perfect then. It is easy to drown in a sea of nostalgia—particularly for a white male American talking about the 1950s.

Recent decades have seen some important improvements in

medical care that have removed many threats to the well-being of children. For example, at the height of the polio epidemic in the United States, in 1951, parents lived in dread as the summer months approached that their child would be struck down. The advent of a vaccination to prevent polio was a cause for celebration (and, having been one of the early "guinea pigs" in the testing of that vaccine, I can well appreciate its significance). By the same token, the decades since the 1950s have seen marked decline in racism and sexism, which constricted the development of identity and the full potential of millions. Sexism limited the choices of girls and women and imposed many costly adaptations (as feminist scholars and firsthand observers have made abundantly clear). Racism, well into the 1950s (and beyond), made a mockery of due process and equality. Blatant racism was uprooted by the civil-rights movement, another real cause for celebration (even though the United States remains a segregated society and the spirit of racism flourishes even as the letter of the law has improved dramatically).

Other forms of blatant discrimination have receded since the 1950s—in the definition and treatment of the handicapped and disabled, in tolerance for dissent, in the acceptance of homosexuals, in the humanization of many hitherto-maligned categories of persons. All this represents cultural progress as I see it, and I salute and appreciate all it. And yet, I still think that the quality of the social environment for children has deteriorated to a degree that I believe it is appropriate to speak of a "socially toxic environment."

Socially Toxic Environment

By the term *socially toxic environment* I mean to suggest that the social context of children, the social world in which they live, has become poisonous to their development. I offer it as a parallel to the environmental movement's analysis of physical toxicity as a threat to human well-being. For example, some evidence indicates that the sperm count of American men has been declining throughout the 20th century in response to the buildup of toxic substances in the physical environment—in the air, the water, and the soil (see Garbarino, 1992). Air quality remains a major problem in many places. Some locales have shown improvement over the past decade, however, as public and professional awareness has led to changes. In the matter of recognizing, understanding, and reversing social toxicity, however, we lag far behind.

The social equivalents of lead and smoke in the air, PCBs in the water, and pesticides in the food chain include violence, poverty and other economic pressures, depression, trauma, despair, nastiness, and alienation. These forces contaminate children and youth and are the elements of social toxicity.

The concept of a "socially toxic " environment is particularly relevant to vulnerable children, just as those who are most at risk in a physically toxic environment are from the most vulnerable groups. When airborne pollution gets really bad, for example, children and the elderly with asthma and other respiratory conditions show its effects soonest and with greatest intensity. This is one of the central elements of my analysis. As the social environment becomes more toxic, it is the most vulnerable children who show the effects first, those who have accumulated the most developmental risk factors. These risk factors include being a single parent, poverty, racism, drug addiction or alcoholism, trauma from violence, and emotional problems that impair parenting.

The accumulation of these risk factors jeopardizes development. As research by Arnold Sameroff and his colleagues (Sameroff et al., 1987) and Carl Dunst and his colleague (Dunst & Trivette, 1992) demonstrates, it is not the presence of any one or even two of these risk factors but their accumulation that developmentally disables children. Such accumulation overwhelms the child—particularly when it occurs without a parallel accumulation of opportunity factors. Once overwhelmed, children are likely to fall prey to the socially toxic influences that surround them.

Intellectual development suffers, and thus children cannot bring cognitive strength to bear in mastering the challenges they face. They learn to devalue themselves and thus lack the reservoir of self-esteem they need to keep positive momentum going in times of difficulty. Impaired parent-child relations alienate and anger children and reorient them to peers and away from socially responsible values.

The context for children's vulnerability is found in the seductive world of television, in the nastiness that results from declining public civility, in the stresses of the modern economy, and in the violence that escalates in many communities. I begin my analysis below with television because it is the most obvious and omnipresent feature of social toxicity.

Television as a Feature of the Socially Toxic Environment

In 1936 British social psychologist T. H. Pear asked, "What differences will television make to our habits and mental attitudes?" (Pear, 1936). Almost 60 years later we are beginning to find out the answer. Television has succeeded beyond its early proponents' greatest expectations in becoming the dominant cultural force in our society. Survey research reports that in any given year only 6% of Americans report having read a whole book. In contrast, virtually everyone watches television. Indeed, television has become the binding force in American culture, perhaps the only common element. But what exactly is common to that experience?

Understanding the consequences of television for childhood and youth is a bit like understanding the effects of smoking on health. While it is difficult to see a simple and direct link between smoking and health, the scientific proof that smoking—even being in the presence of smoking—is bad for your health is clear. After a generation of research and advocacy, this message is now well established.

But smoking was once heavily embedded in our culture. Many years ago, when I was the drama counselor at a summer camp, I often asked children to play the role of an adult in a production. Invariably, their immediate response to being assigned an adult part was to request a cigarette. Smoking was the most visible and unambiguous signal of adulthood. Eradicating smoking may have seemed an impossibility, but now it is a real possibility. There is a lesson in this change in opinion on smoking for our efforts to think about and do something about television.

It is important to remember that the effects of television are difficult to study because it is so deeply embedded in our society and culture (Winn, 1985). What could constitute an appropriate comparison group for studying the effects of television? Those few who do not watch are such a "deviant" minority group that we would be hard pressed to draw any generalizable conclusions from studying them.

And yet, on the basis of historical research as well as my reading of contemporary studies (Garbarino, 1972; National Research Council, 1992; Winn, 1985), I think that television contributes to the social toxicity of the environment for children and families.

Drawing on these sources I see the first consequences of television viewing in its role in transmitting and validating messages about violence in human affairs. The accumulation of hundreds of studies leaves little doubt that watching violence on television has a dangerous effect. One recent analysis (Centerwall, 1992) concludes that the introduction of television in the 1950s eventually resulted in a doubling of the homicide rate. Other studies document a doubling of aggressive behavior among children in the wake of television being introduced into their community (Joy et al., 1986).

A second, much less documented effect of television is its suppression of social interaction in the family and in the community while paradoxically increasing awareness of economic inequalities. A Canadian study (Joy et al., 1986) revealed that, after the introduction of television in a community, face-to-face interaction declined significantly (by about 25%). Others report that high dosages of television viewing result in increased social paranoia—that is, increased fear and distrust of the community.

Furthermore, early research on the introduction of television into families revealed parallel findings. Maccoby (1951) found that 78% of the respondents did not converse during viewing except at specific times, such as commercials. Maccoby wrote, "The nature of the family social life during a program could be described as 'parallel' rather than interactive, and the set does seem quite clearly to dominate family life when it is on." Now, with most households having at least two televisions, this effect may well be even more pronounced.

In another early study, 36% of the respondents said that television viewing was the only family activity participated in during the week (Hamilton & Lawless, 1956). In Maccoby's (1951) study, in response to the question, "Has TV made it easier or harder to take care of the child at home?" 54% said "easier," 33% said "no difference," and only 3% said "harder." But "easier" clearly meant a decrease in interaction: 62% of the mothers said "TV keeps the children quiet." As one mother put it, "It's much easier—it's like putting him to sleep."

My point in citing these data is to suggest that television viewing began to shape and change the social environment of children from its very beginning in the direction of less social interaction. A decade after the introduction of television, Urie Bronfenbrenner (1986) and his colleagues began to detect declining interaction between children and parents. It seems reasonable to expect that as time with adults declines the impact of what children see and hear from television increases.

As television violence increased through the 1960s and 1970s it was doing so in a changed social context, one in which declining adult presence in the lives of children (aided and abetted by television) was setting those children up to absorb the messages of violence. These two features of social toxicity—violent messages and decreased adult influence—work together in a conspiratorial fashion, and today we see the effects of that development.

Nastiness and the End of Childhood

Childhood is a cultural creation, a protected space for children from the economic, political, and sexual affairs of the community. One important element of social toxicity is the erosion of this protected cultural space. Some observers use phrases like "the end of childhood" to refer to this phenomenon, in which children are exposed to and drawn into adult issues and themes well before their time. There are many indications of the phenomenon. For example, as the concept of childhood became established in American culture, clothing marked children as a class distinct from adolescents and adults. Today children wear the sophisticated fashions of adolescents and adults.

Children are certainly "aware" of adult issues like rape, murder, infidelity, and all the other nastiness that adults must contend with or at least acknowledge. I consider these issues part of adulthood. But children's thinking and feeling are different from that of adults—in many ways more concrete, personalized, and limited in its goals and scope. They lack the social roles and personal power to deal with adult issues.

Of course, even many adults sometimes feel over their heads when faced with the problems of the world—war, poverty, injustice, environmental degradation, community catastrophe. I recognize that all too well as someone whose professional life has focused on child abuse, family poverty, and children in war zones. But children face a special challenge because of their relative powerlessness. The Greek philosopher Herodotus recognized the frustration of lacking power when he wrote, "There is no greater sorrow in life than to have an understanding of many things but power over nothing." Children are aware of social problems but powerless. No wonder there is more childhood depression and sadness than before and so many children seem "world weary" at such a young age.

I thought of this situation one day when I was visiting a third-grade classroom in a middle-class elementary school. The children spoke of recent kidnappings of children that had been in the news, of the docudrama programs on television that frightened them, of the soap operas, MTV, and violent movies they watched, of the many experiences of divorce and separation in their lives, of the fact that a third of them went home to no parental supervision after school every day.

And then I asked them to close their eyes and tell me what words, thoughts, and feelings came to them when I said, "Mr. Rogers." I could see the smiles on their faces, the faces of young children recalling positive images: "Kind"; "Good"; "King Friday"; "The Trolley"; "Nice," they said. I had touched something with which they had myriad positive associations.

Then I asked them to close their eyes again and tell me what they thought of when I said, "Beavis and Butt-head." Now the associations, said without hesitation, were of a very different character: "Nasty"; "Mean"; "Fires"; "Rude"; "Hurting people"; "Bad." When we talked about it later they all said that Mr. Rogers was history for them. "He was from our childhood," said an eight-year-old. "Beavis and Butt-head is today."

This experience crystallized for me the fact that one important feature of the socially toxic environment for children is the nastiness to which they are exposed so early in life. Missing children, kidnapped children, abused children, and murdered children are all part of it, of course. A study conducted in Ohio with elementary-school-age children reported that 43% of those in grades 4–6 thought it was "likely" that they would be kidnapped at some point in their lives. Does anyone doubt that today's children are more wary of strangers than were those of a generation ago?

But it is more than the extreme evils listed above that concern me. It is the nastiness that surrounds—and increasingly infuses—children. I objected to the movie *Home Alone* in part because it glorified such nastiness (not to mention its graphic violence). I hear more children using what was formerly called "foul language" in a public and casual way. I think it coarsens them.

The decline in civility (an old-fashioned word, to be sure) is more than shocking. I think it has a negative effect on development by lowering the level of discourse, by provoking a callousness that generalizes, and by eroding the special place in the life of our culture we used to call childhood. Most people now recognize that psychological maltreatment is a real factor in development (Garbarino et al., 1986) and that verbal abuse is part of psychological maltreatment.

A survey commissioned by the National Committee for the Prevention of Child Abuse asked adults, "How likely do you think it is that repeated yelling and swearing at a child leads to long term emotional problems for the child?" Three quarters of the respondents said they thought it was "likely" or "very likely," and I agree. For this reason, I worry about the nastiness of rhetoric in families, in schools, and on the streets. Such nastiness is the last thing children need, especially in the face of so many other challenges, some of which derive from our economic system.

Social Toxicity in Economic Deprivation and the Struggle of Affluence

Whether middle or lower class, children feel acutely the effects of our society's economic life. At the top and at the bottom, the evolution of the American economy over the last few decades has increased social stress on children.

After briefly declining during the war on poverty in the affluent 1960s, poverty among children has increased steadily. This is made all the more troublesome because the development of our strategies for using economic resources on behalf of children has not kept pace with the size and complexity of our economy. Thus, poverty hurts more now that ever before.

While most industrialized societies guarantee all families maternal and infant health care and basic child-support subsidies, ours does not (Miller, 1989). Although the federal budget includes a substantial commitment to entitlement programs, most of this money (five-sixths, according to Fallows, 1982) goes to programs that disproportionately assist affluent adults (e.g., social security), while relatively little goes to families in the service of child welfare-related objectives. This may explain why correlations between measures of income or socioeconomic status and basic child outcomes are often higher in the United States than in other societies (Bronfenbrenner, 1986). Thus, low income is a better predictor of childhood deficits in the United States than in other countries because our social policies tend to exaggerate rather than minimize the impact of family income on access to preventive and rehabilitative services.

The current economic challenges come in the wake of the post–World War II economic track record, which led most Americans, except perhaps the chronically impoverished underclass, to expect material affluence. As a result, many now take for granted as necessities what were considered previously to be luxuries, such as remote-control television and cable services. Television compounds the issue of elevated expectations by making everyone intimately aware of what is possible (and what others have). This combination has become increasingly socially toxic for children, as socioeconomic gaps widen and expectations become inflated and most people's understanding of our economy remains primitive.

Conventional economic theory and research focuses on only one aspect of our economic life, the cash transactions that are counted in compiling measures of the gross national product. But our efforts must begin with the recognition of two economic spheres—the "monetarized," in which money changes hands in the production and distribution of goods and services, and the "nonmonetarized," in which goods and services are produced and distributed without cash transactions (Garbarino, 1992).

Enormous areas of special relevance to children have traditionally existed in the nonmonetarized economy—child care, recreation, entertainment, even health care (as parents took care of minor injuries and illness and provided preventive care). Recent decades have seen more of the daily life of children (indeed, of everyone) becoming part of the monetarized economy, that is, having a dollar price (Giarini, 1980). Massive shifts of activity from one sphere to the other have occurred in recent decades and counted as economic growth. When taken as a whole, however, these shifts often indicate nothing more than shuffling the same resources, and in many occasions they obscure diminished value, a decline in total wealth—particularly when children are concerned.

It is the phenomenology of deprivation that concerns us here. After children have become socialized into a highly monetarized lifestyle (i.e., one in which a high proportion of the activities of day-to-day life involve cash transactions), it is difficult, for cultural and technological reasons, to reenter the nonmonetarized economy. For example, earlier generations used cloth diapers and invested much time and personal energy in their maintainance. Currently, even families with small incomes and limited prospects for earning have come to depend on expensive paper or plastic diapers as a "basic necessity."

Children are also exposed to greater risk by the geographic concentration of economically marginal families as communities become more homogeneous (e.g., through clustering public housing). In Cleveland, for example, from 1960 to 1990, the proportion of poor families who were living in neighborhoods where more than 40% of the other families were poor increased dramatically, from 21 to 61% (Coulton & Pandey, 1992).

As a result of this social-class segregation, poor and middle-class children become strangers, known only through the imagery of television and popular stereotypes. An informal study suggests the impact of this alienation. When I asked a group of 20 middle-class children, "Which would be worse, to be poor or to be blind?" more than half answered they thought it would be worse to be poor.

Beyond the problem of estrangement of children across social-class lines, there is the problem that arises when children are perceived as economic burdens. In a nation where the cost of everything seems to be continually on the rise, most families need two incomes to keep up, although because of divorce and single parenthood increasing numbers of families have only one potential wage earner. Such was not the case in the 1950s, when one income was generally sufficient—in part because of lower and different expectations, in part because more of daily life was "paid for" in the nonmonetarized economy, and in part because of the demographics and financial conditions underlying the post–World War II economy.

Most families with children contained two adults, one of whom was working in the cash economy and both of whom were heavily involved in the nonmonetarized economy.

Now most families depend on the cash economy for meeting almost all their needs, and children are increasingly an economic burden, both directly because of what it costs to raise them and indirectly because of what they "cost" in lost parental income (i.e., time away from the job that over a childhood comes to tens of thousands if not hundreds of thousands of dollars).

The "opportunity costs" of child rearing create another element of social toxicity for children. Children are expected to be ready for out-of-home child-care arrangements as early as possible so that the parents can return to work. Children are left alone more frequently and at younger ages so parents can stay at work because adult supervision is so expensive. They are sent to school when sick, or they return to school sooner than they should because parents cannot afford to leave work to care for a sick child. All this puts pressure on children.

Conventional economic thinking does not consider fully the true costs of caring for children. By distorting our view of the true costs and benefits of family life, it further contributes to the social toxicity of the environment for children. There are limits to the number of children that one caregiver can serve before compromising the children's development. Family day-care providers who serve less-than-affluent families are usually in a difficult position: they cannot generate sufficient income per child served to set a proper limit on the number of children in their care. An analysis conducted in Illinois illustrates this problem (Gilkerson et al., 1987). Workers at a factory studied could afford to pay no more than $30 per week per child for care. A family day-care provider who accepts four children—the approved number—can thus earn only $5,500 per year. Most respond by increasing the number of children cared for to eight and by seeking to stay outside the licensing system. The cost of this pattern of care is borne in decreased developmental prospects for the children. The same analysis concludes that it costs at least $55 per week per child to provide adequate care. The "missing" $25 contributes to the social toxicity of the environment for children who generally experience a lower standard of child care in the monetarized economy than they would in the nonmonetarized economy.

The Decline of Community and the Social Toxicity of High-Risk Neighborhoods

In contrast to the socially rich family environment stands the "socially impoverished" one, in which the parent-child relationship is denuded of enduring supportive relationships and protective behaviors. It is thus deprived of the essential elements, nurturance and feedback systems (Whittacker et al., 1983), of what Gerald Caplan (1974) called "social-support systems." By contrast, the socially rich environment includes people who are what Alice Collins and Diane Pancoast (1976) called "free from drain," individuals who can afford to give to and share with others because the balance of needs and resources in their own personal lives markedly favors others.

They offer "services" to children that do not involve cash transactions. Thus, they stand outside the monetarized human service sector (i.e., the services that involve salaries and wages, prices, and financial contracts) and find nonmonetarized payoff in helping others. They provide "protective behaviors" to children, including keeping an eye on them while they play outside, offering assistance to parents with day-to-day or emergency care, and intervening on their behalf when threatened (even reporting child maltreatment to protective service agencies). These individuals become one aspect of the socially rich neighborhood. One observer puts it this way: "A neighborhood's character is determined by a host of factors, but most significantly by the kinds of relationships that neighbors have with each other. . . . A healthy neighborhood has some sort of cultural and institutional network which manifests itself in pride in the neighborhood, care of homes, security for children, and respect for each other" (Kromkowski, 1976, p. 228).

Socially impoverished neighborhoods, in contrast, lack people who are free from drain and therefore tend to operate on a "scarcity" economy when it comes to social relations (Garbarino & Kostelny, 1992, 1994). Mutuality is suppressed by fears of exploitation and of being a burden and excessively beholding. For example, residents may fear acts of neighboring, such as general offers of shared child care, because the open a Pandora's box of requests and may lead to the expectation of reciprocity—a negative prospect if one distrusts the caregiving practices of one's neighbors.

This social impoverishment can occur independently of economic impoverishment. Thus, even a financially affluent social environment may lack the kind of enduring support systems that adolescents need to provide positive role models, caring adult supervision, and a sense of personal validation. The same may be true for the parents who may feel acute embarrassment in admitting difficulty with their adolescents in a community in which there is a presumption of competence and high expectations for achievement.

Part and parcel of this aspect of social toxicity in the community is the spread of the gun culture. The proliferation of handguns in American communities over the last two decades has been a dramatic development. News stories reporting crime and social disorder stimulate additional gun sales. In New York City, for example, with its population of more than seven million people, there are believed to be a million guns. These guns are reaching the hands of kids with alarming frequency. Surveys report a significant minority of children either regularly or sporadically carrying a weapon to school or in the neighborhood for protection, a "socially contagious" practice.

Concern over guns is an issue not only in the inner city. Among a group of third graders in a middle-class suburban school, most had seen a real gun in the possession of family, friends, or neighbors, and many knew how to get that gun "if they needed it." I think the proliferation of guns is both a cause and a result of the spread of vigilantism, a lack of trust in the authorities and the feeling that one must take matters into one's own hands to be safe. An 11 March 1985 *Newsweek* survey found that 68% of the respondents said they believed vigilantism ("taking the law into one's own hands") was justified "sometimes" (while 3% said "always" and 23% said "never").

When children feel this way as well, and they have access to guns there will certainly be a lot of misery, especially among psychologically vulnerable children. It is no surprise that vulnerable communities are experiencing the most problems. For example, in a study concerning preschoolers in an inner-city public-housing project, the mothers cited "shooting" as their greatest fear for their children (Dubrow & Garbarino, 1989). Others have reported that in such neighborhoods 35% of the kids have witnessed a shooting by the time they reach the age of 15 (Bell, 1991).

In these diminished communities most children have had a first-hand encounter with gunfire, and most teenagers are caught up in the violence. In such environments most women experience their first pregnancy while still unmarried teenagers, living with little prospect of economic self-sufficiency or two-parent family status. Many of these pregnancies result from sexual exploitation by much older men (Barclay-McLaughlin, 1987). These are the environments in which prenatal care is inadequate, intervals between births often too small, beliefs about child care too often dysfunctional, access to and utilization of well-baby care inadequate, early intervention for child disabilities inadequate, and, thus, child mortality and morbidity rampant.

What Is Next?

It is one thing to recognize and analyze the social toxicity of the environment in which children are growing up today. What can we do about it? Answering this question is the goal of the rest of this book. Here let me just cite the general directions of that answer.

Dealing with the social toxicity of the environment for children will require that parents become more astute and that they join together in the public-policy arena to stand for public actions that can reverse the trends. It takes more time, effort, and skill to succeed as a parent today than it did in the past. The social toxicity of the environment demands that parents be more effective in rearing their children to be steady, brave, responsible, and resilient than ever before. It means dealing with the television menace and finding ways to invest the time and supervision that children need (and particularly need to reduce the likelihood of high-risk activities such as sexual activity before the age of 16). It takes a clear understanding of the costs and benefits of activities in the monetarized and the non-monetarized economies.

But it also demands that parents act as citizens to fight the social toxicity itself. It means banding together to refocus television content, insisting on a more civil society in how we treat each other (including how we talk to and about one another), insisting on economic policies that put family well-being first and foremost among political priorities, and having the courage to stop the proliferation of weapons and insist through deed and word on nonviolence as a goal in human affairs. It means speaking out against rabid individualism that flies in the face of children's needs for community. It requires doing all this, and more—an ethic and a politics of caring for the next generation—no matter what the cost. And it means doing so with an appreciation for the persistent role of race and social class in shaping the prospects for children.

Poor and minority families have more children, have them earlier, and have lower life expectancies than do affluent and nonminority families (Wilson, 1987). White life expectancy has increased in recent years—to about 75 years—while black life expectancy has declined to about 69 years. Infant-mortality rates in poor neighborhoods are often six times what they are in affluent neighborhoods (Garbarino & Kostelny, 1993).

The death rate of black children and youths is higher, from all causes, than of white children—for example, in Illinois, 34.8 per 100,000 from accidents for black youngsters 0–4 years old, versus 14.5 per 100,000 for white children of the same age. Homicide (including child-maltreatment fatalities) is three times higher for young black children than for white children. For older children the discrepancy is even greater—seven times higher for black children ages five through 14 than for white children of the same age.

In addition to the economic and demographic polarization discussed above, we can observe several general trends toward community deterioration. In his analysis of why rates of serious depression have increased throughout the 20th century, Seligman (1990) cites the unraveling of community as one cause: at-risk individuals who were supported and sustained by the demands and strong role prescriptions of an earlier era are "set free" by the loosening of community bonds and "permitted" to become depressed. Similar reports have appeared from the former East Germany after the collapse of the Communist regime (Morris, 1991). Morris cites an East German source: "As the economic fallout of unification wears on, and communist social structures continue to fall, Eastern Germans are suffering an increase in mental illness and stress-related disorders."

It is plausible that this social deterioration is the same as that observed in the United States as privatization of community occurs (Garbarino, 1992). Formerly, communities relied on neighbors to augment those few mothers who did work outside of the home in the cash economy. Today, this resource is largely unavailable: in many neighborhoods few adults are both available in residential neighborhoods after school and committed to providing supervision of children. One feature of this phenomenon may be found in a growing impoverishment of time with respect to children in families. More children lack adult supervision after—and often before—school, and they have a greater sense that access to parental time is contingent rather than a "given" (see Garbarino, 1992).

The problem of violence presents further evidence of community deterioration and polarization. While well-functioning families with adequate resources have seen a decline in violence (Straus & Gelles, 1990), high-risk families have evidenced no such decline. In fact, families living in inner-city and rural areas marked by poverty have seen a large increase in violence—for example, a 400% increase in serious assault in Chicago from 1974 to 1990 (see Garbarino et al., 1992). Greater numbers of families live in neighborhoods that are described by residents and observers alike as "war zones" (Kotlowitz, 1991).

All these economic, demographic, and social trends in the United States treated above highlight several important issues of values and ideology: family egalitarianism, social materialism, and the definitions of citizenship for children. Research has shown that egalitarianism within families is associated with lower levels of violence (Straus & Gelles, 1990). Still, authoritarianism remains strong in the form of male domination. Coupled with other sources of stress, such authoritarianism can release violence against women and children. Thus, liberalization within families—but not permissive anarchy—is an important preventative goal. Egalitarian relations between parents are good for children.

Social materialism refers to the "monetarization" of daily life, as I have discussed above. Examples of this monetarization include the establishment of child care in the cash economy, the widespread entry of mothers into the cash labor force, and the movement of recreational and leisure activities into the cash economy. These economic changes put pressure on caregiving for children. They heighten the costs of parenthood—directly in the cash required to "equip and maintain" a child and indirectly in the cash income that parents must forgo to meet child-rearing obligations, both of which conspire against children by increasing the pressure on families and resentment regarding the "burden" of parenthood. This pressure may be particularly intense among those who are frustrated by their limited ability to compete successfully in the cash economy and who may turn this frustration into rejection of and assault against children.

Finally, the trends we have observed highlight the ideological problem we face in responding to children as citizens. Children and child-rearing largely remain private matters in the United States, which means children do not have direct relationships with the community. This lack of relationship puts children in jeopardy because it discourages early, preventative community support.

If the community must wait until there is clear evidence of family dysfunction before becoming involved on behalf of children, the odds of dysfunction increase and the prospects for effective action decrease. Rather, a primary involvement (as is represented, e.g., in a comprehensive, "automatic" home health visitor program that would begin when a woman became pregnant) in the lives of children is needed. Without such a model of child citizenship, children will continue to pay the price of privacy in the form of child maltreatment (Garbarino & Gilliam, 1980).

Our goal must be to prevent the accumulation of risk in the lives of children. Such accumulation tends to overcome resilience and coping and result in developmental impairment. This orientation to prevention is well grounded in research and theory, as it is in moral philosophy.

REFERENCES

Achenbach, T., & Howell, C. (1993). Are American children's problems getting worse? A 13-year comparison. *Journal of the American Academy of Child and Adolescent Psychiatry, 32,* 1145–1154.
Barclay-McLaughlin, G. (1987). *The Center for Successful Child Development.* Chicago: Ounce of Prevention Fund.
Bell, C. (1991). Traumatic stress and children in danger. *Journal of Health Care for the Poor and Underserved, 2*(1), 175–188.
Bronfenbrenner, U. (1986). Ecology of the family as a context for human development research perspectives. *Developmental Psychology, 22,* 723–742.
Caplan, G. (1974). *Support systems and community mental health.* New York: Behavioral Publications.
Centerwall, B. (1992). Children, television, and violence. In D. Schwartz (Ed.), *Children and violence. Report of the 23rd Ross Roundtable on critical approaches to common pediatric problems* (pp. 87–97). Columbus OH: Ross Laboratories.

Collins, A., & Pancoast, D. (1976). *Natural helping networks.* Washington DC: National Association of Social Workers.

Coulton, C., & Pandey, S. (1992). Geographic concentration of poverty and risk to children in urban neighborhoods. *American Behavioral Scientist, 35,* 238–257.

Current Events. (1993). *School violence. 93* (12).

Dubrow, N., & Garbarino, J. (1989). "Living in the war zone: Mothers and young children in a public housing development." *Child Welfare, 68* (1), 3–20.

Dunst, C., & Trivette, C. (1992, March). *Risk and opportunity factors influencing parent and child functioning.* Paper presented at the Ninth Annual Smoky Mountain Winter Institute, Asheville NC.

Fallows, J. (1982). Entitlements. *Atlantic Monthly, 250,* 51.

Garbarino, J. (1972). A note on the effects of television viewing. In U. Bronfenbrenner, (Ed.), *Influences on human development* (pp. 397–400). Hinsdale IL: Dryden.

Garbarino, J. (1992). *Toward a sustainable society: An economic, social and environmental agenda for our children's future.* Chicago: Noble.

Garbarino, J., Dubrow, N., Kostelny, K., & Pardo, C. (1992). *Children in danger: Coping with the consequences of community violence.* San Francisco: Jossey-Bass.

Garbarino, J., & Gilliam, G. (1980). *Understanding abusive families.* Lexington MA: Lexington.

Garbarino, J., Guttmann, E., & Seeley, J. (1986). *The psychologically battered child.* San Francisco: Jossey-Bass.

Garbarino, J., & Kostelny, K. (1992). Child maltreatment as a community problem. *Child Abuse and Neglect, 16,* 455–464.

Garbarino, J., & Kostelny, K. (1993). Neighborhood and Community Influences on Parenting. In T. Luster and L. Okagaki (Eds.), *Parenting: An ecological perspective* (pp. 203–226). Hillside NJ: Erlbaum.

Garbarino, J., & Kostelny, K. (1994). Family-supported community development. In S. Kagan & B. Weissbourd (Eds.), *Putting families first.* San Francisco: Jossey-Bass.

Giarini, O. (1980). *Dialogue on wealth and welfare.* New York: Pergamon.

Gilkerson, L., Nesphachel, S., & Trevino, R. (1987). *Issues in family day care.* Chicago: Erikson Institute.

Hamilton, R., & Lawless, R. (1956) Television within the social matrix. *Public Opinion Quarterly, 20,* 393–403.

Joy, L. , Kimball, M., & Zabrack, M. (1986). Television and children's aggressive behavior. In T. Williams (Ed.), *The impact of television: A natural experiment in three communities* (pp. 303–360). New York: Academic Press.

Kotlowitz, A. (1991). *There are no children here.* New York: Doubleday.

Kromkowski, J. (August, 1976). *Neighborhood deterioration and juvenile crime.* (U.S. Department of Commerce, National Technical Information Service, PB-260 473). South Bend IN: South Bend Urban Observatory.

Maccoby, E. (1951). Television: Its its impact on school age children. *Public Opinion Quarterly, 15,* 423–444.

20

Miller, G. (Ed.). (1989). *Giving children a chance.* Washington DC: Center for National Policy.

Morris, N. (1991, May 23). After unification Germans depressed. *Chicago Tribune.* p. A-35.

National Research Council (1992). *Understanding and preventing violence.* Washington DC: U.S. Government Printing Office.

Pear, T. H. (1936, November 18) What television might do. *Listener.*

Sameroff, A., Seifer, R., Barocas, R., Zax, M., & Greenspan, S. (1987). Intelligence quotient scores of 4-year-old children: Social-environmental risk factors. *Pediatrics, 79,* 343–350.

Seligman, M. E. P. (1990). *Learned optimism.* New York: Knopf.

Straus, M., & Gelles, R. (1990). *Physical violence in American families.* New Brunswick NJ: Transaction.

Whittaker, J., Garbarino, J., & Associates (1983). *Social support networks.* New York: Aldine.

Wilson, W. (1987). *The truly disadvantaged: The inner city, the underclass, and public policy.* Chicago: University of Chicago Press.

Winn, M. (1985). *Children without childhood.* New York: Viking.

The Deterioration of the Family: A Law and Economics Perspective

Allen M. Parkman
University of New Mexico

Family life in the United States has changed dramatically since World War II, with these changes being accepted by most people either fatalistically or optimistically. Often ignored has been the central role of the family in all societies and the societal loss incurred if its importance is reduced (Yorburg, 1983). The vast majority of Americans marry and have children. Although the range of living situations has increased to include single-parent households and homosexual couples, the family continues to be associated with a married couple and, usually, their children, and that will be my focus in this chapter. Few situations have ever seemed as idyllic as the families depicted in television series in the 1950s. The father worked outside the home but was always available at times of family crisis. The mother worked at home and was always a source of wisdom and compassion. The children faced crises, but none were life threatening or irreversible. Teenage pregnancy and drug use were not usual topics on the programs. While these series may not have been totally accurate depictions of the family, they did capture the essence of the family then.

Times have changed.[1] Between 1970 and 1991, the percentage of Americans over 18 years old who were married decreased from 72%

This chapter has benefited from the comments of Natalie Porter.

to 61%. Some of the decrease can be explained by the population bulge of the baby-boom generations. But when the age distribution is standardized to conform to that of 1960, the percentage still decreases from 74 to 63% over the period. Changes in the behavior of individuals were also reflected in the composition of households. Between 1950 and 1991, the percentage of households consisting of married couples fell from 79 to 55%. During the same period, non-family households, consisting mostly of people living alone grew from 10 to 30%. The result was often a family headed by a woman. Since 1950, the percentage of American families headed by women has nearly doubled, to 17%. Many of these women have never been married. Thirty-one percent of one-parent families are now headed by never-married women, in contrast to 6% in 1970. Marriage has become a less attractive alternative for young people as they delay the age at which they marry. Between 1956 and 1990, the median age at first marriage rose from 20.1 to 24.5 years for women and from 22.5 to 26 years for men. Not only has marriage become a less attractive alternative for couples, it has become less stable, as the divorce rate rose from 3.5 per 1,000 in 1970 to 5.3 per 1,000 in 1981, although declining to 4.7 per 1,000 in 1988. Moreover, the quality of life within families has been deteriorating, as measured, for example, by the number of reported cases of child maltreatment. These cases have increased from 669,000 in 1976 to 2,086,000 in 1986.

Typical publications of the groups identifying the deterioration of the family as a problem has been *Beyond Rhetoric*, issued in 1991 by the National Commission on Children, chaired by Senator Jay Rockefeller of West Virginia, and *Families First*, the 1993 report of the National Commission on American's Urban Families, chaired by Governor John Ashcroft of Missouri. These reports stressed three key points (Popenoe, 1994): the American family is not simply "changing," it is growing weaker; the decline in the family is the cause of some of our most urgent social problems; and the heart of the family problem lies in the steady breakup of the two-parent home. Recent polls suggest that these views are shared by many Americans. Meanwhile, academicians such as Coontz (1992), Stacey (1990), and Skolnick (1991) have argued that changes in the contemporary family are not really as bad as have been reported.

While the discussion here concerns the family, I will assume that marriage is generally accepted as a prerequisite for a family. Therefore, changes in the family are often a reflection of a change in the incentives for people to marry and remain married. There are two perspectives for viewing these changes in the attraction of marriage and the family. First, they could be less attractive because of a change in individuals' preferences as is often reflected in an increased emphasis on individual gratification. Many people could be rejecting marriage and a family because it interferes with their perception of their self-interest. Alternatively, preferences could be fairly stable, but the change could be caused by a change in the costs or benefits of marriage and family, leading people to change their behavior. A change in the wages and job opportunities available to women can reduce their incentives to become housewives and mothers, thereby reducing the attraction of marriage to both men and women.

Economic and Legal Analysis

Economics and law provide two valuable tools for analyzing changes in attitude toward marriage. Economics emphasizes behavior based on incentives that reflect the costs and benefits of different activities. Costs and benefits are broad concepts to economists and include psychological as well as financial aspects based on sacrificed, bypassed opportunities. Meanwhile, the law is a major source of changes in those costs and benefits. Alternatively, some schools of psychology emphasize a change in preferences on behavior. Thus, the economic and psychological approaches are interconnected. A change in the cost of an activity induces a behavioral change that can ultimately lead to activities becoming more acceptable, thereby changing individuals' preferences.

My emphasis here is on such changes in incentives based on costs and benefits for marrying and staying married that have occurred over recent decades. An economic framework is used to emphasize that changes in society have reduced the gains from marriage and family for many people and their decision not to marry has increased their welfare and, therefore, that of society. This is especially true for adults who do not want children.

Legal changes have also occurred that have diminished the incentives for adults to commit themselves to a family even when their welfare would be improved by that commitment under different laws. The primary change I am addressing is no-fault divorce. Between 1970 and 1985, every state either replaced or added no-fault grounds to the fault grounds of adultery, desertion, and cruelty. A couple's legal commitment at marriage is based not on their preferences but on a contract created by the state and over which they have little control. Sometimes that lack of control is good because it protects any children of the marriage, but it also can work to the detriment of many couples, especially as concerns the grounds for dissolution of the agreement. Many couples recognize the irreversible costs of one parent, for example, assuming primary responsibility for child rearing and thereby sacrificing or limiting a career. Consequently, they want to make a long-term commitment to each other and their family, a commitment undermined by the contract imposed on them by most states' statutes. All states provide for some form of no-fault divorce that essentially allows either spouse to dissolve the marriage at any time, subject to limited compensation. The no-fault grounds for divorce cannot be changed by the couple, although the state can change them after the couple has married, as it has over the last 25 years.

Let me summarize the primary points that I want to make in this chapter. First, marriage and the family benefit from increased specialization by spouses. The net benefits of specialization during marriage have declined for some people, reducing their incentives to choose marriage and a family. Their not marrying has increased their welfare and, therefore, that of society. Second, the no-fault grounds for divorce have also reduced the incentives for many individuals to commit themselves to marriage and a family. Individuals' response has at times reduced their welfare compared with what it could be under a different legal environment. Third, because self-interest is central to economics, I do not attribute an increase in self-interest to a significant independent force in these changes. The decision to marry and stay married is a selfish choice. Meanwhile, no-fault divorce has reduced the anticipated net benefits from altruistic behavior during marriage, and, therefore, I would expect less altruistic behavior within families.

The following material covers three topics. First, I discuss the economic perspective on why people marry, create families, and sometimes divorce. Then the influence of changes in the legal environment, especially the shift from fault to no-fault divorce, on those decisions is discussed. Last, I present a legal program for increasing the attraction of marriage and a family.

THE ECONOMIC ANALYSIS OF FAMILY FORMATION

During the last few decades, the use of economic analysis has been expanded to many nonmarket activities, including marriage, divorce, and the family (Becker, 1976, 1991; Fuchs, 1983). At a general level, economics is the study of the choices individuals make. The economic perspective assumes that resources are scarce compared with human wants, that these resources can be put to alternative uses, and that people have diverse wants, not all which can be satisfied. It follows that the basic economic problem of every society— and of every individual—is to make choices that allocate the available resources in the most efficient manner to satisfy wants. Especially in the United States, where legal marriage is a monogamous relationship, the need for a person to make a choice when selecting a spouse is obvious: economic analysis can be a valuable tool for comparing alternatives even when they are not denominated in dollars.

Social scientists have long used the economic framework to gain a better understanding of why people make the choices they do. Much of the power of economics to explain human behavior is rooted in the following set of assumptions (Fuchs, 1983). First, people are constantly confronted with the necessity of making choices in their roles, for example, as consumers, workers, and lovers. Many alternatives are mutually exclusive. Second, in making these choices, people try to improve rather than reduce their welfare. The choices are made by comparing the alternative costs and benefits in a context of constraints such as laws, time, abilities, and income, and these choices are described as rational. Third, choices are influenced by the relative sacrifices, or "prices," involved with the different alternatives; these sacrifices can involve money, time, and psychological costs. Fourth, these "economic" decisions are made in an environment influenced by a range of other factors such as religion, social class, and physical and psychological needs. Economists have traditionally assumed that these environmental factors change slowly.

Both psychology and economics attempt to explain and predict human behavior. One critical difference occurs because economists usually assume that preferences are given while psychologists are interested in how preferences are formed and how they change. When economists observe systematic changes in human behavior, they usually investigate whether a change has occurred in the constraints or the relative prices confronting the individuals; people will usually buy less of a good if their income falls or the price of the good rises. Economists assume that tastes and preferences change less quickly than do the prices and the constraints that individuals face. At the same time, different groups can have preferences for different commodities and activities. People in the Southwest eat more green chiles than do people in other regions of the United States, but all consumers, including those in the Southwest, would be expected to buy fewer chiles if their price rose.

Economics has been used to analyze why people marry and create a family and sometimes divorce and dissolve that family (Parkman, 1992b). Since people must marry before they can divorce, I initially will analyze why people marry. The decision to marry consists of two steps: the decision that the individual will be better off married than single and the choice of a particular person as a spouse. Although the sequence is not predetermined, both choices have to be made before someone marries. An understanding of why people marry is important because the incentives that induce people to marry can change so that they no longer want to be married. The result is often a divorce. Economics provides a foundation for understanding these choices.

One has to wonder why it took economists so long to turn their attention to the analysis of marriage. As the study of choice, economics should be a valuable tool for analyzing one of the most important decisions made by individuals. Economic analysis goes far beyond the financial aspects of marriage such as dowries and bride prices noted by historians. It was not until the 1960s, however, that economists started to develop a concerted interest in decision-making outside markets (Becker, 1976, 1991), including marriage.

Marriage in the United States has characteristics that are similar to the other transactions that economists observe. First, it is voluntary and, therefore, it can be assumed that the parties expect that decision to raise their individual welfare above the level that they could attain if they remained single. Second, the parties compete in markets for the best mates. Although economics also can provide insights about homosexual unions and heterosexual relationships that do not result in legal marriage, here I focus on why a man and a woman in the United States choose to marry and establish a family.

THE DECISION TO MARRY

First, the individual must decide that he or she wants to marry. Second, he or she must select a particular mate. These decisions are not necessarily sequential but will be addressed sequentially here with first a look at why people marry. The process by which individuals choose their preferred mate will be discussed later in my discussion of divorce.

Men and women date, enter sexual relationships, and live together; but why do they go a step farther and marry? The economic analysis of the decision to marry focuses on the parties' expectation that marriage will increase their individual welfare—that marriage will expand the "commodities" available to them compared with those available if they remained single. An additional reason for marriage is insurance, if one accepts the element of the marriage vow in which the parties agree to fulfill their duty "for richer or poorer, in sickness and in health" (Cohen, 1987). Of course, love and physical attraction are important factors when selecting the preferred person to marry.

People must find it advantageous to live together before they decide to marry. While recognizing the desire for companionship and sexual attraction, economics also notes that there are gains from living together thanks to economies of scale and specialization. For example, the size of a comfortable house does not normally increase in proportion to the number of occupants; thus, the cost per occupant falls as the number of occupants increases, up to some point. In addition, some commodities consumed in a household are public goods, which are special examples of commodities with economies of scale: a public good has the characteristic that additional people can consume it at little or no additional cost and people cannot easily be excluded from the enjoyment of the commodity. By contrast, a private good is costly to provide to additional people, and people can be excluded from enjoying it. Television sets can be public goods; an apple exemplifies a private good.

The gains from specialization have been the primary focus of economists as they have attempted to explain why people live together and marry. Specialization increases the welfare of individuals by expanding the commodities available to them. Individual welfare is increased through the acquisition or production of commodities. Economic analysis of consumer behavior traditionally focused on the acquisition of goods and services, but economists have come to recognize that individuals do not necessarily receive enjoyment from just the acquisition of goods and services—enjoyment comes from combining goods and services with time to produce commodities (Becker, 1965; Lancaster, 1966). We do not receive enjoyment simply from buying a compact disc but from buying it with money and then listening to it, which requires time. Commodities often can be produced using a variety of time-money combinations. A meal, for example, can consist of an expensive dinner at an elegant restaurant and several hours of time or a picnic in the country costing less money but more time. The enjoyment does not come just from buying the food but from combining the food with time. Commodities produced at home can be an important component of individual welfare; they can be time intensive, including home-cooked meals, an attractive lawn, and caring for children.

The production of these commodities benefits from specialization. We often observe that businesses increase their output and profits by specialization that reduces the time lost as workers move between activities and allows employees to develop the unique skills necessary to perform specific tasks faster. The same principle is appropriate for the production of commodities by consumers. When people specialize, they can become more efficient in the production of commodities. When people cook more frequently, they become better cooks.

COMPARATIVE ADVANTAGE

The activities in which people specialize are often based on comparative advantage. Comparative advantage exists when two people have levels of productivity that vary among activities. The most important of these activities for marriage have traditionally been market work for income and domestic work, especially child care. On the average, men have earned and continue to earn higher incomes than women (O'Neill, 1990). Between 1981 and 1989, the ratio of female wages to male wages increased from .59 to .68 annual full-time earnings. For women and men with similar characteristics, the gap is smaller. However, so long as men continue to outearn women, they will have a comparative advantage in earning income, while the comparative advantage of women will be in domestic work.

While economies of scale and specialization explain why people of either the same or opposite sexes live together, it does not necessarily explain why they have traditionally felt compelled to marry. Although specialization is in the collective best interest of both parties while a relationship lasts, it can be revealed as costly if the relationship ends, especially a relationship of long duration. If the man specializes in income earning, that skill will remain intact if the relationship ends. He would lose his share of the household commodities provided by the woman, but these commodities may have decreased in value after any children have grown up and left home. During the relationship, the woman may have developed skills producing household commodities that do not have substantial value outside the relationship, and her income-earning capacity has deteriorated because of her working at home. She may be worse off if the relationship is dissolved, compared with her situation had she never entered the relationship in the first place. Traditionally, women were reluctant to specialize in domestic work unless they had expected the relationship to last a long time and marriage was associated with that expectation. Since men and women benefited from specialization, both had an incentive to marry.

THE IMPORTANCE OF CHILDREN

We usually associate marriage with a family because most married couples have children. Children are an important source of the gains from economies of scale and specialization. From an economic perspective, children are a public good: they can be enjoyed by both parents at no more cost than if only one parent were present and, if the marriage continues, it is difficult to exclude a parent from that enjoyment. The pressure for a couple to specialize during a relationship grows when they have children. Specialization in rearing children—and the associated costs for the parent who assumes primary responsibility for that role—increases the incentive for the parents to marry. The arrival of children typically results in one party, usually the woman, increasing the emphasis placed on household production. The parents may be tempted to share the responsibility for child rearing, but usually it is less costly to the couple for just one parent to alter his or her employment than for both to alter their employment. Higher-paying jobs often require unexpected overtime and travel. If both parents reject that type of employment, they may be worse off than if only one parent makes that choice. Lower average wages available to women make the mother the lower-cost provider of child rearing. Because that specialization may reduce her potential earnings later, the mother would rationally want a long-term agreement to protect herself from the potential costs of that decision. Although there are various reasons why men and women live together, the desire for children is probably the primary reason they marry.

ASYMMETRIC CONTRIBUTIONS

The incentive for couples to marry can be reinforced by the timing of their contributions to marriage that is strongly influenced by children. The contribution of the primary income-earning spouse, usually the man, often grows over time, while the contribution of the spouse who works at home, usually the woman, can decline after their children have grown. Over the duration of a marriage, the potential contributions of both spouses create the incentive that was the basis for the mutually advantageous exchanges that resulted in the parties' decision to marry, but the asymmetry of their contributions can create incentives in middle age for the income-earning spouse to dissolve their marriage (Cohen, 1987). After the children leave home, husbands may question why they continue to share their income with a woman who they may feel is not providing comparable value to the marriage.

The problems associated with this asymmetry have been recognized by economists in a business setting: when businesses specialize, they often arrange to protect themselves from other firms taking advantage of them through opportunistic behavior (Klein et al.,

1978). For example, a company might build a plant to produce a good that has value to only one buyer. After the construction of the plant, the buyer might be tempted to offer a price for the output of the plant that is only slightly higher than the direct cost of producing the good, a price inadequate to cover all the costs of production. The owner of the plant would be unhappy with that situation, but he would still be better off producing the good and receiving a price greater than the direct cost of production than not producing at all. When producers recognize that opportunistic behavior can occur, they require a long-term contract before the construction of the plant to guarantee a price that covers all its costs. In situations in which these long-term contracts are difficult to draft and enforce, companies have found it attractive to combine all activities within the same firm through vertical integration.

Similar opportunistic behavior can occur during a marriage. In recognition of the potential asymmetry of the timing of the parties' contributions during a marriage, the marriage laws in the United States have historically tried to create a long-term contract to protect the parties, usually women, who specialized in household production. Although the fault divorce laws did not define marriage as a long-term contract, the effect of the fault grounds for divorce was to turn marriage into a long-term arrangement in which a wife who specialized in household production could make that choice with the understanding that compensation would be required as an adjustment for the potential cost that she would incur if the marriage were dissolved.

Because the marriage agreement, even under fault divorce, was not easy to enforce, men and women have adapted to the problems associated with women specializing in household services in other ways. Lloyd Cohen argues that one way society has dealt with the value of the services provided by women in an earlier phase of marriage than those provided by men is reflected in the relative ages of spouses (Cohen, 1987). Women generally marry older men. The effect of this age gap is to make their contributions to marriage more contemporaneous, which increases the period during which women should expect to be widows but decreases the likelihood that their marriages will be dissolved. As the comparative advantages of men and women have been reduced and we find less specialization in marriage, the age gap between men and women at the time of their first marriage has decreased.

Economics thus provides an alternative explanation for marriage being associated with children. Often a man and a woman who are living together decide to marry only when the woman becomes pregnant. A common reason given for this decision is to make the child legitimate. Given the increase in children born to unmarried mothers, legitimacy clearly is not a universal concern. The economic explanation recognizes that the arrival of a child dramatically increases the incentives for one parent to increase his or her specialization in household production if the parents plan to remain together. This specialization has a potential cost to at least one parent for which a long-term marriage contract provides some protection. If the parents do not plan to remain together or the woman will not incur a significant loss in future earnings because of her working at home, then the parents have a smaller incentive to marry even if there is a child.

Before the broad availability of contraceptives, social mores tended to require marriage as a prerequisite for sexual relations. In that environment, sexual relations were almost guaranteed to result in children. If the couple was not married and did not marry, the children could become a burden on the mother and—given her limited employment opportunities—often on society. Society responded by placing a significant social stigma on premarital sex.

IS ECONOMIC ANALYSIS SEXIST?

The economists' emphasis on couple's gaining from marriage based on increased specialization due to comparative advantage can be interpreted as their condoning and encouraging a division of labor based on gender. The present analysis attempts to identify why certain patterns have existed rather than place a value judgment on a particular pattern. The traditional opportunities of men and women in the labor force and at home created incentives for men to increase their income-earning specialization during marriage, while women increased their domestic work specialization. Within this framework, the mother is the preferred provider of child care not because of any biological advantage but because her lower earnings often make her the lower-cost parent to provide those services. This specialization is not absolute. Married men often provide services around the house, and many married women work outside the home. During marriage, however, men and women have tended to increase their specialization compared with when they were single.

Because the goal of family members has been to increase their commodities, both forms of work have traditionally been important. Meals required money provided by the husband and time contributed by the wife. Both inputs were essential, so there was no hierarchy of values placed on the spouses' work. Recently it has become common to treat time spent earning an income as valuable and time expended on domestic work as much less worthy of respect. This may be a self-serving position taken by the more vocal members of society: men—especially married men—and working women. An extension of this thinking places the husband in a position of power in the family because of his increased specialization in income earning. Since married women are working longer hours at home and at a job as their income has risen, one has to question whether income is the source of power within a family. A better explanation of the husbands' power in the past is their greater physical strength rather than their income. Both spouses' work has been and will continue to be an important source of the family's well being.

As women's earnings and opportunities change, we would expect to observe a shift in the roles assumed by spouses during marriage. Over the past few decades, the earnings of women have increased compared with those of men, and the importance of children, measured by the number of children per family, has decreased. The two phenomena are related. Higher earnings available to women can increase the cost of children because of the forgone earnings caused by child-care responsibilities. The higher cost typically reduces the quantity demanded. As these opportunities change, we would expect more wives to become the primary income-earning spouse, while some husbands assume the primary responsibility for child rearing. Since there are gains from specialization, most families do not optimize their gains by dividing these obligations equally. Adults who do not want to specialize will often find marriage less attractive.

Marriage is an attractive institution for both spouses if both expect to be better off married than single. When women were confronted with low wages and limited employment opportunities, marriage with increased specialization in household production was a rational choice for essentially all adult women (Goldin, 1990). Because of women's willingness to specialize, marriage was also attractive for most men who often worked long hours at a job. This situation changed when wages and opportunities for women increased and the availability of domestic labor-saving devices rose. Higher wages increase the opportunity cost—a bigger house, a better car, and more restaurant meals—of the women working at home (Blau & Ferber, 1992). The labor-force participation rate of women rose. If both spouses increase the amount of time that they work outside the home, they reduce the specialization of labor that makes marriage attractive. Particularly important is the increase in the cost of children and a reduction in their demand, since traditionally the mother was the parent who adjusted a career to provide child care. The increase in the job opportunities for women has a potentially dramatic effect on the attraction of marriage by reducing specialization and the attraction of children. Many adults could rationally decide that they had little to gain from marriage (Glick & Spanier, 1980).

In summary, economists note that marriage and a family are not the only choices for adults. Because of economies of scale and specialization, people gain from living together but not necessarily from marrying. Marriage is usually associated with children who magnify the gains through economies of scale and especially specialization, so it has been a choice that traditionally increased most adults' welfare. Changes occur. The increase in women's wages and opportunities and the decline in the demand for children has reduced men's and women's comparative advantage and, therefore, the gains from marriage for some adults. While they date and live together, they have less to gain from marriage.

THE ECONOMIC ANALYSIS OF MARRIAGE DISSOLUTION

A major influence on the attraction of marriage and a family is the rules governing marriage, especially the conditions under which it can be dissolved. Changing conditions can affect the stability of marriage and the laws that control its dissolution. Marriage has become less stable, as evidenced by the increase in the divorce rate. From an economic perspective, a divorce occurs when at least one party after marriage decides that there is no distribution of the future output of that marriage that will make him or her better off compared with the opportunities outside that marriage. Two people marry when both anticipate they will be better off married than single, with the choice of a particular spouse the result of a search process. Sometimes the search that culminates in marriage does not produce the anticipated results. Changes in the anticipated gains from marriage can result from two situations: an unanticipated outcome or the asymmetry of the spouses' contributions.

The choice of an individual to marry is the result of a search that continues while the benefit exceeds the cost: the question is always whether the individual should accept a current candidate or look for a better one. While the expected benefit from continuing to search equals the probability of finding a better mate times the expected increase in welfare from that better mate, the cost of continuing to search for a better mate is the sum of the money, time, and emotional effort of searching plus any welfare forgone by remaining single rather than marrying an available mate. The welfare gains from marriage may be available from several potential spouses. Even after marriage, there can remain a question whether the current spouse is the best mate. The decision to marry a particular person is made with some uncertainty.

Divorce can be caused by the uncertain outcomes that can occur during marriage (Becker et al., 1977). People usually marry with the expectation that their marriage is a lifelong commitment, but at least one party can decide later that he or she would be better off outside that marriage. In the seminal work on this topic, Becker and his colleagues (1977, p. 1143) concluded that the probability of divorce depends on two factors: the expected gain from marriage and the distribution of the unexpected outcomes. The probability of divorce is smaller the greater the expected gain from marriage and the smaller the variability in the outcomes during marriage. People who do not want to specialize and do not appreciate the commodities made available by their spouse do not gain much from marriage. Even if they marry, the marriage is vulnerable. Alternatively, if a couple marries on the basis of certain expectations such as continued good health, a major change in the health of one spouse can increase the likelihood of divorce.

Certain factors have been identified as influencing the amount of the gains from marriage. The increase in specialization during marriage that often accompanies children—which I have already noted—reduces the probability of dissolution. The more people commit themselves to specialized roles, the more they gain from marriage and the more they lose from divorce. And, the more they find they are compatible with their present spouse, the more likely they are to choose to specialize. Less specialization during marriage increases the probability of divorce.

Other factors influence the success of the search process. A better search produces a more predictable outcome during marriage. The people who spend more time and energy on their search will be more likely to find the most desirable mate. For example, people who marry when they are younger than average have significantly higher probabilities of divorce. The amount of search will also vary with its cost. For example, the cost of search is higher in isolated areas than in urban areas.

A larger deviation between actual and expected outcomes during marriage, such as a significant change in the earnings or health of the spouses, will raise the probability of dissolution. This is less likely to occur when the spouses are better matched in attributes such as religion and education. A marriage is also less likely to be dissolved the longer it lasts because people usually discover their mistakes fairly early. People often repeat their mistakes, so the probability of dissolution is higher in subsequent marriages.

Another potential cause of divorce is the asymmetrical timing of the spouses' contributions during marriage, discussed above. During marriage, it has been common for the man to place more emphasis on earning income and for the woman to shift her emphasis toward the production of household commodities. Initially, both the husband and the wife are better off. When their children grow up and leave the home, the value to the man of the household commodities provided by this woman is reduced, even as the value of the market commodities that he brings to the marriage is likely to have increased. He may decide he is better off dissolving the marriage. The man's goal may not be to be single so much as to find a new and more desirable spouse at this point in his life. With a higher income, he may feel that the pool of potential mates is larger than when he first married. Of course, this outcome can also be the result of a flawed search. If the search for a spouse by a woman led her to expect this type of behavior from a man, she would have hesitated to marry him in the first place.

THE DECISION TO DIVORCE

Although uncertain outcomes and asymmetrical contributions can lead to a desire for a divorce, the ultimate decision to seek a divorce is influenced by a comparison of the cost and benefit of dissolving the marriage. The demand for divorce will increase as the cost falls or the benefit rises. One cost is the loss of the commodities produced by the ex-spouse. An additional cost is the emotional strain and financial transfer required to dissolve the marriage. When a spouse who does not want to dissolve the marriage has legal or social protection, part of the cost will be the incentives such as additional property or child custody necessary to convince that spouse not to exercise those rights. The cost shifts over time with changes in laws or social expectations. No-fault divorce significantly lowered the divorcing spouse's cost by reducing the legal protection of spouses who did not want to dissolve their marriage.

The incentive for women, who are more often adversely affected by divorce, to marry and specialize in household production during marriage is in part based on the expected compensation if their marriage is dissolved (Landes, 1978; Parkman, 1992a). Elizabeth Landes found that in states that prohibited alimony there was a lower rate of marriage and a reduced marital fertility rate than in states that did not restrict alimony awards. People marry with certain expectations. A change in the grounds for divorce has a different effect on people already married, under a presumption of the earlier laws, and on those who marry with the expectation that divorces will be governed by the new laws. Historically, women specialized in household production during marriage with the expectation that the fault grounds for divorce provided substantial protection against their marriage being dissolved against their will. A change in the grounds for dissolution came as a surprise to those married women who found themselves worse off after divorce than they would have been under fault divorce. Unmarried women contemplating marriage incorporate the new divorce laws in their decision making. They are less likely to marry and, if they do marry, to specialize in household production during marriage.

This analysis suggests that, while there are reasons for either spouse to want a divorce, the income-earning spouse, who is usually the husband, is the one who is most likely to gain from divorce. The evidence on the party who preferred a divorce, however, is mixed. Because of the negotiated settlements under fault divorce, it was not necessarily common for the filing spouse—usually the wife—to be the one who initiated the divorce. This anomaly resulted from a combination of the fault standards for alimony and the property settlement requiring the plaintiff to be "innocent" and chivalrous (Dixon & Weitzman, 1982).

With no-fault divorce, the filing party was more likely to be the initiating spouse. Dixon and Weitzman found that 22% of the divorces filed in 1968 under fault divorce in Los Angeles were filed by men; in 1977, under no-fault divorce, that figure rose to 36%, still not the majority of divorces. They found that husbands were more likely to file as the marriage lengthened and that husbands who were younger than their wives were more likely to file for divorce. Gunter and Johnson (1978) found that men filed for divorce in 29% of the fault divorce cases in a Florida county; this rose to 68% under no-fault divorce.

Direct evidence is also available on the party initiating the divorce in contrast to filing it. In a recent study by Maccoby and Mnookin (1992) of divorced parents, they find that two-thirds of the divorces were initiated by the wives. Their data from California are similar to those observed by Dixon and Weitzman.

The evidence does not lend strong support to the gains to husbands from divorce. Part of the explanation may lie with interpersonal dynamics within marriage. Goode (1956) argued that, even though it is typically the wife who first mentions divorce in cases of marital conflict, the husband usually was the first to desire it. His behavior, whether intentional or unconscious, may often follow a course that will lead the wife to see divorce as the most viable alternative. Others have pointed out that the prevailing expectation in the history of American divorce is for the man to assume the active role in the provocation for divorce but to take the passive role in the actual initiation of the procedures (Kephart, 1964). Although the issue of who initiates divorce is still subject to debate, few disagree with divorce being a disaster for many divorced women, especially those who were married for a long time.

In summary, people marry when both think that they will be better off married. They divorce when at least one spouse concludes that premise is not true. The legal grounds for divorce have a strong influence on the decision to dissolve the marriage because they influence the cost of divorce.

The Impact of No-Fault Divorce

Most adults continue to want children and generally view marriage as a long-term commitment, yet a major change in the law has reduced the incentives for adults to value family life and make a commitment to it. No-fault divorce has either augmented or replaced the fault grounds of adultery, desertion, and cruelty with incompatibility or irretrievable breakdown. No-fault divorce is both a reaction to the reduced incentives for people to marry and remain married and also a cause of that decline. The shift from fault to no-fault divorce was commonly viewed as desirable, because the new laws removed the hypocritical fault grounds (Weitzman, 1985). In many states, people who benefited from the change were at the forefront of the crusade for it: divorced men and career women. Meanwhile, since the effects have been subtle, those who have been adversely affected were not involved in the debate. Certainly, there was no involvement by economists, who would have recognized the impact of the changed incentives created by this fundamental change in the grounds for divorce.

The impact of no-fault divorce on the family continues to be subtle. Glenn and Weaver (1988) note that between 1972 and 1986 there was a decline in marital happiness without commenting on the change in the divorce grounds during that same period. Few people realize that the grounds for divorce affect their decisions about a family. At the same time, most people, especially women, are aware of the impoverishment of many divorced women and their children. While people may not understand why becoming a homemaker and mother has become more precarious, they know that it is a choice made at great risk. The impoverishment of these women can often be traced to no-fault divorce. Therefore, people are aware of the no-fault divorce's effect without having first-hand knowledge of the statutes themselves.

For most of the history of the United States, divorce—when allowed—was based on the concept of fault, with one spouse required to prove that the other spouse was responsible for the failure of the marriage on the basis of such grounds as adultery, cruelty, or desertion (Glendon, 1989). The legal grounds for divorce and the legal standards for the accompanying property division, alimony, and child support and custody were based on penalizing the party at fault. As divorce became more common, the likelihood increased that the parties had fabricated the evidence to establish those grounds. Under those circumstances, the divorce was often based on mutual consent, with the parties agreeing to their own financial and custodial arrangements. The process of fabrication was straightforward when both parties wanted a divorce. The spouses agreed to a settlement and the evidence necessary to establish the grounds. Then one party accepted the responsibility for the failure of the marriage.

This process became more complicated when only one party initially wanted a divorce. Since the plaintiffs in divorce actions had to be the "innocent party," they either had to have evidence of fault by their spouse or had to persuade their spouse to become the plaintiff in the divorce case. The divorcing spouses usually had to make substantial concessions to the divorced spouses to obtain their cooperation. Wive were often the spouses who initially opposed the divorce because of their increased specialization in household activities during marriage (Cohen, 1987). The concessions at divorce could be an increase in the property settlement, alimony, and child support and custody of the children. In reaching these agreements, the parties could essentially ignore the applicable laws. In a community property state, for example, wives were entitled by law to half the property acquired by the couple during the marriage. If the husband asked for a divorce, the wife could respond by demanding more than half the community property. For the fabricated divorces under the fault standards, the mutual consent of the spouses was far more important than the fault grounds and the legal standards for the arrangements at divorce. In essence, each spouse had a right to specific performance of a continuation of the marriage that could be waived—for compensation.

Even with the negotiating power provided by the fault grounds for divorce, injustices still occurred because some spouses were so humiliated or harassed that they did not use the protection available. Nothing is worse for someone's self-esteem than knowing that he or she is no longer loved. One reaction is to attempt to sever the relationship as soon as possible. The ability to thwart the divorce was often ignored by divorced spouses. The divorce represented their only opportunity to receive compensation for the services provided during the marriage often based on their sacrificed career. Alternatively, some spouses could be physically and psychologically harassed into cooperating in a divorce. Even with the problems of humiliation or harassment, it cannot be denied that fault divorce gave substantial power to a spouse who did not want a divorce. Whether the spouse exercised that power was up to him or her.

The introduction of no-fault divorce was a radical change in those procedures. California adopted the first unequivocal no-fault divorce statute in 1969 when it established irreconcilable differences and incurable insanity as the only grounds for divorce. During the next 16 years, the other 49 states, Puerto Rico, and the District of Columbia passed statutes that either made incompatibility and irretrievable breakdown the only grounds for divorce or added them to the existing fault grounds. In most states, no-fault divorce meant that a divorce could be obtained by just one spouse. The divorce settlement continued to be subject to outdated legal standards for the property division, alimony, and child support and custody. These laws usually provide for a return of any separate property, an equal division of narrowly defined marital property, short-term rehabilitative spousal support, and child custody and support. Typically ignored are many costs of divorce, such as sacrificed careers if a spouse had worked at home and the psychological costs incurred by the divorced spouse and the children.

No-fault divorce has created its own frustrations, because of the belated recognition of the power that the fault grounds gave to spouses who did not want to divorce. The no-fault grounds for divorce dramatically reduced the negotiating power of those people, which would be less important if the parties had not altered their activities because of the marriage. Such was not usually the case, since the benefits of marriage increase from the spouses' increasing their specialization. This specialization can result in costs for at least one spouse if the marriage is dissolved, costs that are not accurately reflected in the legally required arrangements at divorce since any restrictions that a spouse imposed on his or her career is seldom a basis for substantial compensation.

Recognizing these costs, individuals who might have assumed a primary role working at home during marriage have taken steps to protect themselves from the potential adverse effects of divorce. Married women, for example, have dramatically increased their work outside the home (Parkman, 1992a). It has been shown that more capable women have the most to lose from becoming a homemaker. In addition, married women are working more hours at home and at jobs outside the home (Parkman, 1994). Both these changes have made marriage less attractive for women and often for men.

REMEDIES FOR BREACH OF A CONTRACT

Because marriage has all the elements of a common-law contract— offer, acceptance, and consideration—a valuable technique for analyzing the shift from fault to no-fault divorce is to examine the effect of a move from specific performance to damages as the remedy for the breach of a contract. Contract remedies create incentives for parties to make decisions that increase social welfare (Posner, 1992). To an economist, the outcomes are efficient. When two parties enter into a contract, it is reasonable to assume that both expect to be better off because of the contracted transaction. Contracts that involve future activities can be subject to unforeseen changes. The normal remedy of damages confronts the parties with the option of either performing under the contract or paying damages. If the seller's costs rise so that the buyer can acquire the contracted goods from another source at a lower price than the seller's costs, society is better off if the buyer buys from the alternative source. The law requires the seller to compensate the buyer for the difference between the contract price and the price paid. Meanwhile, the supplier has avoided incurring the higher costs of production.

Specific performance is an alternative remedy that requires the parties to perform under the terms of the contract or face contempt of court. It is used as the remedy for the breach of a contract for unique goods such as real estate and it also encourages efficient outcomes (Kronman, 1978). Being a right rather than an outcome, it can be relinquished, usually for compensation. When a breach is worth more to the breaching party than performance is to the victim, specific performance creates incentives for the parties to reach a settlement that leaves them better off. Specific performance forces the parties to identify their costs and benefits from not performing. The costs associated with nonperformance when the good is unique are the value of the good to the buyer and the expense of finding an alternative. These costs usually cannot be estimated by anyone other than the parties, who have incentives to make that calculation to decide whether there is a basis for a negotiated settlement. Specific performance has the disadvantage that it can increase the costs of settlement negotiations, which are a deadweight loss since the costs incurred by one party do not confer benefits on the other.

Because the decision to dissolve a marriage (and therefore a family) involves costs and benefits, social welfare is improved when the remedies encourage divorce only when the net benefits are positive. The fault grounds for divorce provided the spouses with a legal right to specific performance of the marriage agreement, especially the right to certain standards of conduct and a continuation of the marriage. If a spouse breached the agreement by adultery, cruelty, or desertion, the innocent party could, but did not have to, sue for divorce. The spouses who committed the breach could not use their acts to initiate a divorce. If a spouse initiated a divorce based on the fault grounds and relied on the courts to decide the financial and custodial arrangements, the remedy was liquidated damages based on the reliance interest of the innocent spouse (Brining & Carbone, 1988). The actual divorce arrangements, however, were often more generous to the divorced spouse on the basis of private agreements ratified by the courts rather than independent determinations by them. Since the outcome was voluntary, one must conclude that the parties felt that it was preferable to any alternative: it was welfare enhancing.

A SHIFT TO LEGAL STANDARDS

With the introduction of no-fault divorce, the importance of private arrangements changed dramatically. In most states, one spouse could get a divorce without the agreement of the other. In contrast to the situation under the fault grounds, the financial and custodial arrangements at divorce were more likely to be based on the legal standards. It was unlikely that negotiated settlements would differ dramatically from what the parties could expect from litigation. Because of the increase in employment and marriage opportunities for divorced women, the courts under the reliance interest generally provided more limited awards for divorced women (Weitzman, 1985). Without any grounds for divorce, the parties who did not want a divorce were in a much weaker position to negotiate settlements that were a substantial improvement over the award that they could expect from litigation. At divorce, a spouse who worked at home during the marriage could expect to receive a property settlement that returned his or her separate property and gave him or her approximately half the tangible property acquired during the marriage, perhaps some rehabilitative support, and some child support until the children reached adulthood. In general, the effects of the marriage on the homemaker's career and any psychological costs are ignored. These arrangements are similar to liquidated damages under contract law.

The damage remedy for breach of contracts will produce excessive and inefficient breaches that reduce social welfare when the damages are less than the loss experienced by the nonbreaching party (Bishop, 1985). If the divorcing spouse is confronted with costs that are less than those of all affected parties, then the probability increases that a divorce will occur when the net benefits are negative. Under the Coase theorem, this would not occur when the costs and benefits consist of private goods that can be converted to common units (e.g., dollars) and transaction costs are zero (Coase, 1960). Under those circumstances, if the costs of a choice exceeded the benefits, the parties have an incentive to negotiate an outcome that rejects the choice. However, the benefits of marriage and the costs of divorce may be public goods, valued in heterogeneous units, and the transaction costs associated with divorce can be substantial (Parkman, 1993; Zelder, 1993). The losses experienced by the divorced spouse, especially one who increased his or her specialization in household production during marriage, and any children are often underestimated (Parkman, 1987). The probability increases that a divorce will occur when the net benefits to all affected parties are negative: the divorce reduced social welfare.

Recognizing the reduction in the protection provided investments in increased specialization in domestic work, the spouse who would normally have assumed that role became more reluctant to assume it, which in turn reduced the gains from marriage and a family for all parties. Fewer people married, and among those who did marry the likelihood increased that they would find that marriage did not increase their welfare. Marriage and a family became less attractive and less stable.

In summary, changes in basic economic conditions have worked to reduce the attraction of family life to some adults. Usually, their decisions to delay or refrain from marriage have increased social welfare. Some people reacted to these changes by advocating more flexible grounds for divorce. The result was the change in the divorce grounds from fault to no fault in all states. Unfortunately, this shift has created substantial, unintended results, the most important of which is the reduction in incentives for people to make choices during marriage with potential long-term costs that have reduced the attraction of marriage and family life. With the no-fault divorce laws, it is potentially costly for spouses to sacrifice opportunities to increase or maintain their marketable skills so as to emphasize domestic work during marriage. This change in attitude makes marriage less attractive to both men and women.

The Alternative to No-Fault Divorce

If no-fault divorce has had such a perverse effect on families, what alternatives would encourage family formation? The most important incentive for family formation is protection for long-term commitments. No-fault divorce provides little protection for this commitment. Although there has been some dissatisfaction with no-fault divorce (Kay, 1990; Weitzman, 1985), alternative grounds for divorce have not received much attention (Parkman, 1992b). Further reflection reveals that there are compelling reasons for considering the agreement of both spouses—mutual consent—as a basis for divorce. The incorporation of compensation for a sacrificed career into the property considered at divorce would still not recognize all the costs incurred by divorced spouses and their children, since many of these costs are difficult to estimate and the spouses' situations may be unique. Specific performance is the preferred remedy for breaches of contracts involving unique items, mainly because of the problems associated with estimating damages under such circumstances. Social welfare might be improved by making the dissolution of marriage subject to specific performance as well. The effect would be to limit divorces to situations involving mutual agreement by the spouses. Then a divorce would only occur when the collective benefits exceeded the costs. Although the divorced spouse may have initially preferred the continuation of the marriage, a compensation package of property and child custody may be possible that would increase his or her welfare compared with any alternative arrangement, given the preferences of the divorcing spouse.

THE COST OF DIVORCE

Mutual consent would increase the incentives for the spouses to recognize and value the benefits and costs of divorce, including both financial and psychological factors. Some divorce costs that go beyond the sacrificed human capital that are currently ignored under no-fault divorce are lost companionship, the search for a new spouse or companions, and the disruption in the lives of the children. The fact that the divorcing spouse no longer wants to be married to the divorced spouse usually reduces the value the divorced spouse places on his or her companionship, but that companionship may retain substantial value to the divorced spouse lost if the marriage is dissolved.

Divorce also imposes a search cost on the divorced spouse. The marriage was the result of a search process by the spouses. At divorce, the divorcing spouses have decided that they want out of their current marriage. This choice might mean that they are no longer interested in being married to anyone, although it is common for divorced people to remarry. The divorcing spouses may have decided that their costs of searching for a new spouse will be low or zero. Some middle-aged men feel that their experience and higher income make them more attractive mates than when they were younger. They believe that with limited searches they can find a better mate than their current spouse. Of course, sometimes, they have already located this alternative spouse and their search costs are zero. No matter whether the divorcing spouses incur new search costs, they impose costs of a new search on the divorced spouses. For some divorced spouses seeking a new mate, the costs of these new searches are so high that they never remarry. These search costs recognize that one cost of marriage and divorce is the sacrificed opportunity to have married someone else earlier. Even if the divorced spouse has no desire to remarry, there are costs in establishing a social life that compares favorably to the marriage.

A major cost of divorce is imposed on the children. The courts attempt to recognize the financial costs of divorce on the children, but other costs to the children are often ignored. Clearly, it is not in the best interest of the children to force antagonistic parents to live together, but there are situations in which the parents do not hate each other but are no longer as strongly attracted to each other as they once were. The children would be much better off in this environment than being shuffled between the parents. The cost of the divorce to children is often underestimated by the divorcing spouse, who usually sees the children as well adjusted to the new situation. This is especially a problem if the new household has only one parent.

Mutual-consent divorce forces the parents to address the costs incurred by their children because of divorce. These costs go far beyond just maintenance, which is covered by child support. If the divorcing spouses are forced to recognize the full costs of their divorce, some parents could probably make their marriage work and thereby provide benefits to their children. The parents, usually the mothers, who expect custody of the children after divorce are most likely to recognize the costs that the children will incur. If the children are less happy after divorce, their attitudes will influence the welfare of the custodial parent. These changes in the welfare of the children and of the custodial parent are costs. The custodial parent has incentives to consider these costs when deciding to divorce. These companionship, search, and children's costs would be difficult for anyone other than the spouses to estimate and include in any award at divorce.

Mutual consent is not a perfect solution. Like specific performance, it can result in excessive performance if one party wants to ignore the costs of performance, which can occur when a spouse—

basing a decision on spite—is opposed to a divorce under any circumstances. Economists have noted the fundamental rationality of individuals' decisions even when dealing with emotional issues such as marriage and divorce. In most divorces, at least one spouse initially wanted the marriage to continue (Wallerstein & Kelly, 1980), but when the collective benefits of divorce exceed the costs, social welfare is increased by a divorce. Under those circumstances, the parties have incentives to construct an agreement that leaves them both better off. The large number of divorces based on mutual consent under the fault grounds illustrates the willingness of spouses to negotiate even under trying conditions.

This point can be illustrated by two examples. A husband who did not initiate the divorce may feel that he is no longer strongly attracted to his spouse, he can find a living situation just as attractive with a limited amount of effort, and his children would not be adversely affected by a divorce. He might therefore be willing to reach a divorce agreement at a small cost to the party who initially wanted the divorce. Social welfare would be improved by allowing the divorce. Alternatively, he might still be strongly attracted to his spouse, feel that only a long and costly search would find another comparable spouse or situation, and believe that his children would suffer in comparison with the quality of life that is still possible if the parents stay together. He might under those circumstances ask for a level of compensation that the other spouse is unwilling to pay. In other words, the party who wants the divorce does not value the divorce as much as the other spouse and the children value the continuation of the marriage. In this case, social welfare is improved by continuing the marriage.

A ROLE FOR FAULT DIVORCE

Fault grounds for divorce may still serve a useful purpose when someone is "driven out" of a marriage instead of than "wanting out." Mutual consent would not provide a solution for the situation in which one spouse is the victim of acts such as cruelty or adultery but the "guilty" spouse does not want a divorce. Courts during the era of fault divorce showed little skill, however, at deciding these cases. Often the grounds given for fault divorce were hypocritical and the marriage had failed for other reasons. And even when the fault grounds could be proved, the reasons a marriage failed were probably much more complicated than just the acts that established the grounds. Even when the grounds for divorce are mutual consent, the spouses cannot be forced to live together. Subject to financial obligations to the other spouse and the children, a spouse who felt that he or she was being driven out of a marriage could leave the other spouse. The spouse who left just could not marry another person. Because of these concerns, however, fault grounds such as cruelty and desertion based on a high standard such as clear and convincing evidence could be added to mutual consent as a basis for divorce.

A ROLE FOR NO-FAULT DIVORCE

Mutual-consent divorce gives substantial power to spouses who do not want a divorce. To limit abuse of this power, it might be attractive to allow no-fault divorce when the potential costs of divorce are likely to be low, as they usually are early in a marriage and when there are no children. Therefore, no-fault divorce might be allowed during the first year of marriage or until the wife becomes pregnant, whichever comes first. Later, divorce would only be granted on the basis of mutual consent or fault.

If people considering marriage knew that mutual consent was the only, or one of several, grounds for divorce, that knowledge might increase the incentive for them to negotiate premarital or postmarital agreements. Neither fault divorce nor no-fault divorce provided marrying individuals with the opportunity to construct their own grounds for the dissolution of their marriage. With mutual-consent divorce, the dissolution of marriage would be based on the parties' criteria rather than those of the state. Under those circumstances, the parties might be more inclined to specify their own grounds at the time of marriage. For example, some might feel that adultery should be a ground for dissolution, but others might not.

The important thing to recognize about mutual-consent divorce is its ability to encourage the long-term commitment that has traditionally generated the gains from marriage. It would increase the potential costs of divorce encouraging people to approach marriage with more care. Because it would make marriage more attractive for people who want to make it a long-term commitment, the marriage rate could increase and the quality of marriage and family life should improve.

Conclusion

The family has always served a central role in all societies. It is not an absolute, however, but the result of people making welfare-enhancing decisions. Along with the desire for companionship and sexual attraction, most adults have found marriage attractive because it increases their welfare because of their increased specialization. This specialization has been based on the parties' comparative advantage, with men traditionally increasing their specialization outside the home and women inside the home. The increase in the opportunities outside the home for women and men inside has reduced the comparative advantage of men and women and, therefore, the gains from specialization for some people. This is especially true because children have become more expensive based on sacrificed earnings and, therefore, less attractive. To the extent that fewer marriages are a response to the reduced net benefits of marriage, social welfare has been increased. The change in the divorce grounds from fault to no fault has had an additional and detrimental effect on the attraction of marriage. The costs of divorce have been decreased, often resulting in one in which the net benefits to all affected parties are negative. These divorces reduce social welfare. This potential outcome for marriage has dynamic effects as people become less willing to commit themselves financially and psychologically to a relationship that would benefit from that commitment. Couples cannot alter the marriage agreement imposed on them by statute and, therefore, they cannot create a long-term legal commitment. The decline in the attraction of marriage and a family due to no-fault divorce has reduced social welfare. A combination of mutual consent, fault, and no-fault grounds as the basis for the dissolution of mature marriages would increase social welfare by encouraging people to make a long-term commitment to their marriage.

NOTE

1. The data used here are contained in the *Statistical Abstract of the United States* for various years. The *Abstract* provides citations to the original sources.

REFERENCES

Becker, G. S. (1965). A theory of the allocation of time. *Economic Journal, 75,* 493–517.
Becker, G. S. (1976). *The economic approach to human behavior.* Chicago: University of Chicago Press.
Becker, G. S. (1991). *A treatise of the family* (enlarged ed.). Cambridge MA: Harvard University Press.
Becker, G. S., Landes, E. M., & Michael, R. (1977). An analysis of marital instability. *Journal of Political Economy, 85,* 1141–1187.
Bishop, W. (1985). The choice of remedy for breach of contract. *Journal of Legal Studies, 14,* 299–320.
Blau, F. D., & Ferber, M. A. (1992). *The economics of women, men, and work* (2nd ed.). Englewood Cliffs NJ: Prentice-Hall.
Brinig, M. F., & Carbone, J. (1988). The reliance interest in marriage and divorce. *Tulane Law Review, 62,* 855–905.
Coase, R. H. (1960). The problem of social costs. *Journal of Law & Economics, 3,* 3–44.
Cohen, L. (1987). Marriage, divorce, and quasi rents; or, "I gave him the best years of my life." *Journal of Legal Studies, 6,* 267–304.
Coontz, S. (1992). *The way we never were.* New York: Basic.
Dixon, R. B., & Weitzman, L. J. (1982). When husbands file for divorce. *Journal of Marriage and the Family, 44,* 103–115.
Fuchs, V. R. (1983). *How we live: An economic perspective on Americans from birth to death.* Cambridge MA: Harvard University Press.
Glendon, M. A. (1989). *The transformation of family law.* Chicago: University of Chicago Press.
Glenn, N. D., & Weaver, C. N. (1988). The changing relationship of marital status to reported happiness. *Journal of Marriage and the Family, 50,* 317–324.
Glick, P. C., & Spanier, G. B. (1980). Married and unmarried cohabitation in the United States. *Journal of Marriage and the Family, 42,* 19–30.
Goldin, C. (1990). *Understanding the gender gap.* New York: Oxford University Press.
Goode, W. J. (1956). *Women in divorce.* New York: Free Press.
Gunter, B. G., & Johnson, D. P. (1978). Divorce filing as role behavior: Effect of no-fault law on divorce filing patterns. *Journal of Marriage and the Family, 40,* 571–574.

Kay, H. H. (1990). Beyond no-fault: New directions in divorce reform. In S. D. Sugarman & H. H. Kay (Eds.), *Divorce reform at the crossroads* (pp. 6–36). New Haven CT: Yale University Press.

Kephart, W. M. (1964). *The family, society, and the individual.* Boston: Houghton-Mifflin.

Klein, B., Crawford, R. G., & Alchian, A. A. (1978). Vertical integration, appropriable rents, and the competitive contracting process. *Journal of Law and Economics, 21,* 297–326.

Kronman, A. T. (1978). Specific performance. *University of Chicago Law Review, 45,* 351–382.

Lancaster, K. (1966). A new approach to consumer theory. *Journal of Political Economy, 74,* 132–157.

Landes, E. M. (1978). Economics of alimony. *Journal of Legal Studies, 7,* 35–63.

Maccoby, E. E., & Mnookin, R. H. (1992). *Dividing the child.* Cambridge MA: Harvard University Press.

O'Neill, J. (1990). Women and wages. *American Enterprise, 1*(6), 25–33.

Parkman, A. M. (1987). Human capital as property in divorce settlements. *Arkansas Law Review, 40,* 439–467.

Parkman, A. M. (1992a). Unilateral divorce and the labor-force participation rate of married women, revisited. *American Economic Review, 82,* 671–678.

Parkman, A. M. (1992b). *No-fault divorce: What went wrong?* Boulder CO: Westview.

Parkman, A. M. (1993). Reform of the divorce provisions of the marriage contract. *BYU Journal of Public Law, 8,* 91–106.

Parkman, A. M. (1994). *Why are married women working so hard?* Unpublished manuscript.

Popenoe, D. (1994). Family decline and scholarly optimism. *Family Affairs, 6,* 9–10.

Posner, R. A. (1992). *Economic analysis of law* (4th ed.). Boston: Little, Brown.

Skolnick, A. (1991). *Embattled paradise.* New York: Basic.

Stacey, J. (1990). *Brave new families.* New York: Basic Books.

Wallerstein, J. S., & Kelly, J. B. (1980). *Surviving the breakup.* New York: Basic.

Weitzman, L. J. (1985). *The divorce revolution.* New York: Free Press.

Yorburg, B. (1983). *Families and societies* (rev. ed.). New York: Columbia University Press.

Zelder, M. (1993). Inefficient dissolutions as a consequence of public goods: The case of no-fault divorce. *Journal of Legal Studies, 22,* 503–520.

Community, Family, and the Social Good: The Psychological Dynamics of Procedural Justice and Social Identification

Tom R. Tyler
University of California, Berkeley
Peter Degoey
University of California, Berkeley

My fellow Americans, we can cut the deficit, create jobs, promote democracy around the world, pass welfare reform and health care, pass the toughest crime bill in history, but still leave too many of our people behind. . . . Our problems go way beyond the reach of government. They're rooted in the loss of values, in the disappearance of work and the breakdown of our families and our communities. . . . So I say to you tonight, let's give our children a future. Let us teach them to obey the law, respect our neighbors, and cherish our values.
—President Bill Clinton, State of the Union Address, 1994

President Bill Clinton's remarks suggest that social values are important to the attainment of societal objectives. Like President Clinton, many Americans believe that it is important to nurture the types of social values that they believe will lead individuals to want to act in the interests of their society—to behave in a socially responsible manner. But are social values important in the promotion of social good? Economists have argued they are not and have focused instead on changing behavior through the use of incentive mechanisms. This chapter argues that social values are, in fact, important.

How can social values contribute to the social good? President Clinton identifies two arenas in which social values play an important role: the community and the family. Community psychologists have addressed the issue of social good in the community mainly by focusing on the design of alternative strategies to improve the quality of life for the disadvantaged (Chavis, 1993; Levine & Perkins, 1987). Social good in families has been predominantly investigated by family psychologists interested in the use of therapy in the prevention of family breakdowns (Kaslow, 1990).

In this chapter, we attempt to tie these disparate approaches to the promotion of social good together by viewing the dynamics of social good through a social-psychological lens. In doing so, we respond to the current recognition by community and family psychologists that social psychology can provide them with the strong theoretical base to further their respective disciplines (Kaslow, 1991; Levine & Perkins, 1987). But more important, we believe that a "boundary-spanning approach" (Masters & Yarkin-Levin, 1984) to studying the dynamics of social good in both communities and families can further the science of social psychology as well. Two studies will be presented that explore our ideas.

Concern for the Social Good in Community and Family

The first setting we will consider from a social-psychological perspective is communities in the midst of resource shortages. Such communities are the focus of the literature on social dilemmas. Most social scientists, including both economists and psychologists, have stipulated that, in social-dilemma situations, self-interested actors are presented with an interesting paradox. Each community member has an individual incentive to act in his or her short-term self-interest and maximize his or her use of a scarce communal resource, but all members are better off if they refrain from doing so and instead act in their community's and/or their own long-term interests (Dawes, 1980; Edney, 1980; Messick & Brewer, 1983).

The classic example of a social-dilemma situation is the "tragedy of the commons" identified by Hardin (1968). In that hypothetical situation, self-interested farmers each increased the number of sheep they placed in a common community pasture until the pasture was overgrazed and eventually destroyed, leading to the death of many sheep. Recent examples of real-world social dilemmas are scarcities of water and fresh air, problems of traffic congestion, and the depletion of the ozone layer. Resource scarcities have been widely studied in laboratory as well as natural settings (see Martin, 1989, for a bibliography of more than 5,000 case studies).

How can communities effectively deal with social dilemmas? One way is for community members to voluntarily take individual, helping actions—an *individual*-level solution to social dilemmas. For example, in communities threatened by scarcities, people can exercise individual restraint—using less water, food, and/or gasoline. The suggestion that such voluntary efforts can be central to the maintenance of social good is also contained in political statements, such as President George Bush's suggestion that the United States benefits from "one thousand points of light"—to wit, individual people working to help their communities.

Our concern in this discussion is with a second, more social, type of responsibility—deferring to the collective decisions of the group. This is a *social* solution to social dilemmas. Collective decision-making structures, such as authority structures, rules, and sanction systems, are key features of groups ranging from the highly formalized and hierarchical legal and political system, through less structured managerial authority systems, to the more informal authority structures found in families. Collective decision-making structures regulate the behaviors of group members.

In the social-dilemma literature, collective decision-making structures have mainly been examined in terms of people's willingness to create group authorities (Messick et al., 1983; Rutte & Wilke, 1984; Samuelson, 1991; Samuelson & Messick, 1986a, 1986b, in press; Samuelson et al., 1984; Wit, 1989). The creation of authorities, however, is not a magical solution to group problems. Typically, people are sensitive to the efforts of others to control or restrict their behaviors and will resist the influence of external rules or structures on their lives (Thibaut & Walker, 1975). Hence, it is important to examine the conditions under which community members will pledge their support to authorities. The antecedents of people's willingness to defer collective decision-making powers to group authorities are the focus of this analysis.

While our comments have focused directly on communities in times of conflict, they also apply to family settings. Irrespective of their degree of formality and hierarchy, authorities are strongly dependent on the cooperation of group members (Tyler & Lind, 1992; Yamagishi, 1988). A focus on family dynamics, especially in times of conflict, is crucial because of their recognized centrality to the development of social values that may underlie both individual and social actions for the collective good. Attachment theorists, for example, have argued that the quality of interactions between caregivers and infants in stressful situations become coded into "working models" of relationships that determine to a large degree how people interact with others over time (Bowlby, 1988; Bretherton, 1985). Respect for rules in the family and a willingness to resolve family conflicts in a mutually beneficial manner have also been recognized as important precursors to obedience to rules in adolescent and adult life—that is, to accepting social solutions to social problems. Family dynamics, for example, have been found to have an important effect on crime and juvenile delinquency (Wilson, 1993). Hence, the second setting that will be considered from a social-psychological perspective is families in times of conflict.

The Legitimacy of Authorities

In democratic societies, voluntary compliance is crucial to the success of authorities. People must take on the obligation to obey authorities themselves. They may accept authority, but they do so reluctantly. Studies of organized groups suggest that support for authority structures is a dynamic process in which choices among forms of authority are continuously modified and that group authorities often have difficulty maintaining the support necessary to facilitate compliance with the rules they create (Buckley et al., 1974; Edney & Harper, 1978). Similar concerns apply to both community and family settings. In both settings, people resist the restriction of their behavior by authorities.

One key factor enhancing the likelihood of the voluntary acceptance of authority is views about the legitimacy of authorities. Authorities viewed as legitimate are better able to secure voluntary compliance with rules (Tyler, 1990) and are more likely to be able to maintain group support for their actions (Kelley & Mirer, 1974).

A review of the extant literature on authority-follower relations indicates that several aspects of legitimacy are important (Tyler, 1990). First, people's feelings of trust in the competence and honesty of authorities may contribute to a willingness to contribute to the social good. Second is people's willingness to voluntarily accept the decisions made by authorities. Finally, a third important aspect of legitimacy involves feelings of obligation to follow rules that the authorities implement. Research suggests that each of these aspects of legitimacy is linked to actual behavior (Tyler, 1990; Tyler & Lind, 1992), with people who feel that an authority is more legitimate actually deferring to that authority to a greater degree.

The Antecedents of Legitimacy of Authorities

INSTRUMENTAL COMPLIANCE STRATEGIES

One approach to gaining legitimacy is instrumental. Authorities seek to shape the behavior of group members by altering the rewards and punishments associated with resource use. In experimental studies, rewarding actions that benefit group interests and punishing those that do not have been shown to be effective in influencing individual behaviors (Yamagishi, 1986). Kelman (1958) labels these actions "compliance" effects.

Despite their theoretical possibility, the actual implementation of compliance strategies has proved to be problematic in real communities and real social dilemmas (Yamagishi, 1988). To implement compliance strategies, communities must have resources available to enforce the rewarding and sanctioning of individual behaviors. Paradoxically, such resources are least likely to be available when they are most needed—that is, in times of resource scarcity and social conflict (Tyler, 1990). In the case of the 1975 oil crisis, for example, the economic problems developing from the resource scarcity limited the ability of the government to mobilize additional economic resources to develop solutions for the problem (Sears et al., 1978).

A second approach to altering the payoff structure of self-interested behaviors in social-dilemma situations is instituting what is referred to as a "market" system of community-resource management. Freeing the price of a scarce community resource will manipulate public demand to match the available supply of that resource. For example, a community might induce a lower rate of power consumption by raising the price of electricity during peak hours or in times of scarcity until demand and supply are equal.

Unfortunately, research has shown that price changes alone will not lead directly to efficient resource consumption (Phillips & Nelson, 1976). Furthermore, regulating or restricting individual access to a common community resource is often impractical or impossible, a situation labeled the "nonexcludability" of a public good (see Weimer & Vining, 1992). Resistance to market solutions in public-good shortages is also often high because of feelings that a basic right to access to common community resources is jeopardized for groups lacking in money, such as the poor and/or minorities.

In other words, not only are short-term self-interested behaviors on the part of individuals problematic in social-dilemma situations, but community strategies aimed at influencing the payoff of such behaviors are problematic as well. If nothing else, practical issues have complicated the implementation of such strategies and suggest the need for other mechanisms. Beyond these practical problems, an increasingly large literature is developing that questions the self-interested model of human motivation on theoretical grounds (see Mansbridge, 1990).

Incentive-based behavior has also been explored within other settings, such as the family. This literature begins with the writings of behaviorists (Skinner, 1953, Watson, 1924) and is more broadly found in the literatures on learning theory and, within policy studies, in literature on deterrence (see Gibbs, 1975, 1986; Melton & Saks, 1986, Zimring & Hawkins, 1973). In these literatures scholars argue that people are influenced by the incentives within their environment.

Learning theory has been under increasing attack for saying little about how individuals function in a complex, social environment (Bronfenbrenner, 1979). Furthermore, the intensive resource demands required for continual monitoring and rewarding of behavior produce the same type of strain on informal groups such as the family as that produced on larger social groups. Within the family the inadequacies of learning models are illustrated by their inability to explain the development of social values, while the high rate of teenage pregnancy illustrates that, although children's behavior may be controllable while they are in their homes, behavior in peer-group contexts is typically not effectively monitored and depends on the children's personal values, beliefs, and feelings.

In both community and family settings, then, the instrumental approach has been found to be limited in value, both on practical and theoretical grounds. As a consequence, psychologists have focused on social motivations for behavior. This chapter suggests two social mechanisms through which concern for the social good—and the legitimacy of authority—can be enhanced: identification with a social group and the perceived fairness in which group authorities make decisions.

SOCIAL IDENTIFICATION

The question of how people develop social motivations is hardly a new one within psychology. In his classic discussion of human motivation, Freud (1960) argued that a core issue in socialization is understanding how people develop social motivations to control the operation of self-interest. Freud coined the concept of the "superego," an internalization of and identification with the values of authority figures. He suggested that the development of the superego reflects the need for restraints on more primary motivations of individuals to act in their self interest. As William Damon notes: "Classic Freudian theory . . . holds that morality is a necessary part of civilized social living . . . but that submission to moral standards will inevitably conflict with some deep inclinations of the self" (Damon, 1984, p. 110).

Social motives have recently been similarly emphasized in discussions of families in crisis and the origins of crime and juvenile delinquency (Wilson, 1993). Such social motives do not develop out of incentive-based strategies (Rushton, 1980) but through a capacity "for being affected by the feelings of others" (Wilson, 1993, p. 30). Similarly, theories on attachment developed by Bowlby (1982) suggest the importance of having a strong and affectionate emotional bond between children and parents for social interactions later in life. Strong identification with moral values and beliefs have also been linked, for example, to the willingness of Christians to rescue Jews during World War II (London, 1970, Oliner & Oliner, 1988), and to participation in the civil-rights movement (Rosenhan, 1970).

The psychology of attachment to communities has been investigated under the rubric of social identification. Social-psychological theories such as social-identity theory (Tajfel, 1978) and self-categorization theory (Turner et al., 1987) propose that people who identify with groups develop psychological attachments to them and internalize the groups' values and goals into their self-concepts. These attachments alter the basis of their attitudes and behaviors. In particular, people become motivated to act on behalf of their group (Tyler & Dawes, 1993). Studies show that, when individuals identify with a community, they tend to engage in cooperative behavior in social-dilemma situations (Brewer, 1979; Brewer & Kramer, 1986; Dawes & Thaler, 1988; Dawes et al., 1988, 1990; Edney, 1980; Kramer & Brewer, 1984, 1986; Tyler & Dawes, 1993; Wit, 1989).

This identity perspective of the social good can again be contrasted with an instrumental view. It has also been suggested that group-oriented behaviors in social-dilemma situations are influenced by people's expectations about whether other community members will reciprocate restraint in the use of a scarce resource (Brann & Foddy, 1988; Brewer, 1981; Brewer & Kramer, 1986; Kramer & Goldman, 1988; Kramer et al., 1989; Messick et al., 1983). Identification with a community and expectations of reciprocity do not represent similar psychological concerns. The former reflects an emotional bond that people feel toward their community, while the latter may reflect an instrumental concern that people feel about the probable consequences of their behavior. However, they are both aspects of a sense of belonging to a community. Similarly, identification with one's parents and the belief that they would help one in times of need are two aspects of the sense of belonging to a family.

Whether social identification also leads to greater feelings of the legitimacy of group authorities has not been previously examined. However, some social-identity researchers have acknowledged that "the leader [or authority] is the individual who is the best exemplar of all the group's characteristics and thus best represents the group, or *is* the group" (Hogg & Abrams, 1988, p. 114, italics in original). In other words, social identification may act as a motivation to support a group authority because that authority often acts as a representative of groups.

PROCEDURAL JUSTICE OF GROUP AUTHORITIES

In contrast to the influence on authority legitimacy of informal connections between individuals and the groups to which they belong, views about legitimacy may also be influenced by the more formal aspects of authority structures within groups. These aspects are the subject of the procedural-justice literature, which demonstrates that people's reactions to rules and decisions are affected by the manner in which those rules and decisions are made and communicated (Tyler & Lind, 1992). People are more willing to obey decisions made on behalf of the group if those decisions are made in ways viewed as fair. Hence, authorities gain legitimacy through the actions that they take—if those actions are judged to be fair.

Procedural-justice evaluations have been found to influence the perceived legitimacy of authorities in legal (Tyler, 1984, 1990), political (Tyler & Caine, 1981; Tyler et al., 1985), and managerial (Alexander & Ruderman, 1987; Folger & Konovsky, 1989) settings. They have also been found to affect people's willingness to voluntarily accept the decisions made by authorities in those settings (see Lind & Tyler, 1988). Similarly, procedural justice is a key antecedent of rule-following behavior (Tyler, 1990). Finally, previous studies have found that people continue to care about procedural justice even when authorities' decisions are of substantial importance to them. Procedural justice is the key antecedent of willingness to accept decisions among people who are involved in lawsuits over large amounts of money (Lind et al., 1991), and among people who face the risk of substantial prison terms (Casper et al., 1988).

Little research has been conducted that explores the link between the legitimacy of authority and procedural justice in family settings. Wilson (1993), however, suggests that the human sense of justice has its "source in the parent-child relationship, wherein a concern for fair shares, fair play, and fair judgments arises out of the desire to bond with others" (p. 70). The conclusions of the procedural-justice literature also have their roots in earlier literatures. Piaget's (1965) idea of moral autonomy, for example, is built on the suggestion that children learn about justice by finding that long-term interactions can only be maintained when everyone involved adheres to common rules of fair conduct. The Freudian idea of "value internalization" also suggests that people's sense of self is linked to adhering to ethical and societal values. At least one empirical study supports the suggestion that interpersonal relationships among adults are governed by a need for procedurally fair behavior (Barrett-Howard & Tyler, 1986). Other studies suggest that parental fairness is related to psychological well-being and self-esteem in young adulthood (Joubert, 1991; Roberts & Bengton, 1993).

COMPARISONS BETWEEN COMMUNITY AND FAMILY SETTINGS

This chapter suggests that both identification with a group and the perceived procedural fairness of authorities that operate within a group will matter in the community and family arenas. The two domains differ in many ways, however, and one way to view these differences is the type of relationship that exists between group members, the group authority, and the group itself.

First, consider the domain of families. The nature of social relations within families has long been recognized by psychologists to be a key antecedent of social motivations. Inspired by Freud, a vast literature on socialization has examined the development of identification with and internalization of common group norms and values that lead children to be concerned about others. Identification and internalization refer to an emotional and cognitive connection between people on the basis of their judgment that others share similar values and goals. Identification and internalization of commonly held values can be said to produce "trust" in social relations: participants in the social relationship can be expected to behave in predictable, mutually beneficial ways.

Because social bonds are strong in family settings, it is predicted that identification will play an especially important role in family support for authorities (typically parents). In community settings emotional bonds are less clear. Moreover, similarity in terms of values and goals is also less clearly defined in the community, which suggests that identification will be less able to produce trust in community settings than in family settings. In other words, when individuals move in the life course from being a family member to being a community member, alternative sources of trust in social relations need to be found.

The views about the fairness of the procedures used by community authorities are one alternative source of legitimacy and trustworthiness. Zucker (1986) suggests that the production of trust in economic exchanges has moved from traditional connections between individuals with extensive personal connections and knowledge of each other to institutional arrangements and formalized social structures. This change mirrors the transition of individuals from family to community settings over the life course.

Although Zucker (1986) does not directly address the issue of procedural fairness, she does suggest that institutional arrangements, with clearly defined procedural norms and rules of conduct, have supplanted personal relations as a source of trust. Shapiro (1987) also suggests that societies can control trust relationships that are not embedded in personal relationships by creating authorities constrained by procedural norms. One such procedural norm is the fairness of decision-making procedures. Arts and van der Veen (1992, p. 163) make the connection between procedural justice and institutional arrangements more explicit in an examination of the work of Max Weber. They suggest Weber argued that "the question of which rules, procedures and organizations are used to guarantee justice in society"—procedural justice—"is the central issue" in the study of bureaucratic administration. Hence, we predict that procedural justice is particularly important in the community setting. The perceived fairness in which procedures are carried out may provide information about the trustworthiness of authorities. Because of the diffuse nature of community membership (individual group members may freely choose to exit or join a community), we expect social identification to have a relatively lesser influence on support for authority in that setting.

Empirical Studies

CONTEXTS OF THE STUDIES

The social dilemma we will discuss is a naturally occurring one—the California water shortage. As a consequence of population growth, the politics of water distribution (Kahrl, 1982; Reisner, 1986), and five years of drought, California experienced widespread water shortages in 1991. These shortages forced many areas of the state to enact water conservation measures, ranging from voluntary guidelines to mandatory use restrictions, enforced by heightened price rates for overuse and, in some cases, fines for water misuse. The study was conducted in San Francisco, whose residents were engaged in voluntary efforts to conserve water as well as being subjected to regulations imposed by a locally appointed water authority, the Public Utilities Commission (for a more detailed discussion of the study, see Tyler and Degoey, 1994).

In addition, we extend our analysis of mechanisms that facilitate social good within the family. Families differ from a community in the midst of a social dilemma in several ways. First, it is less clear that family members lose from self-interested behavior. The particular irony of social dilemmas is that social actors themselves, as well as groups, lose from self-interested actions. In other situations selfish behavior may actually pay off. Hence, the family is a more interesting arena because a selfish actor could feel that he or she might gain through self-serving behavior. If social motivations are shown to be important in such an arena, they may have broader applicability.

The family study examines the views of college students about the actions of their parents. In the study, college students at the University of California, Berkeley, completed a questionnaire, as part of a course requirement, about a recent experience with one or both of their parents. While the use of college students as respondents has sometimes been criticized (Sears, 1986), it seems quite appropriate within this context. College students are still connected with their parents, both emotionally and cognitively. However, they are sufficiently independent to be able to voluntarily determine the degree to which they will defer to their parents' decisions and the rules of their family.

MEASURES

The operationalization of all the variables used in these studies are outlined in the Appendix to this chapter. The perceived legitimacy of authorities was assessed in terms of feelings of trust in authorities, willingness to accept their decisions, and feelings of obligation to follow group rules. An overall legitimacy index that included these three aspects was created as well. Subjects' bonds to their groups were assessed in terms of group identification and expectations of reciprocity. Satisfaction with an authority's decisions and perceived procedural fairness constituted evaluations of authorities in the two settings.

VIEWS ABOUT LEGITIMACY OF AUTHORITY IN COMMUNITY AND FAMILY SETTINGS

The antecedents of deference to collective authority structures was first explored within a community setting.[1] The antecedents of such voluntary deference are examined in Table 1. The results indicate that the actions of authorities influence all three aspects of legitimacy: trust, willingness to voluntarily accept decisions, and willingness to obey rules. In particular, judgments about the fairness of group decision-making procedures shape people's willingness to defer to group authorities ($\beta = .53$, $p < .001$) for the overall legitimacy index. Outcome satisfaction had no significant influence ($\beta = .06$, NS). Further, legitimacy was influenced by identification with the community ($\beta = .18$, $p < .001$), but not by expectations of reciprocity ($\beta = -.06$, NS).

Table 2 extends the analysis to the arena of the family. Again, the antecedents of collective deference to authority are explored.[2] However, in this case, the individuals studied are not restraining their consumption of scarce commodities, as was true in the social dilemma studied in the community. Instead, they are proactively behaving out of concern not just with themselves but with their families.

The results in Table 2 are similar to those already outlined in the community case. Procedural justice influences legitimacy ($\beta = .32$, $p < .001$), as does community identification ($\beta = .42$, $p < .001$). Finally, outcome satisfaction has a small influence ($\beta = .14$, $p < .05$), and expectations of reciprocity have none ($\beta = .07$, NS).

THE INDIVIDUAL, THE FAMILY, AND SOCIAL GOOD

Table 1

Antecedents of the Legitimacy of Community Authorities

	Trust in Authorities	Willingness to Voluntarily Accept Decisions	Feelings of Obligation to Obey Rules	Overall Legitimacy Index
Community relations:				
Community identification	.06	.10[a]	.16[b]	.18[c]
Expectations of reciprocity	−.05	.09	−.10	−.06
Authority evaluations:				
Outcome satisfaction	.06	.11	.05	.06
Procedural justice	.50[c]	.32[c]	.18[b]	.53[c]
Adjusted R-squared (%)	27[c]	16[c]	6[b]	32[c]

$n = 214$ Note. Entries are beta weights.   [a]$p < .05$. [b]$p < .01$. [c]$p < .001$.

Table 2

Antecedents of the Legitimacy of Parental Authorities

	Trust in Parents	Willingness to Voluntarily Accept Decisions	Feelings of Obligation to Obey Rules	Overall Legitimacy Index
Family relations:				
Family identification	.49[c]	.13[b]	.54[b]	.42[c]
Expectations of reciprocity	.05	.03	.03	.07
Parental evaluations:				
Outcome satisfaction	.00	.22[c]	−.02	.14[a]
Procedural justice	.27[c]	.37[c]	.01	.32[c]
Adjusted R-squared (%)	42[c]	36[c]	30[c]	52[c]

$n = 317$ Note. Entries are beta weights.   [a]$p < .05$. [b]$p < .01$. [c]$p < .001$.

The findings of both studies support the suggestion that people's self-interested motivations can be supplemented by social motivations. These motivations influence the willingness of individuals to voluntarily defer to the judgments of group authorities. Two mechanisms are recognized: group identification and fair decision-making procedures. Those who more strongly identify with their group and those who feel that group authorities make decisions fairly are more willing to defer to those decisions, irrespective of whether the authority's decisions were favorable to them or not.

These findings replicate the procedural-justice effect found in many other studies of governmental authority (Tyler, 1990; Tyler & Lind, 1992) but make a new contribution in terms of parental authorities. The findings also extend the social-identity literature to include the effects of group identification on support for group authorities.

Comparison across the two arenas supports our predictions as well. Both in absolute terms and relative to the influence of social identification, procedural justice is more central to the legitimacy of authority in community settings. In family settings, where emotional bonds are stronger, procedural-justice concerns and social identification play a similar role in the perceived legitimacy of authorities (the difference between the effects of social identification and procedural justice on the overall legitimacy index is nonsignificant).

It is important to note that procedural-justice effects are especially strong in community settings. When people do not know one another well, they are more likely to focus on the appearance of justice in group decision making. When people have close emotional links, as children have with their parents, those links significantly affect reactions to parental decisions. However, even in family settings, procedural justice has an influence. In fact, even in families it continues to dominate willingness to voluntarily accept decisions.

The Psychology of Procedural Justice

AUTHORITY BEHAVIORS AND PROCEDURAL JUSTICE JUDGMENTS

The studies showed that social motivations, rather than instrumental concerns for access to resources or favorable decisions, drive deference to collective decision-making structures. Furthermore, the studies showed that the social setting (community or family) has an important influence on the relative importance of procedural justice and social identification. These two findings can also be explored in terms of the antecedents of procedural-justice judgments.

In the procedural-justice literature, two psychological models have been proposed: the instrumental-control model of Thibaut and Walker (1975) and the relational model of Tyler and Lind (1992). Thibaut and Walker (1975) not only demonstrated the importance of procedural justice in shaping people's evaluations of government authorities; they also proposed that people's procedural justice judgments reflect their evaluations of their control over receiving favorable decisions. In Thibaut and Walker's model decision and process control are distinguished. Decision control refers to control over authorities' decisions. Process control ("voice") refers to control over the presentation of information to authorities in the decision-making process. They argue that people prefer direct control but must sometimes relinquish it. If they must do so, they attempt to retain as much indirect control, that is, control through evidence presentation, as possible. Thibaut and Walker's model is an instrumental one, linking procedural-justice judgments to people's concerns about having control (Thibaut & Walker, 1975).

Tyler and Lind (1992) propose an alternative, relational, model of procedural justice. They argue that procedural-justice evaluations primarily reflect a person's judgments about their relationship to authorities. Tyler and Lind (Tyler, 1989; Tyler & Lind, 1992) demonstrate that the neutrality and trustworthiness of authorities and the standing people perceive themselves to have with authorities influence judgments of procedural justice.

Since procedural judgments can themselves be both instrumental and relational in character (Tyler, 1989; Tyler & Lind, 1992), it is important to examine what aspects of procedures influence judgments about their fairness. Five aspects of procedures are considered: outcome favorability; control; neutrality; trustworthiness; and standing. Judgments about outcome favorability are instrumental in character, while judgments about neutrality, trustworthiness, and standing are relational. Control judgments contain elements of both models and differ psychologically in different settings. As before, we predict that the social, relational factors of procedural-justice judgments play a dominant role in both the community and family settings.

But how would the relational factors differ across settings? In the community setting, the relationship with the authority is impersonal—community members seldom, if ever, interact with the community authority. Hence, we predict that group members are particularly concerned about their interests being equally considered against other group members—neutral treatment—in the community setting. In the family setting, however, children have long-term, deep personal connections to their parents. Indicators that they are respected individuals and that their parents can be trusted may be particularly salient to children in the personal interactions of the family setting. Hence, we predict that judgments about respectful treatment ("standing") by trustworthy parents will dominate concerns for equal and neutral treatment in the family setting.

Table 3 presents the results of an analysis of the psychology of procedural justice in community and family settings. The findings suggest that, in both settings, relational concerns are important to the psychology of justice. Control judgments do not play a significant role (β = .03 and -.03, NS). As predicted, however, the same relational factors are not important in both settings. The neutrality of authorities is the strongest influence in community settings (β = .44, p < .001), while trustworthiness and standing play only a marginal role (β = .14, p < .01; .12, p < .01, respectively). In the family, this situation is reversed: judgments about the trustworthiness of parents and standing (both β = .35, p < .001) dominate judgments about neutrality (β = .07, NS).

The studies show that procedural-justice judgments are defined by people's relational judgments concerning their social bond with authorities. People's concerns are not simply with judgments about their own self-interest: when judgments about the favorability of government decisions are controlled for, strong relational influences on the evaluation of the fairness of procedures and of the legitimacy of authorities remain, in both community and family settings. These findings provide strong support for Tyler and Lind's model (Lind & Tyler, 1988; Tyler, 1989; Tyler & Lind, 1992).

Interestingly, the same relational concerns do not predominate in both settings. In communities, people focus most heavily on issues of neutrality. This seems reasonable given that citizens have no directly personal connection with the authorities involved. In families, where personal connections are direct and strong, people focus on trustworthiness and standing. This differential pattern within the relational model supports the previously outlined suggestions and provide an important extension of Tyler and Lind's model.

It is also important to note that the nature of people's instrumental concerns is not the same in the two settings. In both community and family settings, control judgments are strongly linked to relational concerns (both average r = .63). In community settings, how-

Table 3

Authority Evaluations as Antecedents of Procedural Justice in Community and Family Settings

	Procedural Justice of Authority in the Community	Procedural Justice of Authority in the Family
Authority evaluations:		
Outcome satisfaction	.22[c]	.27[c]
Control	.03	−.03
Neutrality	.44[c]	.07
Trustworthiness	.14[b]	.35[c]
Standing	.12[b]	.35[c]
Adjusted R-squared (%)	53[c]	77[c]

Note. In the family study, $n = 323$. In the community study, $n = 239$. Entries are beta weights.
[a]$p < .05$.   [b]$p < .01$.   [c]$p < .001$.

ever, outcome favorability and control are only moderately related ($r = .30$), while in family settings they are more strongly related ($r = .60$). It may be that citizens recognize they are unlikely to have any role in shaping political decisions and view control as a more symbolic or relational issue—that is, having the opportunity to present evidence (process control). Children, on the other hand, view control over family decisions (decision control) as an actual possibility. Hence, whether such control is shared is more strongly linked to the actual favorability of the outcomes obtained.

THE JOINT INFLUENCE OF SOCIAL IDENTIFICATION AND PROCEDURAL-JUSTICE JUDGMENTS

It is important to recognize that the two mechanisms underlying concerns for the social good—social identification with groups and perceived procedural justice of group authorities—are not necessarily distinct. In fact, it would not be surprising that social identification and procedural justice interact, since we hypothesized that both are linked to the social bonds between individuals. In the case of social identification, people may defer to authorities because of an emotional bond felt toward their community. In the case of procedural justice, people may defer to authorities because of relational judgments about neutrality, trustworthiness, and standing. Alternatively, it can be hypothesized that people defer to authorities on the basis of instrumental motives. People may cooperate on the basis of their beliefs that others will reciprocate their efforts, making it less likely that others will act as "free riders" or they may cooperate because authorities give them favorable decisions.

Our concern is with the relationship between the two mechanisms, that is, with the possibility that the instrumental and/or relational aspects of each mechanism interact. In particular, we test the hypothesis that people who identify with their group evaluate justice issues differently. The suggestion of an interaction is not unique. Discussions of value socialization often intertwine with consideration of rule application and empathy. As already noted, Wilson (1993) links the development of the "human sense of fairness" to the consistent application of rules in the parent-child relationship. Similarly, the literature on prosocial behavior finds that the emotional bond between children and parents is a crucial antecedent of sympathy for others and willingness to act on their behalf. For example, the literature on delinquency suggests that both the existence of a social bond between parents and children and the consistent application of rules ("procedural fairness") are necessary to avoid delinquency in children (West & Farrington, 1973; Wilson & Herrnstein, 1985).

The suggestion of an interaction can be tested on two levels. First, the effects of an interaction between identification and procedural justice on the perceived legitimacy of group authorities can be explored. Second, the effects of an interaction between social identification and the relational aspects of procedural justice on overall judgments of procedural justice can be examined. The possibility of an interaction effect between identification and evaluations of the fairness on perceived legitimacy is tested in the interaction analysis shown in Table 4. That analysis examines whether people are especially likely to regard authority as legitimate if they both identify with their group and regard group procedures as fair. The results support this interaction finding in the community setting, but not in families ($\beta = .17$, $p < .05$; and $\beta = .09$, NS, respectively). Hence, there is some support for the predicted interaction in one setting.

To test the second interaction possibility, overall indicators of the instrumental and relational aspects of procedural justice were

Table 4

Antecedents of Legitimacy in Community and Family Settings: Interactions between Authority Evaluations and Group Relations

	Community	Family
Main effects:		
Group relations:		
Social identification	.32^c	.40^c
Expectations of reciprocity	.06	.12^a
Authority evaluations:		
Procedural justice (PJ)	.42^b	.31^c
Outcome satisfaction (OS)	.09	.14^a
Interactions:		
PJ x identification	.17^a	.09
OS x identification	−.01	−.09
PJ x reciprocity	−.06	−.02
OS x reciprocity	.09	.01
Adjusted R-squared (%)	30^c	52^c

Note. In the family study, $n = 323$. In the community study, $n = 239$. Entries are beta weights.
$^a p < .05.$ $^b p < .01.$ $^c p < .001.$

constructed. Based on factor analyses, control judgments in the community study were included in the relational factor, while in the family study they were included in the instrumental factor. An interaction analysis was performed, exploring the influence of instrumental and relational aspects of procedural justice; social identification and reciprocity judgments; and the interaction between the two.

The results of the analyses are shown in Table 5. The analyses of main effects suggest again that, as expected, relational concerns are central to the definition of procedural justice in both settings. Interaction analyses further suggest that those who identify more strongly with their community or family placed greater weight on relational aspects of procedural justice when making procedural-fairness judgments. The link between social identification and relational aspects of decision-making procedures is particularly strong in the community setting. Finally, those people who identify more closely with their families define procedural justice less strongly in instrumental terms.

In addition to finding that identification affects the way people evaluate the fairness of procedures, it is also interesting that there are no interactions involving the expectation of reciprocity from oth-

Table 5

*Antecedents of Procedural Justice in Community and Family Settings:
Interactions between Procedural Judgments and Group Relations*

	Procedural Justice of Authority in the Community	Procedural Justice of Authority in the Family
Main effects:		
Group relations:		
Social identification	.35[c]	.07
Expectations of reciprocity	.06	−.01
Procedural justice judgments:		
Instrumental judgments (I)	.21[c]	.20[c]
Relational judgments (R)	.47[c]	.75[c]
Interactions:		
I x Identification	−.01	−.16[a]
R x Identification	.40[c]	.16[a]
I x Reciprocity	−.04	.2
R x Reciprocity	.12	−.07
Adjusted R-squared(%)	63[c]	75[c]

Note. In the family study, $n = 323$. In the community study, $n = 239$. Entries are beta weights.
[a]$p < .05$.   [b]$p < .01$.   [c]$p < .001$.

ers. In other words, the instrumental judgment—whether others will reciprocate one's efforts—does not affect how people evaluate the criteria used to assess the fairness of the authorities being dealt with.

Discussion

SOCIAL GOOD IN COMMUNITY AND FAMILY SETTINGS

The central concern of this chapter is the nature of social good in two important social settings, the community and the family. As President Clinton suggested in his 1994 State of the Union Address, government can provide incentives, create job training, and pass tough crime bills, but it is the breakdown of the social fabric of our communities and families that affects us most. This chapter explored concerns for the social good in terms of views about the legitimacy of authority in community and family settings—that is, feelings of trust in the honesty and competence of authorities, feelings of obligation to abide by rules that authorities enact to guide our communities and families, and a willingness to voluntarily accept the decisions of authorities.

The findings clearly suggest that social mechanisms, not incentive strategies that reward or sanction individuals' pursuits of self-interests, underlie the perceived legitimacy of authorities. Two social mechanisms were explored: identification with a group and judgments about the fairness in which authorities make decisions. In both the community and the family, social identification and procedural justice had a strong effect on the willingness to defer to group authorities. The favorability of the authorities' decisions carried little weight in this matter.

The procedural-justice findings of this study have clear implications for authorities—whether formal government authorities or parents—seeking ways to legitimate their actions. Such authorities should make their decisions in ways that the people affected by them will view as fair. As previous studies have suggested, people are more open to restrictive governmental decisions than is often recognized, provided that those decisions are made in fair ways. These findings suggest that authorities gain support through following fair decision-making procedures.

The findings regarding procedural-justice effects in the family study echo the suggestion that juvenile delinquency is linked to the lack of consistent (i.e., "fair") disciplinary procedures (Wilson, 1993). While it has been recognized that adolescent behavior is shaped by the way parents administer discipline, disciplinary procedures have not been thought of within a procedural-justice framework. Such a framework provides a number of suggestions concerning how discipline can be administered in ways that children will regard as just—enhancing their commitment to following family and other types of rules. Treatment with respect and in a trustworthy manner may contribute to such commitment.

The question of why procedural justice matters still remains, however. At least two answers may be proffered. Procedural justice may be important because agreements on what constitutes fair procedure may give a sense of security or continuity to individuals. They can believe that, even if a one-time decision is not favorable to them, the use of fair procedures will produce a reasonable—"just"—

number of fair decisions in the long run. Fair decision-making procedures may also be important, however, because they contribute importantly to a person's sense of personal fulfillment within their community or family. While people join groups for positive reasons—to gain a social identity and to facilitate long-term exchange gains, for example—they tend to remain insecure and fearful. They fear that they are being disadvantaged relative to others, that they are "suckers" (Tyler & Dawes, 1993). If people feel that the procedures of allocation and dispute resolution being used are fair, their fears of exploitation are minimized. They can believe that, in the long run, their identity as worthy group members will not be jeopardized by deferring to group authorities.

It needs to be recognized, however, that procedural-justice evaluations are based on the *views* people have of third-party procedures and, as such, are vulnerable to manipulation and distortion. The subjectivity of people's views of the procedures used by the Public Utilities Commission, the community authority studied, illustrates this point: only 18% of all respondents felt they actually knew "a great deal" or "something" about the commission's procedures, while 74% reported they viewed those procedures as fair. Of course, children are much more familiar with the procedures used by their parents but are still vulnerable to manipulation as well. The possibility of promoting the acceptance of an unfavorable outcome by presenting it as having been made through the use of fair procedures has already spawned a literature on "impression management" for business managers (see, e.g., Greenberg, 1990).

The other social mechanism explored in this chapter was identification with the social group. As with procedural justice, that mechanism is contrasted with the instrumental mechanism embodied within expectations that others will reciprocate cooperative behavior. Again, the findings outlined suggest the importance of this second social mechanism. Identification influences legitimacy independently of the influences of the instrumental mechanism represented by reciprocity.

These latter findings make the "community" the focus of concern. In contrast to the formal structures of government, community-identification effects may be responsive to informal connections to other people or groups in the community. Hence, the enhancement of community identification, for example, through the creation of small community and neighborhood organizations, may prove to be paramount in conserving a common community resource or resolving a conflict.

The family is also a community, and the findings of this study have similar implications for the family. Informal efforts to create emotional bonds within the family should lead to a willingness to defer to the judgments of parents taking on the value of helping the family. Such emotional bonds are important because those linked emotionally will want to help others with whom they identify. Hence, they will willingly defer to the decisions of family authorities—parents.

Interestingly, these suggestions link the implications of these studies to early studies of social change conducted during World War II. In a famous series of studies, social scientists attempted to determine how housewives might be encouraged to feed their families intestinal meats—an unappetizing food that they would primarily serve out of patriotic motives (Lewin, 1947). Lewin argued that commitment to honor a group consensus was key to behavior change. What is striking about this early work is the focus on creating identification with a group—group cohesiveness—and with group decisions, through public commitment, as a mechanism for encouraging deference to group decisions. These early insights are reflected in the focus on identification with the group that is outlined here.[3]

Recognizing the importance of emotional bonds with others in the community and family highlights the potential harm of weakened social networks. In the community, neighborhood networks are weakening, while broken homes and the decline of extended families are weakening emotional bonds within the family. At a time when society is seeking social mechanisms that enhance social motivations to aid the community, one of those mechanisms—social identification—is weakening as a force within both communities and families. Fortunately, our studies point to a second social mechanism that may replace the need for strong emotional bonds within a community—procedural fairness of a group authority. When community members could not rely on their social bonds with other members when deciding on supporting social solutions to their problems (we suggested that information about similarity in goals and values, which may enhance trust in social relations, was not as strongly available in the community setting as it was in the family setting), they put more weight on the fairness of community authorities.

A word of caution is in order here, however. To maximize the identification effects examined in this study, respondents were allowed to self-define their community. This is especially important in the case of communities, although it played a role in the family study as well: not all children defined their biological parents as their "family." In the community study, different respondents could imagine their block, their neighborhood, their church, or the greater Bay Area as their subjective community. Hence, this study provides no information about how people choose the communities with which they identify. The studies' findings are especially striking, however, because they demonstrate that identifications with several social groups can generalize to a willingness to undertake actions on behalf of an entire city.

Research has not yet clearly established how social identifications are formed. Specific social identities may be activated at some times and not at others (Brewer, 1991). People may identify with a community because it is small (Olson, 1965), because community members are in proximity or feel close to one another, or because they share a common fate (see Tajfel, 1982; Turner et al., 1987; Wit, 1989, for discussions of these factors). It is essential that the processes through which identification is activated be more fully explored in future research.

THE PSYCHOLOGY OF PROCEDURAL JUSTICE

A second central concern of this chapter is to understand the psychology of procedural justice. This was explored in two different ways: first, we examined which aspects of authority evaluations contribute to views about procedural fairness; and second, we examined whether judgments about procedural fairness and feelings of identification with a group are linked.

In regard to the question of which aspects of authority evaluations contribute to procedural-fairness judgments, we contrasted the traditional control model of Thibaut and Walker (1975) with the recently developed relational model of Tyler and Lind (Lind & Tyler, 1988; Tyler, 1989; Tyler & Lind, 1990). Traditional control models give an instrumental explanation for procedural-justice effects, while the relational model links procedural-justice judgments to noninstrumental issues. Again, the key to differentiating between these models is to examine why people are concerned about fairness. The relational model of procedural justice received strong support in both the community and family setting. People care more about their social bond to an authority than about their perceived control over the decision-making process or the outcomes of that process. Relational concerns were found to affect both overall judgments of fairness and the perceived legitimacy of a group authority.

Interestingly, the various relational aspects of authority evaluations—neutrality and trustworthiness of the authority and perceived standing with the authority—were not found to carry equal weight in the two settings examined. Neutral treatment was the dominant determinant of procedural-justice judgments in the community setting, while treatment with respect by trustworthy authority dominated procedural-justice judgments in the family setting. These findings represent an important extension of the relational model of Tyler and Lind, suggesting that relational bonds between individuals and authorities that determine procedural justice judgments are influenced, in part, by the social setting.

Future research remains to determine whether the differences between the community and family setting that we hypothesized to cause the different emphasis on aspects of authority evaluations are indeed responsible. We suggested that a lack of personal relationships and direct interactions with a group authority leads individuals to focus on the neutrality of that authority, while in the reverse, we hypothesized that direct personal interactions and long-term relationships with an authority lead to an emphasis placed on respectful and trustworthy authority behaviors. One possible setting in which these hypothesized effects can be examined is a work organization. Temporary workers in such a setting, for example, may be more sensitive to the perceived neutrality of their supervisor because they have not developed a long-term relational bond with that supervisor. Permanent workers, who have developed a personal relationship with their supervisor, may place a premium on respect and trustworthiness. Similarly, line supervisors may need to be more concerned about the respect they accord to their immediate subordinates, while departmental heads may be held more accountable for their perceived neutrality.

Finally, we examined whether social-identification and procedural-justice judgments interact. We suggested that, since both identification and procedural-justice judgments reflect a social bond between individuals, they may be related. Support for our suggestion was found mostly in the community study: respondents who identified more closely with their community defined the meaning of procedural fairness in more strongly relational terms. Moreover, respondents who identified more closely with their community *and* thought the community authority acted in a procedurally fair way were more willing to pledge their support to that community authority.

These findings provide strong support to our suggestion that procedural-justice judgments are noninstrumental in nature. Furthermore, expectations of reciprocity were not found to interact with procedural-justice judgments in either of the settings. Expectations of reciprocity represent instrumental concerns underlying social attitudes toward the community, because they reflect that people will engage in cooperative behaviors when they view such restraint as a more profitable long-term course of action (Brann & Foddy, 1988; Brewer, 1981; Kramer & Goldman, 1987; Kramer et al., 1989; Messick et al., 1983).

In summary, the findings outlined provide strong support for arguments about the importance of social values in shaping people's views about the legitimacy of authorities within both community and family settings. In both settings noninstrumental mechanisms are found to have an important role in legitimizing authorities.

APPENDIX: MEASURES

The community. In the community study, respondents were told that the survey was conducted by the University of California, Berkeley, and that their answers would help us understand how the water shortage should be handled. All response items were assessed using four-point Likert-type scales. Respondents were also offered a "don't know" option. "Don't know" responses were treated as missing values in the analyses. Reliabilities of the scales are reported in terms of Cronbach's alpha coefficients.

The Legitimacy of the Public Utilities Commission. Respondents were asked about their general feelings about the legitimacy of their local water authority, the Public Utilities Commission. Three aspects of legitimacy were assessed. These three elements of legitimacy were previously identified as central to the legitimacy literature (Tyler, 1990) and were operationalized here as they have been in prior studies of legitimacy. The three aspects of legitimacy were found to be related, albeit weakly (mean $r = .15$, $p < .01$).

Trust in the Public Utilities Commission. The questions used were drawn from the "trust in government" scale (Tyler, 1990). Respondents were asked to agree or disagree with the following statements: "The commission does its job well"; "The decisions made by the Public Utilities Commission are too influenced by political pressures"; "The Public Utilities Commission can be trusted to make decisions that are good for everyone"; "Government rules about water conservation work well"; and "Rules about water conservation are too influenced by political pressures" ($\alpha = .76$).

Willingness to accept Public Utilities Commission decisions. Respondents were asked, "If the PUC asked people to voluntarily reduce water use, would you do so?"

Perceived obligation to obey government rules. Respondents were asked to agree or disagree with the following statements: "Respect for government authority is an important value for people to have"; "People should obey laws even when they go against what they think is right"; and "Disobeying the law is seldom justified" ($\alpha = .61$).

Evaluations of the Public Utilities Commission. Respondents were asked about their general feelings about how the commission makes its decisions and their evaluations of those decisions. They were also asked to consider a situation in which they personally went to a commission's meeting to advocate some policy or position. The procedural-justice questions are centered around this hypothetical event and focus on the respondents' feelings about their perceived control over the commission's decision making, the neutrality of the commission, the trustworthiness of its members, and the respect with which the board treats its constituents.

Outcome satisfaction. Outcome satisfaction was assessed using four items: "Past water conservation decisions made by the Commission have been vary favorable to you and to the other members of your household"; "In the past, the Commission has allocated you enough water"; "Past water conservation decisions of the Commission have been very fair to you and to the other members of your household"; and "In the past, the Commission has allocated water fairly in your community" ($\alpha = .83$).

Procedural fairness. Respondents were asked two questions about their overall justice judgments of the Public Utilities Commission: "How fair are the procedures the Commission used to make its policies?" and "Suppose you went to an open meeting of the Commission: Would you agree or disagree that the Commission would make its decisions in a fair way?" ($\alpha = .69$).

Control. Respondents were asked: "Suppose you went to an open meeting of the Commission: Would you agree or disagree that . . . the decisions of the Commission would be influenced by your views?"; "the Commission would give you plenty of opportunity to make your arguments and be heard?"; and "the Commission would consider the views you expressed to them?" ($\alpha = .77$).

Neutrality. Respondents were asked: "Suppose you went to an open meeting of the Commission: Would you agree or disagree that . . . the members of the Commission would be honest in the things they said and did?"; and "the Commission would get the information needed to make good decisions?" ($\alpha = .64$).

Trustworthiness. Respondents were asked: "Suppose you went to an open meeting of the Commission: Would you agree or disagree that . . . the Commission would give your views as much consideration as the views of others?"; and "the Commission would treat you fairly?" ($\alpha = .50$).

Standing. Respondents were asked: "Suppose you went to an open meeting of the Commission: Would you agree or disagree that . . . the Commission would respect your rights as a citizen?"; and "the Commission would treat you politely?" ($\alpha = .61$).

Community Attitudes. Assessing respondents' attitudes toward their community requires an effort to deal with the meaning of community to individual respondents. In this study respondents were asked to define "community" using their own subjective reference points; a common definition of community was not presented. The advantage of this approach is that each subject is responding through an individual subjective framework, thinking about whatever he or she considers their community. Two aspects of people's identification with their self-selected community were assessed.

Community Identification. For the purposes of this study, we have combined two aspects of people's attitudes toward their community (identification with a community and feelings of pride in a community). While these two aspects of community attitudes can be separated (see Tyler & Degoey, 1994), they are highly correlated ($r = .57$). Respondents were asked to agree or disagree with the following statements: "There are many people in your community whom you think of as good friends"; "You could ask many of the people in your community to help you if you needed help"; "Many of them have similar values to yours"; "I am proud to tell my friends about the community I live in"; "I often talk about my community to others as a great place to live"; and "The community I live in is important to the way I think of myself as a person" ($\alpha = .84$).

Expectations of reciprocity. The operationalization of expectations of reciprocity is based on Messick et al. (1983). Respondents were asked, "If the government urged people to voluntarily use less water, how likely is it that people in your community would do so?" and "If there were rules telling people how much water they can use, how likely is it that people in your community would voluntarily follow those rules?" ($\alpha = .69$).

The family. In the family study, students were told that the researchers were interested in how they and their parent(s) resolve conflicts. They were asked to describe a major conflict involving them and their parent(s) and to report their feelings and thoughts about this conflict. The questions regarding parental decision making focus on this event. Respondents were also asked to describe how they generally feel about their parents and their family and how they generally behave toward them. All response items were assessed using seven-point Likert-type scales. Scale reliabilities are reported using Cronbach's alpha coefficients.

Legitimacy of Parents. As in the community study, three aspects of students' views about the legitimacy of their parent(s) as the appropriate decision makers in their family were assessed. These three aspects were moderately interrelated (mean $r = .33$, $p < .001$).

Trust in parents. Students were asked eight questions: "When you think about your parent(s), to what extent do you . . . trust them?"; "respect them?"; "feel similar to them?"; "feel they deserve your support?"; "like them?"; "feel loyal to them?"; "feel satisfied with them?"; and "feel they are the appropriate decision makers in your family?" ($\alpha = .91$).

Willingness to accept parental decisions voluntarily. Students were asked about their willingness to accept their parent(s)' decisions using six items, the first five focusing on the dispute they were considering: "How willing were you to voluntarily accept the decisions your parent(s) made?"; "To what extent did you follow those decisions even when others were not around?"; "To what extent did you go along with your parent(s)' decisions?"; "To what degree did you willingly embrace the solution that you and your parents arrived at?"; "If this problem were to occur again in the future, how willing would you be to see it resolved in a similar way?"; and, more generally, "When you think about your parent(s), to what extent do you accept their decisions voluntarily?" ($\alpha = .80$).

Perceived obligation to conform to family rules and expectations. Six questions assessed the degree to which students felt their behaviors toward their family are generally in line with family expectations and rules: "How frequently do you act according to what your family expects of you?"; "Do you try hard to be punctual about arriving on time for appointments with your family members?"; "To what extent do you follow your family's customs and rules in your life?"; "How hard do you try to avoid creating problems for your family?"; "How hard do you try to respect the rights of your family members?"; and "To what extent do you inform your family of actions on your part that may affect them before initiating those actions?" ($\alpha = .78$).

Evaluations of Parental Decision Making. Students were asked to report how they felt about the outcome of their conflict with their parent(s), and the fairness of the way their parents handled the conflict.

Outcome satisfaction. Outcome satisfaction was assessed using ten items: "Overall, how satisfied were you with the outcome?"; "How favorable was the outcome to you?"; "Compared to the situation before you talked to your parent(s), how much better or worse was the situation after the conflict was resolved?"; "How does your outcome compare to the outcome you expected when you first started discussing the problem with your parent(s)?"; "How does your outcome compare to the outcomes other people generally receive when they go to their parent(s) with similar problems?"; "How does your outcome compare to the outcomes you generally received when dealing with your parent(s)?; "Given the rules in your family, did you get more or less than you feel you deserved?"; "How fair was the outcome you and your parent(s) settled on?"; "How does the outcome you received compare to what you feel you deserved in this situation?"; and "How much did you gain or lose?" (α = .92).

Procedural fairness. Overall views about the fairness in the way conflicts are resolved were assessed using a three-item scale: "Overall, how fairly were you treated by your parents?"; "How fair was the way your parents tried to resolve the conflict?"; and "How fair were the ways your parents handled the conflict?" (α = .93).

Control was assessed by asking respondents: "How much opportunity were you given to describe your point of view?" and "How much influence did you have over the decisions made?" (α = .64).

Neutrality was assessed by asking respondents, "Did your parents get all the information they needed to make good decisions?"; "How hard did they try to bring the issues out into the open?"; "How honest were your parents?"; and "Did the methods used by your parents favor one person over another?" (α = .60).

Trustworthiness was assessed by asking respondents, "How much consideration was given to your views?"; "How hard did your parents try to do the right thing?"; "How hard did your parents try to take account of your needs?"; and "How hard did your parents try to be fair to you?" (α = .89).

Standing was assessed by asking respondents, "How politely were you treated by your parents?"; "How much concern did your parents show for your rights?"; and "How respectful was your parents' treatment of you?" (α = .88).

Family Attitudes. As in the community study, two aspects of students' emotional bonds to their family—identification and pride— were combined to form an eight-item identification scale. Expectations that family members will come to each other's aid were also assessed.

Family identification. Respondents were asked, "How similar are the things you and your family want out of life?"; "How important is your family to the way you think of yourself as a person?"; "How often do you think of yourself as a 'family member'?"; "How much do you talk up your family to friends as a great family to be a part of?"; "How proud are you to tell others that you are a part of this family?"; "Would it be very hard to find another family that you would like as much to be a part of as this family?"; "If someone praises one of your family members, to what extent does that feel like a personal compliment to you?"; and "How similar are your values and those of your family?" ($\alpha = .89$).

Expectations of reciprocity. Respondents were asked: "Can you count on your family to help you if you need it?"

NOTES

1. Although it is outside the scope of this chapter, it would also be possible to examine the antecedents of individual actions to aid the group. When their community was faced with the water shortage citizens could respond by voluntarily conserving water. An examination of the antecedents of that behavior among those people who felt that conserving water would help with the water shortage ($n = 300$) suggests that identification matters. The focus on a subset of respondents was chosen since psychological research has generally found that those people who feel a sense of "personal agency," believing that their actions can influence personal and community problems, are more likely to act on their feelings (Ajzen, 1985, 1988; Ajzen & Madden, 1986; Bandura, 1986; Kerr, 1989; Olson, 1965; Samuelson & Biek, 1991). In fact, many people in the community studied did report conserving water. An examination of the antecedents of that behavior suggests that identifying with the community influences conservation behavior ($\beta = .13$), as does the belief that others will conserve—reciprocity expectations ($\beta = .25$). In other words, both the emotional bond people have with their communities and their instrumental beliefs about what others are likely to do shaped people's individual actions in response to the water shortage.

2. As in the community study, it is also possible to consider the antecedents of the willingness to act voluntarily in ways designed to help the family (individual action). If such actions are considered, it is found that, as in the community study, identification with one's parents influences whether people indicate acting in ways designed to aid their families ($\beta = .43$, $p < .001$). In this situation neither expectations of reciprocity nor judgments about the decision-making characteristics of authorities were important.

3. More recently, Kerr and Kaufman-Gilliland (1994) have extended the work of Lewin by examining the influence of group discussion on coopera-

tion within social dilemmas. They argue that while discussion enhances cooperation it does not do so through the mechanism of changing group identity—a conclusion contrary to that reached here.

REFERENCES

Ajzen, I. (1985). From intentions to actions: A theory of planned behavior. In J. Kuhl & J. Beckmann (Eds.), *Action control: From cognition to behavior* (pp. 11–38). Berlin: Springer.

Ajzen, I. (1988). *Attitudes, personality, and behavior*. Milton Keynes, England: Open University Press.

Ajzen, I., & Madden, T. J. (1986). Predictions of goal-directed behavior: Attitudes, intentions, and perceived behavioral control. *Journal of Experimental Social Psychology, 22*, 453–474.

Alexander, S., & Ruderman, A. (1987). The role of procedural and distributive justice in organizational behavior. *Social Justice Research, 1*, 177–198.

Arts, W., & van der Veen, R. (1992). Sociological approaches to distributive and procedural justice. In K. Scherer (Ed.), *Justice: Interdisciplinary perspectives* (pp. 143–176). Cambridge: Cambridge University Press.

Bandura, A. (1986). *Social foundations of though and action: A social cognitive theory*. Englewood Cliffs NJ: Prentice-Hall.

Barrett-Howard, E., & Tyler, T. R. (1986). Procedural justice as a criterion in allocation decisions. *Journal of Personality and Social Psychology, 50*, 296–304.

Bowlby, J. (1982). *Attachment and loss* (2nd ed.). New York: Basic.

Bowlby, J. (1988). *A secure base: Parent-child attachment and healthy human development*. New York: Basic.

Brann, P., & Foddy, M. (1988). Trust and consumption of a deteriorating common resource. *Journal of Conflict Resolution, 31*, 615–630.

Bretherton, I. (1985). Attachment theory: Retrospect and prospect. In I. Bretherton & E. Waters (Eds.), *Growing points in attachment theory and research*. Monographs of the Society for Research in Child Development, 50 (pp. 3–35). Chicago: University of Chicago Press.

Brewer, M. B. (1979). In-group bias in the minimal intergroup situation: A cognitive-motivational analysis. *Psychological Bulletin, 86*, 307–324.

Brewer, M. B. (1981). Ethnocentrism and its role in interpersonal trust. In M. B. Brewer & B. E. Collins (Eds.), *Scientific inquiry and the social sciences* (pp. 345–360). New York: Jossey-Bass.

Brewer, M. B. (1991). The social self: On being the same and different at the same time. *Personality and Social Psychology Bulletin, 17*, 475–482.

Brewer, M. B., & Kramer, R. (1986). Choice behavior in social dilemmas: Effects of social identity, group size, and decision framing. *Journal of Personality and Social Psychology, 50*, 543–549.

Bronfenbrenner, U. (1979). *The ecology of human development: Experiments by nature and design*. Cambridge MA: Harvard University Press.

Buckley, W., Burns, T., & Meeker, L. D. (1974). Structural solutions of collective action problems. *Behavioral Science, 19,* 277–297.

Casper, J. D., Tyler, T. R., & Fisher, B. (1988). Procedural justice in felony cases. *Law and Society Review, 22,* 483–507.

Chavis, D. M. (1993). A future for community psychology practice. *American Journal of Community Psychology, 21,* 171–181.

Damon, W. (1984). Self-understanding and moral development from childhood to adolescence. In W. M. Kurtines & J. L. Gewirtz (Eds.), *Morality, moral behavior, and moral development* (pp. 109–127). New York: Wiley.

Dawes, R. (1980). Social dilemmas. *Annual Review of Psychology, 31,* 169–193.

Dawes, R. M., & Thaler, R. (1988). Anomolies: Cooperation. *Journal of Economic Perspectives, 2,* 187–197.

Dawes, R. M., Van de Kragt, A. J. C., & Orbell, J. M. (1988). Not me or thee but we: The importance of group identity in eliciting cooperation in dilemmas situations. Experimental manipulations. *Acta Psychologica, 68,* 83–97.

Dawes, R. M., Van de Kragt, A. J. C., & Orbell, J. M. (1990). Cooperation for the benefit of us—not me, or my conscience. In J. Mansbridge (Ed.), *Beyond self-interest.* Chicago: University of Chicago Press.

Edney, J. J. (1980). The commons problem. *American Psychologist, 35,* 131–150.

Edney, J. L., & Harper, C. S. (1978). The commons dilemma: A review of contributions of psychology. *Environmental Management, 2,* 491–502.

Folger, R., & Konovsky, M. (1989). Effects of procedural and distributive justice on reactions to pay raise decisions. *Academy of Management Journal, 32,* 115–130.

Freud, S. (1960). *The ego and the id* (J. Riviere, Trans.). New York: Norton. (Original work published 1923).

Gibbs, J. P. (1975). *Crime, punishment, and deterrence.* New York: Elsevier.

Gibbs, J. P. (1986). Deterrence theory and research. In G. B. Melton (Ed.), *The law as a behavioral instrument* (pp. 87–103). Nebraska symposium on motivation (1985). Lincoln: University of Nebraska Press.

Greenberg, J. (1990). Looking fair versus being fair: Managing impressions of organizational justice. *Research in Organizational Behavior, 12,* 111–157.

Hardin, G. (1968). The tragedy of the commons. *Science, 162,* 1243–1248.

Hogg, M. A., & Abrams, D. (1988). *Social identifications.* New York: Routledge.

Joubert, C. E. (1991). Self-esteem and social desirability in relation to college students' retrospective perceptions of parental fairness and disciplinary practices. *Psychological Reports, 69,* 115–120.

Kahrl, W. L. (1982). *Water and power.* Berkeley and Los Angeles: University of California Press.

Kaslow, F. W. (1990). *Voices in family psychology.* Newbury Park CA: Sage.

Kaslow, F. W. (1991). The art and science of family psychology: Retrospective and perspective. *American Psychologist, 46,* 621–626.

Kelley, S., & Mirer, T. W. (1974). The simple act of voting. *American Political Science Review, 68,* 572–591.

Kelman, H. C. (1958). Compliance, identification, and internalization: Three processes of attitude change. *Journal of Conflict Resolution, 2,* 51–60.

Kerr, N. L. (1989). Illusions of efficacy: The effects of group size on perceived efficacy in social dilemmas. *Journal of Experimental Social Psychology, 25,* 287–313.

Kerr, N. L., & Kaufman-Gilliland, C. M. (1994). Communication, commitment, and cooperation in social dilemmas. *Journal of Personality and Social Psychology, 66,* 513–529.

Kramer, R. (in press). Helping the group or helping one's self? Cognitive and motivational determinants of cooperation in resource conservation dilemmas. In D. Schroeder (Ed.), *Social dilemmas.* New York: Praeger.

Kramer, R., & Brewer, M. (1984). Effects of groups identity on resources use in a simulated commons dilemma. *Journal of Personality and Social Psychology, 46,* 1044–1057.

Kramer, R. and Brewer, M. (1986). Social group identity and the emergence of cooperation in resource conservation dilemmas. In H. Wilke, D. Messick, & C. Rutte (Eds.), *Experimental Studies in Social Dilemmas* (pp. 205–234). Frankfort: Peter Lang.

Kramer, R., & Goldman, L. (1988). *Expectations that bind: Group-based trust, causal attributions, and cooperative behavior in a commons dilemma.* Unpublished manuscript, Stanford University.

Kramer, R., Goldman, L., & Davis, G. (1989). *Social identity, expectations of reciprocity, and cooperation in social dilemmas.* Unpublished manuscript, Stanford University.

Levine, M., & Perkins, D. V. (1987). *An ecological perspective on behavioral understanding.* New York: Oxford University Press.

Lewin, K. (1947). Group decision and social change. In T. M. Newcomb & E. L. Hartley (Eds.), *Readings in Social Psychology* (pp. 330–344). New York: Holt.

Lind, E. A., Kulik, C. T., Ambrose, M., & Park, M. (1991). *Outcome and process concerns in organizational dispute resolution.* Working paper, American Bar Foundation.

Lind, E. A., & Tyler, T. R. (1988). *The social psychology of procedural justice.* New York: Plenum.

London, P. (1970). The rescuers: Motivational hypotheses about Christians who saved Jews from the Nazis. In J. Macauley & L. Berkowitz (Eds.), *Altruism and helping behavior* (pp. 241–250). New York: Academic Press.

Mansbridge, J. J. (1990). *Beyond self-interest.* Chicago: University of Chicago Press.

Martin, F. (1989). *Common pool resources and collective action: A bibliography.* Workshop on political theory and policy analysis. Indiana University, Bloomington.

Masters, J. C., & Yarkin-Levin, K. (1984). *Boundary areas in social and developmental psychology.* Orlando FL: Academic Press.

Melton, G. B., & Saks, M. J. (1986). The law as an instrument of socialization and social structure. In G. B. Melton (Ed.), *The law as a behavioral instru-*

ment (pp. 235–278). Nebraska symposium on motivation (1985). Lincoln: University of Nebraska Press.

Messick, D. M., & Brewer, M. B. (1983). Solving social dilemmas. *Annual Review of Psychology, 40*, 45–81.

Messick, D. M., Wilke, H., Brewer, M. B., Kramer, R. M., Zemke, P. E., & Lui, L. (1983). Individual adaptations and structural change as solutions to social dilemmas. *Journal of Personality and Social Psychology, 44*, 294–309.

Oliner, S. P., & Oliner, P. M. (1988). *The altruistic personality: Rescuers of Jews in Nazi Europe*. New York: Free Press.

Olson, M. (1965). *The logic of collective action*. Cambridge MA: Harvard University Press.

Phillips, N., & Nelson, E. (1976). Energy savings in private households: An integrated research program. *Journal of the Marketing Research Society, 10*, 180–200.

Piaget, J. (1965). *The moral judgment of the child* (M. Gabain, Trans.). New York: Free Press. (Original work published 1932).

Reisner, M. (1986). *Cadillac desert*. New York: Viking.

Roberts, R. E. L., & Bengton, V. L. (1993). Relationships with parents, self-esteem, and psychological well-being in young adulthood. *Social Psychology Quarterly, 56*, 263–277.

Rosenhan, D. (1970). The natural socialization of altruistic autonomy. In J. Macauley & L. Berkowitz (Eds.), *Altruism and helping behavior* (pp. 251–268). New York: Academic Press.

Rushton, P. (1980). *Altruism, socialization, and society*. Englewood Cliffs NJ: Prentice-Hall.

Rutte, C. G., & Wilke, H. A. M. (1984). Social dilemmas and leadership. *European Journal of Social Psychology, 14*, 105–121.

Samuelson, C. D. (1991). Perceived task difficulty, causal attributions, and preferences for structural change in resource dilemmas. *Personality and Social Psychology Bulletin, 17*, 181–187.

Samuelson, C. D., & Biek, M. (1991). Attitudes toward energy conservation: A confirmatory factor analysis. *Journal of Applied Social Psychology, 21*, 549–568.

Samuelson, C. D., & Messick, D. M. (1986a). Alternative structural solutions to resource dilemmas. *Organizational Behavior and Human Decisions Processes, 37*, 139–155.

Samuelson, C. D., & Messick, D. M. (1986b). Inequities in access to and use of shared resources in social dilemmas. *Journal of Personality and Social Psychology, 51*, 960–967.

Samuelson, C. D., & Messick, D. M. (in press). When do people want to change the rules for allocating shared resources? In D. Schroeder (Ed.), *Social dilemmas*. New York: Praeger.

Samuelson, C. D., Messick, D. M., Rutte, C. G., & Wilke, H. (1984). Individual and structural solutions to resource dilemmas in two cultures. *Journal of Personality and Social Psychology, 47*, 94–104.

Sears, D. O. (1986). College sophomore in the laboratory: Influences of a narrow database on social psychology's view of human nature. *Journal of Personality and Social Psychology, 51*, 515–530.

Sears, D. O., Tyler, T. R., Citrin, J., & Kinder, D. R. (1978). Political system support and public response to the energy crisis. *American Journal of Political Science, 22*, 56–82.

Shapiro, S. P. (1987). The social control of impersonal trust. *American Journal of Sociology, 93*, 623–658.

Skinner, B. F. (1953). *Science and human behaviors.* New York: Macmillan.

Tajfel, H. (1978). *Differentiation between social groups.* London: Academic Press.

Tajfel, H. (1982). *Social identity and intergroup relations.* Cambridge: Cambridge University Press.

Tajfel, H., & Turner, J. C. (1986). The social identity theory of intergroup behavior. In S. Worchel & W. G. Austin (Eds.), *Psychology of intergroup behavior* (2nd ed.) (pp. 7–24). Chicago: Nelson-Hall.

Thibaut, J., & Walker, L. (1975). *Procedural justice.* Hillsdale NJ: Erlbaum.

Turner, J. C., Hogg, M., Oakes, P., Reicher, S., & Wetherell, M. (1987). *Rediscovering the social group: A self-categorization theory.* Oxford: Basil Blackwell.

Tyler, T. R. (1984). The role of perceived injustice in defendant's evaluations of their courtroom experience. *Law and Society Review, 18*, 51–74.

Tyler, T. R. (1989). The psychology of procedural justice: A test of the group value model. *Journal of Personality and Social Psychology, 57*, 830–838.

Tyler, T. R. (1990). *Why people obey the law.* New Haven CT: Yale University Press.

Tyler, T. R., & Caine, A. (1981). The role of distributional and procedural fairness in the endorsement of formal leaders. *Journal of Personality and Social Psychology, 41*, 642–655.

Tyler, T. R., & Dawes, R. (1993). Fairness in groups: Comparing the self-interest and social identity perspectives. In B. Mellers & J. Baron (Eds.), *Psychological Perspectives on Justice* (pp. 87–108). Cambridge: Cambridge University Press.

Tyler, T. R., & Degoey, P. (1994). *Collective restraint in a social dilemma situation: The influence of procedural justice and community identification on the empowerment and legitimacy of authority.* Unpublished manuscript.

Tyler, T. R., & Lind, E. A. (1992). A relational model of authority in groups. In M. Zanna (Ed.), *Advances in experimental social psychology* (Vol. 25, pp. 115–191). New York: Academic Press.

Tyler, T. R., Rasinski, K., & McGraw, K. (1985). The influence of perceived injustice on support for political authorities. *Journal of Applied Social Psychology, 15*, 700–725.

Watson, J. B. (1924). *Behaviorism.* New York: Norton.

Weimer, D. L., & Vining, A. R. (1992). *Policy analysis: Concepts and practice.* Englewood Cliffs NJ: Prentice Hall.

West, D. J., & Farrington, D. P. (1973). *Who becomes delinquent?* London: Heinemann Educational.

Wilson, J. (1993). *The moral sense*. New York: Free Press.

Wilson, J., & Herrnstein, R. J. (1985). *Crime and human nature*. New York: Simon & Schuster.

Wit, A. P. (1989). *Group efficiency and fairness in social dilemmas: An experimental gaming approach*. Unpublished doctoral dissertation, University of Groningen, Groningen, Netherlands.

Yamagishi, T. (1986). The provision of a sanctioning system as a public good. *Journal of Personality and Social Psychology, 51*, 110–116.

Yamagishi, T. (1988). Seriousness of social dilemmas and the provision of a sanctioning system. *Social Psychology Quarterly, 51*, 32–42.

Zimring, F. E., & Hawkins, G. J. (1973). *Deterrence: The legal threat in crime control*. Chicago: University of Chicago Press.

Zucker, L. G. (1986). Production of trust: Institutional sources of economic structure, 1840–1920. In B. M. Staw & L. L. Cummings (Eds.), *Research in organizational behavior* (Vol. 8, pp. 53–111). Greenwich CT: JAI.

Social or Individual Orientation? Dilemmas in a Post-Communist World

Mati Heidmets
Tallinn Pedagogical University

What is social good, and how can it be integrated with personal fulfillment? This question, on which this book is focused, was central not only to Soviet psychology but also to daily life in the former Soviet empire. Although the Communist system has collapsed, those of us who live in the East are still looking for the answer.

Such inquiry is important not only to a better understanding of the human condition but also to the social transformation that we are hoping to achieve. For decades, people in Eastern Europe experienced one model of social relations, guided by a particular interpretation of social good and a particular prescription of means to personal fulfillment. Now we are experiencing a new model. Not only new political and economic structures but also new patterns of individual-societal relationships are being introduced.

In a sense, life in the former Communist world has been a massive two-stage social experiment: First, build a society to conform strictly and systematically to a particular ideology, then rapidly tear it down and reconstruct society to match a markedly different social paradigm. Social scientists might find this real-life experiment exciting. It is hard to imagine a richer opportunity to test theories about social change and adaptation.

In fact, however, neither Eastern European nor Western social scientists have had much to say about this period of dramatic transition from one system of political economy to another. Such a contribution may be too much to ask. Understanding this transformation requires one to act simultaneously as insider and outsider—fully aware of the extraordinary changes in daily life but also fully objective in describing the new social reality. The role of dispassionate participant-observer is an especially difficult one to sustain during a time of great social and political turmoil and acute economic hardship. Even if it were possible to fulfill such a role, the number of active researchers in the social sciences in the former Soviet Union has shrunk as business opportunities have proven to be effective lures and as government support for research, especially on microlevel social phenomena, has dwindled.

With these caveats, I intend to address the thematic question of this book primarily from the "social" side: How is social good perceived? How are motives to promote social good injected into personal life? What are the effects of these social constructions?

I have chosen such a perspective in part because of my background. I grew up in a society in which the dominance of "social" over "individual" was taken as an indisputable principle of morality and social reality. I have also adopted such a starting point because it seems more intellectually challenging; I suspect that problems of motivation for social good are more basic and also more controversial than questions about the routes to personal fulfillment.

The Dominance of "Social" Over "Individual": The Communist Model

THE GUIDING PRINCIPLES OF COMMUNIST LIFE

As social animals, human beings throughout history have been faced with needs, constraints, and compulsions related to the social bodies to which they belong. The question of social good is historically, culturally, and developmentally relative. Social good is manifested first and foremost as a problem of competence and authority: Who will decide what is socially good or necessary? When power is vested in a particular individual or entity, that agent or group must then resolve the technical problem of transforming the needs of society into individual behavior.

The Communist experiment presents one definition of social good and the prescription of mechanisms for achieving it. I begin with this approach not to demonstrate my skill in social criticism but instead to identify some problems experienced under Communism that are surprisingly similar to those faced by contemporary Western societies.

The foremost principle in the Communist model is that social good is superior to individual fulfillment. "Social," it is argued, is more important than "individual"; it has been so throughout human history, and it will determine humanity's common future. In this context, "social" means the whole society, as represented by state authority. The practical import of this conceptualization is that individual needs, goals, and actions are subordinated to social needs and goals as defined by the state authorities (politicians and bureaucrats).

In this model, the individual is not the only loser. The welfare of intermediate social units like families, neighborhoods, and communities is also perceived as less important than the good of the whole society, as expressed in the state. In Communist ideology, the intermediate units were conceptualized as gradually losing their significance across human history; such a diminution of importance also became an everyday reality under Communist governments.

The authorities understood well that the key to placing individuals at the service of the state was the development of a mentality in which people identified the needs and goals of society as their own. As we all now know, political force was the initial means of achieving such an identification. This direct subjugation of individual will to the power of the state was reinforced by more subtle means. All domains of public life—the mass media, education, even housing—were used as tools to channel personal motivation toward social good as proclaimed by the state.

COMMUNIST HOUSING POLICY

Housing serves as a good example. During the first two decades of Soviet rule, the development of a physical environment appropriate for the expected new life-style was viewed as an urgent problem. After considerable debate, housing communes were determined to be the best reflection of the new relation between the individual and the society as well as the best means to stimulate the growth of such a social order. Six principles were adopted as bases for living in communes (Heidmets, 1993; Khazanova, 1980): First, housing should be collective. Thousands of people would share the same place of residence, and private housing should be abolished. Second, communal spaces should predominate within housing units. Private space would be kept to a minimum (usually limited to 6–10 m² for private family bedrooms). Third, the commune itself should have large spaces for shared use. The commune would include facilities for residents to eat, wash, read, and play together. Fourth, care of children should be communal. Children would live in dormitories, where they would be supervised by specialists, and they would play and study together in child-care centers and schools within the commune. They would see their parents only during communal leisure-time activities. Fifth, housing should be egalitarian. All families would have the same type of accommodations, and all would have the same access to areas of communal use. Finally, housing should be owned collectively. Housing would be constructed by the state and given to the residents who would assume collective ownership.

Early Soviet housing policy thus reflected the prevailing ideology of relations between the individual and the society. Communal housing was a materialization of Communist ideology: the suppression of individuality and family relations, the "liberation" of children from their parents, support for—indeed, establishment of—the life of the group, and limitation and standardization of personal consumption of goods and services. A collectivist life-style was further intended to be a tool in the development of socialist behavior and mentality—the transformation of motivation—across domains of life. Group interdependence manifested in personal dependency became the norm.

Only a few communes of the ideal described above were actually built before World War II. Thus, there is little direct evidence about their effects. After World War II, a modified version of the collectivist housing program was initiated. The idea of communal living was transformed into the construction of enormous high-rise apartment complexes throughout the Soviet Union during the 1960s, the 1970s, and the 1980s.

Although clearly less utopian in form, the Soviet apartment complexes were based on the same principles as the early communes. The state, as the embodiment of the whole society, was supposed to know what was best; it was further obligated to take care of the individuals within the society. Accordingly, the state *gave* the apartment complexes to the residents; nothing was asked of them while the complexes were being planned and built. Moreover, the residents had a duty to adapt themselves to the prescribed social arrangement.

Whether this policy was good is difficult to answer. Although the personal accommodations were small, millions of people had electricity, central heating, and running water for the first time. At the same time, the long-term social harm in the growth of a culture of dependency was undeniable.

Whatever the balance between short-term benefits and long-term harm, the housing policy reflected the struggle that occurred throughout the Soviet era between, on the one side, the motivation for personal expression and identity and, on the other, the state's goal of suppression of individuality to promote standardized lifestyles and subordinate individual desires to the good of the society. Of course, the outcome of this struggle actually was often compromise, as illustrated by the movement in housing policy from "pure" communes to a kind of semi-communal living. Indeed, study of such compromises between "social" and "personal" in Soviet history—for example, the development of ways to evade prohibitions on private ownership—might be instructive in approaching the central problem in this book.

PERSONALITY IN SOVIET SOCIETY

Sometimes, however, compromises did not occur. Collectivization was often pursued quite aggressively. Individuals became more and more dependent, and the state assumed greater responsibility for everyday life. This submersion of the individual within the whole was acceptable to many people. Communism ultimately provided a more or less stable social environment and engendered a sense of security and predictability.

By the 1970s, many Soviet people really did identify themselves with the society as a whole, and the mental structures that the authorities sought did emerge. In exchange, in effect, for loss of freedom and individual identity, people obtained a sense of social support, a guarantee of provision of basic physical needs by the state, and a belief in a predictable, relatively secure future. McDonald's and a free press were not in that imagined future, but their absence was offset by plenty of Russian ice cream and guaranteed employment and housing.

An important, perhaps even crucial factor in building this collective vision was a strong, officially cultivated opposition to the rest of the world. When one's personal livelihood is so clearly tied to the welfare of the society as a whole, both objectively and subjectively, then it is easy to fear the threat presented by those who not only are outside that collective but also challenge its goodness.

In this context, it should come as no surprise to find that most Soviets accepted the former regime and that many today look nostalgically to the Soviet era. Having experienced the benefits bestowed by the state and having divided the world mentally into "us" and "them," many former Soviets are at best confused by the new ordering of relations between the individual and the society.

THE PERSON-SOCIETY DILEMMA IN SOVIET SOCIAL SCIENCE

Although many citizens approved of the Soviet order and the government pronounced that the relative emphasis of "personal" and "social" was balanced, intellectuals typically realized that the level of personal subjugation present in the Soviet empire was neither necessary nor desirable for social good. How then did Soviet social scientists approach the problem? Doing so was not easy. Opposing the official view meant loss of research opportunities; embracing it meant a loss of intellectual integrity and feigned ignorance of easily available evidence.

The approach that was most likely to prove both politically and intellectually acceptable was historical analysis, which avoided contemporary ideological pressure but enabled examination of fundamental problems of social exchange. Accordingly, the theories of personal-social relations that are most interesting to me were presented by Soviet psychologists and sociologists, such as N. Gumilev, I. Kon, and B. Porshnev, who focused on the historical development of such processes.

One insight from that tradition was that "social" has been dominant over "individual" throughout history. The principal actors in society have always been the collective units: tribes, clans, communes, and families. As members of such groups, individuals were "not autonomous parts of the community but elements of the indivisible whole, unable to survive outside the community" (Kon, 1978, p. 128). Dependence on the group meant full identification with it— in which the subject thinks of himself or herself not as "I" but "we." Mental construction of the world has been typified throughout history by differentiation between others and *us*, strangers and us, and enemies and us, not others and *me*. This dichotomy stands as "a universal principle of emerging human communities during all our history" (Porshnev, 1979, p. 88).

According to this view, issues about personal fulfillment are relatively new. Throughout most of history, life was dominated by the pursuit of social good, as defined by the tradition and interests of the tribe. Only in modern times have individuals acted autonomously with recognition of the self and personal strengths and limitations. The European Renaissance established the "tendency to consider the individual self as the highest moral and social value . . . with common acceptance of the right (and even obligation) to fully realize one's potential" (Kon, 1978, p. 138). Thus the dominance of individualism—conscious motivation to achieve personal fulfillment and self-actualization—has been a feature of only the last historical epoch.

Assuming the validity of this historical analysis, one still may ask about the significance of social forces during an era in which the pervasive view is that human behavior results from autonomous action stimulated by motivation for individual gratification. The Soviet historicists reply that the importance of collective interests and communal responsibilities has not diminished. The growth of individualism has been accompanied by *expanding* interdependence as society has become global, with multinational corporations, everbroadening political alliances, and international environmental problems.

The modern dilemma arises, therefore, from contradictory historical trends toward autonomy of individuals and interdependence of individuals, groups, communities, and nations. Are these trends compatible? When individual behavior is oriented toward personal goals, who represents the interests of the complex, powerful new "wholes"? What will happen to individuals amid these new concentrations of economic and political power, which may be more dangerous simply because of their enormous scope and resources?

One way to resolve the historical contradiction is the Soviet approach: Push everyone into a high-rise apartment complex and then enforce a centrally determined allocation of resources and establishment of group activities. Give clear priority to social good, and constrain the individual.

The disastrous results of the Soviet experiment are evident to everyone, but what are the alternatives? Is Western liberal democracy strong enough to keep social good and personal fulfillment in balance if both forces continue to strengthen?

Looking from the East to the West: Old and New Hesitations

THE SEARCH FOR A NEW MODEL

In answering the above questions, it is important to recognize that the Communist regime achieved some compatibility of individual strivings with social goals for some time. The price for doing so was quite high, however—too high for the Soviet empire to survive.

Now, as Eastern European nations look for a new model to guide public policy, we inevitably turn to the West to find a more human approach to social life and a better resolution of the contradiction between individualism and interdependence. From the perspective of post-Communist uncertainty, how does the West look?

A political system emphasizing individual liberty combined with an economic system featuring a free market no doubt maximizes economic efficiency. Wealth grows, and society develops, when the prevailing ideology gives free rein to individual desires and pays little attention to social needs.

Having a habit of skepticism about attractive schemes, some in the East are questioning, however, the price of accepting the individualist model. If we adopt the Western approach, can we be sure that we will not face convulsions similar to those that we have experienced in the past few years? Although the Western liberal democracies are far more self-regulatory and adaptable than the Communist system, they also appear to have some inherent limitations that are causing some skepticism and fear in Eastern Europe.

ILLUSORY HAPPINESS

In Russian intellectual culture, a primary source of skepticism is the concept of personal fulfillment, in particular, capitalism is seen as leading people to seek happiness in the wrong places. Self-gratification is unlikely to provide real fulfillment because "the essence of humanity lies in a field of interpersonal relations, rooted in experiences of interpersonal oneness" (Kon, 1978, p. 23). In short, although the people in the West are moving quickly, they are moving in the wrong direction.

Some scholars are adding loss of motivation to the list of "direction issues." German Diligensky (1991), a Russian philosopher, sees an apocalyptic crisis in Western civilization: "This crisis means that goals and motives, which have organized this [Western] social system have lost their meaning and importance. . . . The whole system determining human motivation and behavior is crumbling. Paradoxically, individual liberty itself is dispersing the values and meaning of life" (p. 37).

The idea is that the unfettered pursuit of self-interest inevitably brings increased alienation and loss of motivation. While the complicated world of Russian interpretations of the meaning of life and the path to happiness is beyond the scope of this chapter, I do think that the basic point of the Russian critics is worth pondering. Maybe such strange issues as "direction of movement" and "seeking of meaning for the endless circles of production and consumption" remain open for discussion, especially in societies in which basic physical needs are satisfied for most people and those whose lives are most comfortable are sometimes the ones searching for goals and meaning. Reading the other chapters in this volume, I am reminded of the aspects of life in Western democracies that are sometimes described as postmodern: the decline of social bonds and structures, such as family, neighborhood, and community.

THE NEW DEPENDENCY

Although the Russian criticism is provocative, my own concern is focused on a more concrete and urgent issue: the risk of dependency. The Western model of society is based on a perpetual cycle of production and consumption of wealth. The inevitable outcome is a new "nature," an artificial environment. This constructed world grows and multiplies, maybe even faster than our ability to comprehend and interpret it (see Moiseev, 1993).

Humankind is increasingly free from nature but dependent on technology. This dependency is most striking and most problematic in the West, where it is most developed. It hides grave risks not only to the physical ecology but also to the social ecology. Individuals are increasingly less capable of adapting successfully by themselves. We need professional specialists to assist us in managing the new environment.

Perhaps the best analysis of this "new and risky dependence" has been presented by Ulrich Beck (1992), a German sociologist, who points out several features of modern societies that create and exacerbate this risk. First, individualism means that everyone is so unconstrained by social structures that they must "construct their own biographies." Alone, each person must face the labor market "with all its attendant risk, opportunities, and contradictions" (Beck, 1992, p. 92).

Second, people are being liberated from traditional social networks. We are observing a "social transformation . . . in the course of which people will be set free from the social forms of industrial society—class, stratification, family, gender status of men and women—just as during the course of the Reformation people were released from the secular rule of the church in the society" (Beck, 1992, p. 89).

Third, this "liberation" is matched by increasing dependency on "institutions and actors, who may well be—and are arguably increasingly—alien, obscure, and inaccessible" (Beck, 1992, p. 4). Beck is referring to the emergence of something similar to that which I have described as the new "whole," a level of social organization that is beyond the state, a hardly definable socioeconomic system. Individual existence in a context of such a "whole" means more rules, limitations, and needs in order to avoid the risks that are inevitable in a highly complicated world.

At the psychological level, this new dependence is experienced as fear: "If . . . the driving force in the class society can be summarized in the phrase 'I'm hungry,' then in the risk society it is expressed in the statement 'I'm afraid'" (Beck, 1992, p. 49). If people who are hungry are motivated to obtain things (foods, shelter, and clothing), then the people from the world of fear are afraid of losing what they have. The way to reduce that fear is to surrender some personal freedom by following the demands of the new social organism.

In the context of social-personal exchange, this experience is reflected in a new social dependency. The demands of the "social" are no longer overt and obvious, as under the Communist regime, but instead covert and subtle. That subtlety makes it easier to ignore the existence of the dependency, but it also obscures the problem and makes coping with it harder.

Similar conclusions have been reached by ecologists concerned with sustainable development. Noting the growth orientation of Western society, they conclude that "sustainable growth in a finite environment is a logical impossibility, but there is no contradiction in sustainable development" (Rees, 1991). Given ecological, technological, social, and political realities, change from an orientation toward growth to an orientation toward development inevitably results in some subordination of individual freedom to pursuit of communal social goals. The result must be changes in lifestyles and consumption patterns—changes that are hardly popular.

Do these insights forecast a return to Communism or at least to a strong central power that can represent the interests of the new whole and implement strategies to protect them? Even the most rational Weberian bureaucracy lacks the capacity to balance personal and communal needs in the complex contemporary world. Beck argues that such an accommodation should be made by society itself through public discussion and grassroots political activity: "only if medicine opposes medicine, nuclear physics opposes nuclear physics, human genetics opposes human genetics . . . can the future that is being brewed in the testtube become intelligible and evaluable by the outside world" (Beck, 1992, p. 234).

Of course, one might be skeptical about the capacity of society to manage the new situation. Moiseev (1993), for example, reaches a quite different conclusion: "To create a new moral imperative . . . for global society has become a most urgent task for civilization. . . .

Trying to understand the possible basis for this new morality, I have to return to the basic principles of Christianity. . . . And I'm doing this not as a Christian, but as a natural scientist, who has all his life tried to discover the mechanisms of development and self-organization in nature, the processes where we now observe the fatal imprints of ourselves" (p. 14).

To juxtapose Beck's and Moiseev's views, we in the East now have a choice of large-scale grassroots debate or revealed truths, radical rationalism or religious revival. These are the new dilemmas and fears of the (capitalist?) future against the backdrop of the ruins of a failed system.

Conclusions

East and West may be converging in a social transformation based in our common dependency. We must move in a far more "social" direction than has been typical in the West, but we must do so in a way that is more sensitive to individual needs than was present under the Communist regime.

The role of social good under our former Communist government and perhaps in our future (postcapitalist?) society can be summarized as follows:

- Who defines social good?
  The past: The state (through proclamations by the authorities)
  The future: Society (through public discussion)
- What is the social good?
  The past: Movement to the ideal state
  The future: Solving contemporary problems
- How is the social good achieved?
  The past: Through use of force and propaganda
  The future: Development of a consensus through public discussion
- What does the society expect of individuals?
  The past and the future: Identification
- What are the obstacles to achievement of social good?
  The past: Alienation and inefficiency
  The future: The intractability of socioeconomic problems

The only similarity of these two models is that the "whole" is able to sustain itself only if individuals identify with its goals and ideals. Just as the Communist system focused on the development and maintenance of a particular worldview, the new society can function only in a regime of public participation in the pursuit of social good. Thus, some shifts in personal-fulfillment strategies should be expected.

The significance of personal fulfillment in the (Communist) past and the (postcapitalist?) future might be summarized as follows:

- Who defines personal fulfillment?
  The past: Society, represented by the state
  The future: The market
- What is its content?
  The past: Serving social goals
  The future: Satisfying personal needs
- How is it achieved?
  The past: Work and collective action
  The future: Personal success
- What does the individual expect of society?
  The past: Stability and certainty
  The future: Freedom from restraint
- What are the obstacles to achievement of personal fulfillment?
  The past: Dissonance between social and personal needs
  The future: The market cycle and related risks

Such comparisons are highly simplified, but they can illuminate some unexpected similarities or hidden controversies. One is identification and identity formation, a topic of increasing importance and controversy in both the East and the West. How can identification with the global society be obtained if it will affect individual interests and lifestyles, sometimes painfully, especially in the wealthiest countries? Can social identification still be achieved in former Communist countries in which people are impatiently awaiting rapid economic growth—a goal that appears to be related to individual freedom to pursue self-interest? Can individual liberty be preserved in a world that is increasingly interdependent?

Although the Eastern European experience makes the social cost of extreme communalism clear, I agree with Doyal and Gough that an accommodation of individual and social interests is possible only if the goal of self-fulfillment is tempered by strong moral principles that take global consequences into account: "There is a firm moral case for a global conception of need and of just ways of meeting needs—a case which is buttressed by the growing and probably irreversible interdependencies in the modern world. . . . Optimizing need satisfaction on a world scale ultimately entails some system of global authority to enforce global rights to need satisfaction. . . . In transition to this system, there must be an awareness among the citizens of the privileged parts of the world that we have some responsibility for the global order" (Doyal & Gough, 1991, p. 294).

REFERENCES

Beck, U. (1992). *Risk society: Towards a new modernity.* London: Sage.
Diligensky, G. (1991). End of history or change of civilizations? *Voprosy Filosofii, 3,* 14–35.
Doyal, L., & Gough, I. (1991). *A theory of human need.* London: Maximillian.
Heidmets, M. (1993). Mass housing areas and their young inhabitants: The situation in former Soviet territories. In K. Ekberg & P. E. Mjaavatn (Eds.), *Children at risk: Selected papers* (pp. 78–85). Trondheim: Norwegian Centre for Child Research.
Khazanova, V. (1980). *Soviet architecture: The first decade.* Moscow: Nauka.
Kon, I. (1978). *Discovering the self.* Moscow: Politizdat.
Moiseev, N. (1993). The 21st century world and the Christian tradition. *Voprosy Filosifii, 8,* 3–14.
Porshnev, B. (1979). *Social psychology and history.* Moscow: Nauka.
Rees, W. (1991, September). *Understanding sustainable development.* Paper presented at the conference on Sustainable Development and the Future of Cities, Dessau, Germany.

Social Networks and Family Violence in Cross-Cultural Perspective

Jill E. Korbin

Case Western Reserve University

One of our deeply cherished beliefs is that the family is a place of comfort, love, and safety—a refuge from the cruelty of the larger outside world. This conventional wisdom springs not from fantasy or wishful thinking but from human experience. Even in the worst of circumstances, most families take good, or at least adequate, care of their members to protect them and to enhance their survival, comfort, happiness, and well-being. Yet even in the best of circumstances, some families maltreat their members.

It is no longer novel or startling, as it was a mere 15 or 30 years ago (Adelson, 1961; Elmer, 1960; Kempe et al., 1962; Straus et al., 1980), to point out that violence occurs among family members. The various forms of intrafamilial maltreatment were first identified as matters of public and professional concern in Western nations, in particular in the United States. Historical and policy analyses (e.g., Gelles, 1987; Gordon, 1988; Lynch, 1985; Nelson, 1984; Pleck, 1987) show that intrafamilial violence is not a new problem but that the framing of the issue took on a new light as efforts were made to promote public awareness and to construct appropriate social and legal policies.

With the recognition that the family is a place of danger for some rather than a universal place of safety for all, questions arose as to whether intrafamilial maltreatment was an aspect of human nature or simply a concomitant of many of the ills of Western societies. Attention therefore turned to cultures very different from Western societies. The cross-cultural literature has fueled speculation about human motivations and cultural factors that promote or prevent violence and maltreatment.[1] The cross-cultural record is rich, even though relatively little attention has been directed specifically or systematically at family violence.

This chapter first briefly summarizes the cross-cultural literature concerning the occurrence of different forms of family violence. It then turns to a discussion of what our understanding of family violence looks like if we put social networks at the core. While child maltreatment is the focus, other forms of familial violence are included in the discussion.

The Cross-Cultural Occurrence of Family Violence

While intrafamilial violence is relatively rare in some societies, its existence is recognized in almost all cultures (Counts et al., 1992; Korbin, 1981, 1987; Levinson, 1988). Contrasting views of the "pristine" state of human social life in which family members are either treated with unfailing kindness and respect or treated with brutality are not borne out by the cross-cultural record. Rather, the picture is more complex.

A major problem in cross-cultural comparisons is that of cultural equivalence. That is, how are behaviors and their consequences made meaningful within their cultural contexts and how can this be translated across cultural boundaries? Examples of practices that would be differentially defined as child abuse or neglect by different cultural groups are abundant in the cross-cultural record (Finkelhor & Korbin, 1988; Garbarino & Ebata, 1983; Gray & Cosgrove, 1985; Green, 1982; Hong & Hong, 1991; Ima & Hohm, 1991; Korbin, 1981, 1987; Scheper-Hughes, 1987). While anthropology has generally stressed cultural relativity, increased attention has been directed to cultural practices that even in context may be detrimental and harmful (Edgerton, 1992; Keesing, 1982).

Estimates of the incidence and prevalence of family violence hinge on valid and reliable definitions. *Culture, family,* and *intra-*

familial violence are all difficult to define. They are political as well as social and scientific terms that have varied across time. The difficulty in defining these terms is compounded by the fact that they are heterogeneous and not unitary phenomena. Not all countries have comparable reporting systems, and among those that do, report data have been subject to bias. However, the question of relative incidence and prevalence is important to consider, in large part because questions of relative magnitude have contributed to the search for cultural differences in the etiology of maltreatment.

The following sections are a brief summary of the evidence for the occurrence of different forms of family violence in cross-cultural perspective.

CHILD MALTREATMENT

Among Western countries, and within multiple-jurisdiction countries like the United States, child-maltreatment statistics are difficult to compare across differing systems of reporting and record keeping. Moving beyond Western nations, definitional issues of cultural equivalency exacerbate the difficulties in comparisons of the frequency of child maltreatment. Hoping to avoid the pitfalls of cultural differences in definitions of child maltreatment, Levinson (1988, 1989) examined physical punishment of children in a sample of 90 small-scale and peasant societies.[2] Physical punishment of children occurred in 74.4% of the societies studied. The intracultural variability is even more interesting than the overall prevalence cross-culturally. Physical discipline was regularly or frequently used in 34.4% of societies and was rarely or never employed in 26.5%. Behaviors coded as physical punishment (including spanking, slapping, beating, scalding, burning, pushing, and pinching) overlap somewhat with both mild and severe behaviors included in the Conflict Tactics Scales (Straus et al., 1980) and with behaviors that have the potential for causing injury and therefore of being implicated in child-abuse reports in the United States.

Despite increasing international awareness, child abuse and neglect are often difficult to recognize or make sense of in small populations. Because child maltreatment is a low base-rate behavior, it may be rare in a small population during the one or one-and-a-half years of fieldwork that is traditional in anthropology. Among the Inuit, for example, Graburn (1987) observed a few cases of what could be described as the classic battered child. These cases were not only rare, but they also contradicted past literature on Inuit peoples and Graburn's overall impression of nurturing, indulgent, and nonpunitive Inuit parenting. Descriptions of these cases were not published until well after Graburn's fieldwork (Graburn, 1987), thereby leaving intact a literature that would lead one to believe that child abuse was almost nonexistent among Inuit peoples living in traditional circumstances (Briggs, 1975; Graburn 1987). Similarly, in my own fieldwork among rural Hawaiian-Polynesian-Americans, child maltreatment seemed so aberrant from the larger pattern of loving and attentive care of children that the few cases that came to my attention also did not find their way into the literature for many years (Korbin, 1990a).

On the other hand, Levy (1964) recognized the newly identified "battered-child syndrome" (Kempe et al., 1962) among the Navajo. Twins, about whom there was traditional ambivalence, showed a pattern in which one or both were unlikely to survive.

The frequency of child maltreatment is also difficult to assess in societies with high infant-mortality rates and high mortality rates for those under five. Neglect as a component in differential child survival may be difficult to distinguish from disease or malnutrition in individual cases, even though demographic analyses have yielded categories of children at risk (e.g., Das Gupta, 1987; Scrimshaw, 1978). Some children may fail to receive the level of care required to ensure their survival, but the cause of death may be attributed to factors beyond parental control. While her analysis has generated controversy (Nations & Rebhun, 1988), Scheper-Hughes (1992) has described a pattern of classification of child illness in a Brazilian favela that allows parental withdrawal of care from children who are thought to be unlikely to thrive. Nuitini and Roberts (1993) described a pattern in Tlaxcala, Mexico, in which the deaths of infants were attributed to being "sucked" by the *tlaheulpuchi* (blood-sucking witches), even though many in the community suspected that mothers or other members of the household were involved in the infant deaths. The cultural belief in witches, then, afforded a cultural explanation that relieved parents of culpability. Our cultural construction of ideal mothering and child death may similarly confound accurate identification of child fatalities. As but one example, publication of a case report of one mother with several children whose deaths were diagnosed as sudden infant death syndrome (SIDS) led to murder charges being filed against her some years later (Pinholster, 1994).

An additional problem in estimating the cross-cultural incidence and prevalence of child maltreatment is reporting bias by race and social class (Newberger et al., 1977). Hampton and Newberger (1985), in a reanalysis of the National Incidence Study (National Center on Child Abuse and Neglect, 1981), found that class and race were the best predictors of whether an incident was reported by hospitals. Impoverished black families were more likely to be reported than affluent white families, even if the severity of the incident was comparable. O'Toole, Turbett, and Nalepka (1983) found that vignettes were more likely to be identified as abuse if a lower-class caretaker was involved. A recent study found that drownings were more likely to be reported to child protection services if, among other variables, the family was nonwhite and poor (Feldman et al., 1993).

Reporting bias is evident not only in the United States. A government report in New Zealand in the early 1970s (Fergusson et al., 1972) indicated that Polynesian (primarily Maori) children were vastly overrepresented in child abuse and neglect reports. Polynesian children, who accounted for approximately 10% of the child population of New Zealand, constituted more than half of the children reported as not being properly supervised. In part, this high reporting rate was the result of cultural conflict in the definition of child maltreatment, because the Polynesian practice of sibling caretaking was misunderstood. In the indigenous setting, sibling caretaking is highly valued by both children and adults and is central to Polynesian socialization patterns (Gallimore et al., 1974; Korbin, 1990a). However, in the move to urban settings, Maoris often find themselves in the poorest sections of the city in substandard housing that is more prone to fire, on streets with fast-moving cars, and isolated from a larger supportive network of kin. Sibling care taking in this changed setting may indeed pose increased risk to children of accident and injury (Ritchie & Ritchie, 1981). Twenty years later Kotch and his colleagues (Kotch et al., 1993), found that Polynesian children, particularly Maori and Samoan children, are still more likely to have injuries and fatalities attributed to maltreatment than are white children.

SPOUSAL VIOLENCE

In contrast to child maltreatment, which may be rare in some smaller-scale societies, spousal violence may be so ubiquitous in many societies that the ethnographer treats it as a regularity of culture. This may account for the fact that, despite its prevalence, spousal violence has been relatively ignored in the anthropological literature (Counts et al., 1992; Erchak, 1984). Spousal violence is often a matter of anecdote in the cross-cultural literature. Elizabeth Fernea (1965) accompanied her husband to a village in the Middle East while he conducted his dissertation fieldwork in anthropology. She was advised by the women who befriended her to scream at least occasionally from behind her courtyard walls so that others would believe that her husband beat her and thus loved her. Similarly, Hawaiian-Americans expressed the belief about marital relations as, "No fight, no love" (Ito, n.d.).

Wife beating is the most common cross-cultural form of intrafamilial violence. In Levinson's (1988, 1989) study of 90 non-Western small-scale and peasant societies, women were the most common recipients of family violence. Wife beating was reported in 84.5% of these societies (Levinson, 1988, 1989). As was the case with physical punishment of children, the intracultural variability is even more interesting than the overall prevalence of wife beating. Wife beating occurs in all or almost all households in 18.8% of societies and rarely or never in 15.5%. Thus, even where wife beating is tolerated, some men do not beat their wives. And even where wife beating is strictly forbidden, some men nevertheless are violent toward their wives.

In comparison, husband beating was present in fewer societies in Levinson's (1988, 1989) study, and occurred in those societies in which wife beating was found (even if the two did not occur simultaneously). Husband beating occurred in 26.9% of societies, but in only 6.7% of societies was it found in a majority of households. Husband beating was rare or absent in 73.1% of societies.

What has been termed *mutual combat,* in which both husbands and wives are violent toward one another, occurred in only four of Levinson's 90 societies (Levinson, 1988, 1989).[3] In an Australian Aboriginal community, however, Burbank (1992) recorded 58 fights between men and women over an approximately 19-month period. It was possible to determine the initiator of 37 of these altercations:

women initiated 17 and men 20. As in mutual combat as described by Straus and his colleagues (Straus et al., 1980), women were more likely than men to be injured.

SIBLING VIOLENCE

Sibling violence is the most frequent form of intrafamilial violence in the United States, with prevalence among 82% of siblings (Straus et al., 1980). In Levinson's cross-cultural study, however, sibling violence occurred in 43.7% of societies and was routine in only 22.9%. In the United States, sibling aggression may be the training ground for intrafamilial violence, Straus et al. (1980) have argued. In other societies, particularly those with extended households that punish child-on-child aggression more severely (Minturn & Lambert, 1964), sibling violence may be less frequent, as will be discussed below. Since there was information on sibling violence in only 48 of Levinson's 90 societies, another possibility is that sibling violence went unrecorded by Western ethnographers who consider sibling violence, as reflecting sibling rivalry, to be a commonplace and normal part of development.

ELDER MISTREATMENT

Cross-cultural gerontology has sought to address the myth that, in smaller-scale, simple societies, elders are venerated and invariably treated well (Foner, 1984; Glascock & Feinman, 1981; Goldstein et al., 1983; Tout, 1989). The treatment of elders varies across cultures. In some foraging societies living in precarious environments, elders may be required to commit suicide or wander away from the group to a certain death when they can no longer keep up with or contribute to the group. In other foraging societies, elders are carried when they can no longer walk and are cared for well, even in times of famine (Myerhoff, 1978). In a study of 42 developing cultures, Glascock and Feinman (1981) found 16 cases in which elders were abandoned and another 26 cases in which they were killed. In Levinson's (1989) cross-cultural sample, however, violence toward elders was rare.

As the above discussion indicates, violence within the family occurs in various forms and across a wide range of cultural contexts. The next section of this chapter suggests some factors that contribute to or prevent violence among family members in diverse cultural contexts.

Social Networks and the Etiology of Family Violence

Colin Turnbull, an anthropologist who studied the Mbuti of the Ituri Forest in Zaire, wrote of a couple who became engaged in a serious argument. Among the Mbuti, the hut is symbolic of social relationships. If an argument or dispute arises between two households, a woman may simply move the doorway of their home to face away from the offending neighbor. In this particular instance, the angry wife began tearing down the leaves that formed the walls of their dwelling. Her husband ridiculed her, leaving her no option but to continue tearing down their hut. All the leaves had been removed, and she began to take out the framework of sticks. Once the hut was completely dismantled, the wife would have no choice but to return to her parents' home. Suddenly, the husband suggested to the wife that she did not need to wash the sticks, just the leaves. The couple then took the leaves from their home to the stream and diligently washed each one. The wife replaced the leaves, restoring their hut, and all was well: "For several days women talked politely about the insects in the leaves of their huts, and took a few leaves down to the stream to wash, as if this was a perfectly normal procedure. I have never seen it done before or since" (Turnbull, 1961, pp. 132–133).

I begin this section with this story not as an example of non-violent conflict resolution juxtaposed against the prevalence of family violence in other societies. In the context of Mbuti society, this incident threatened the very existence of a marriage. Rather, this story highlights the importance of a social network not only in providing the parameters of acceptable disputes and the scrutiny to keep an altercation within acceptable bounds but also in endorsing the couple's way out of their difficulty. That the other women engaged in the wholly unnecessary act of washing the leaves of their huts brought an altercation back from the brink of marital destruction.

The cross-cultural literature is a rich source, what anthropologists call "the natural laboratory," for generating and testing hypotheses about human behavior. If a variable or a constellation of variables are associated with intrafamilial violence, then they should hold both across and within cultural contexts. In this chapter, I focus on what our understanding of intrafamilial violence looks like if we put social networks at the core. The goal of this discussion is to move beyond consideration of the motivations of individuals in isolation from the broader social context. It is not to suggest that attributes of networks in and of themselves sufficiently explain the presence or absence of family violence.

"It takes a village to raise a child" has become a cliché of the need for broader social responsibility for children. The village, while important, is not a panacea; the statement depends on what kind of village. The village must have the resources to provide a supportive context for child rearing. There must be sufficient consensus to provide a nexus of individuals to assist with child rearing. And the village must have the moral authority to establish and enforce standards of good care and bring back into line those who deviate too greatly from the continuum of acceptable or tolerable behavior. We need to understand better not only the motivation of the perpetrator to be aggressive and the motivation of the recipient to tolerate this aggression but also the motivations of the wider network of individuals surrounding the persons engaged in violence.

A useful starting point is Gelles's (1983) straightforward statement proposing an exchange or social-control theory of intrafamilial violence: "People hit and abuse other people because they can" (p. 157). The statement is correct if others will not intervene and if the target of the aggression has little power or recourse to retaliate, as well as if they have more to gain from the violent behavior than they do from nonviolence. The cross-cultural literature can help us to understand why family members can hit or maltreat one another as well as under what conditions they do or do not maltreat one another.

It has been suggested (e.g., Garbarino & Crouter, 1978; Garbarino & Kostelny, 1992; Garbarino & Sherman, 1980) that the presence of social networks and social supports to children and families, and a positive balance between supports and strains, is important to child well-being and the prevention of child maltreatment. The cross-cultural literature strongly supports the position that social networks provide an important protection from child maltreatment (Korbin 1981, 1987) and spousal violence (Counts et al., 1992). At the same time, the notion of social networks as an unfailing remedy for child maltreatment has been thoughtfully challenged (e.g., Thompson, 1992).

Not all networks are good networks and not all network involvement is positive (e.g., Thompson, 1992). Proximity or frequency of contact with kin, friends, or neighbors does not necessarily mean that those individuals will be helpful or supportive. Further, if individuals in one's network are themselves abusive or neglectful, this may reinforce maltreating behaviors and attitudes. Potentially abusive or neglectful parents may take solace or comfort in the idea that they are not "bad" parents but simply behave like everyone else around them (Korbin, 1989).

For example, among women incarcerated for fatal child maltreatment, I was initially puzzled by the women's reports of active social networks and a high level of perceived social support. Some women reported seeing friends on a daily basis, sharing meals, and watching one another's children. In each case of fatal maltreatment, a professional, neighbor, relative, or friend knew about prior incidents of abuse of the child. A major factor in perpetuating the abuse up to the fatality was the reassurance the woman received from her social network that she was a "good mother" and not an abusive parent (Korbin, 1989).

Our thinking about the construct of social support needs to expand to examine how social networks and perceived social supportiveness can exacerbate the risks for adverse outcomes such as child maltreatment. A high level of perceived support sustained, probably unintentionally, these women in their pattern of abusive behavior. In contrast, a low level of perceived support that did not bolster the woman's self-concept as a good mother but that might have acted against the continuing abuse would have not been perceived as supportive.

The question must also be posed as to whether one's social network can exacerbate the risk for child maltreatment. Some networks are composed of problematic individuals who support and reinforce one another's attitudes and behaviors. These women reported that their friends and siblings exhibited parenting skills and attitudes much like their own. One woman and her siblings all hit their own children. However, none would have dared to intervene in the parenting behavior of another, because they were fearful that the adult would turn on them or that their own abusive behavior would be reported. Further, since they all behaved similarly, the force leveled at their children was perceived as within the normal range.

Networks do not necessarily have complete knowledge of their members' behavior. Because family violence occurs in private, not all incidents are necessarily known. Specific incidents, then, could be seen as aberrations rather than regular behavior and thereby rationalized away.

INTERVENTION BY OTHERS

The privacy and isolation of nuclear families in the United States and Western countries in general has been suggested to be the essence of why intrafamilial violence can occur and continue unchecked (e.g., Garbarino, 1977). The implication is that the intervention of others would prevent the maltreatment. However, even if others intervene, they may be ineffective. A few examples illustrate the point.

In November 1987, national attention was riveted on a seven-year-old girl, Lisa Steinberg, who had been beaten to death by her adoptive parents. The story became even more compelling as neighbors and others testified that they had seen the small girl with bruises and injuries, had heard yelling and screaming from the apartment, and in some cases had called social services or the police.

In the recent case of two 10-year-old British boys found guilty of kidnapping and killing a toddler, the police investigation identified approximately 30 adults who had seen the three children. Some observed the older boys dragging along a crying toddler, and some witnesses noticed a bruise on the toddler's forehead. They were told by the older boys that the toddler was their younger sibling or that he was a lost child that they were taking to the police station (Schmidt, 1993).

In contrast, in the rural Hawaiian community where I conducted ethnographic fieldwork for a period of years, one morning I was casually watching young children playing in the ocean with a rubber raft. An older brother of about eight years of age began teasing his younger brother of about four years of age, saying that he was going to dump him over, push him out to sea, take the raft away and leave him, and so on. Because the younger boy was not in danger (in my estimation), I did not intervene. Instead, I retained the stance of the impartial and nonintrusive observer, with an eye to writing up ethnographic fieldnotes later. After a few moments, the older boy stopped teasing the younger, and all the children moved back into the shallow water. An older couple had been watching from a distance, but felt no need to intervene because I, an adult, was nearby. Indeed, they praised me for making the older boy stop teasing his brother. They dismissed my claim that I had not intervened as indicating appropriately modest and non-self-aggrandizing behavior. These are only anecdotes and individual incidents, but they reflect larger societal and cultural proclivities toward intervention.

In smaller-scale closely knit societies, intervention is most often in the domain of kin and neighbors, who are often one and the same. In larger, more heterogeneous, and more anonymous societies, families may be embedded in networks of known individuals who will intervene. If not, individuals less well known to the family or unknown bystanders must fill this role. The willingness of unknown and/or unrelated others to intervene on behalf of children has not been well studied with respect to child maltreatment. The literature in social psychology on "bystander behavior" (e.g., Baumeister et al., 1988; Dovido, 1984; Tice & Baumeister, 1985) may be relevant to the well-being of children. It identifies situational factors (e.g., presence of others, appearance of person in need of help) and individual characteristics (e.g., personality factors, leadership position) that promote altruistic or prosocial intervention in public in simulated circumstances or emergencies in which there is little risk to the intervener.

Davis (1991) interviewed 37 individuals (involved in 50 incidents) who had initiated an encounter in response to public punishment of a child. Most individuals who intervened were women addressing a punishing mother. Those who intervened received a hostile response from the punishing parent and a mixed reaction from individuals in their own networks. For example, one woman's husband warned her to stay out of the conflict, that she was lucky that the parent did not turn around and hit her. Indeed, "there is a common shift in interactive focus from the wrongful treatment of the child to the deviant involvement of the stranger" (Davis, 1991, p. 242).

This situation is borne out in our current study of neighborhood conditions related to reported rates of child maltreatment in Cleveland, Ohio (Coulton et al., in press; Korbin & Coulton, 1994). Neighborhood residents ($N = 121$) believe that they are living in vastly changed circumstances from their own childhoods. Preliminary analysis indicates that 88.4% ($n = 107$) felt that someone would have made them behave when they were children if their parents were not present. The overwhelming tenor of their remarks was that any adult had the authority to enforce good behavior. Any adult who observed their misbehavior could reprimand or sometimes physically punish them. Whether or not the other adult took direct action, their parents were likely to be informed of their misbehavior. A common response was that they would have been disciplined twice, first by the intervening adult and then again by their parents for behaving badly enough to warrant another adult's attention. To paraphrase one resident, "The parent would punish the child and thank the neighbor."

In contrast, fewer than one-third of residents (32.1%; $n = 36$) reported that someone would intervene today if a child was misbehaving. Residents expressed the belief that parents would take the child's side. They also were apprehensive that the child's parents would be angry at them for intervening and the parents might retaliate verbally or physically. Disturbingly, a degree of the hesitancy to intervene was also tied to fear that children and adolescents would verbally assault them or physically retaliate against them or their property.

To paraphrase the comments of one neighborhood resident: "Before, neighbors treated all children like their own. Now no one would step in. People don't want to step on other people's toes. And if they do step in sometimes the kids, or even the parents get nasty. Just a few days ago, there was a woman walking down the sidewalk by our house. She had a little boy with her who was throwing rocks at our dogs. I told the boy to stop it, and the mother turned around and said all kinds of words I can't repeat. Then the little kid repeated exactly what she said!"

THE BROADER CONTEXT

Cross-culturally, social networks provide assistance to parents with child-care tasks and responsibilities, and parents are more likely to display warmth rather than rejection toward their children if others are available to assist with child-care tasks (Minturn & Lambert, 1964; Rohner, 1986). Networks further provide options for redistribution of children. Children who are not wanted by their parents can be absorbed into other households where they are wanted for their economic or emotional contributions. Mechanisms such as child lending, fostering, and informal adoption allow redistribution of children on a temporary or permanent basis.

Informal child lending may ease the stress of children who tax scarce family resources. In some African-American communities in the United States, children may be redistributed among a network of households, depending on the need for child helpers and the available resources. If one family is temporarily low on resources, the child may go to live for a few weeks with an "aunt" who is in a better position (Stack, 1974).

A focus on social networks, however, must consider the context in which networks of kin and neighbors must function. Ongoing epidemiological and ethnographic research on neighborhood factors associated with reported rates of child maltreatment in Cleveland has identified macrosocial factors that predict variation in rates of child maltreatment (Coulton et al., n.d.; Korbin & Coulton, 1994). Variation in rates of reported child maltreatment in Cleveland's urban neighborhoods is related to structural determinants of community social organization: economic and family resources, residential stability, household and age structure, and the economic isolation of neighborhoods. Neighborhoods characterized by poverty, excessive numbers of children per adult residents, high population turnover, and female-headed households are more likely to have higher rates of reported child maltreatment. These factors also predict variation in rates of other deviant behavior or family and child problems, including violent crime, drug trafficking, juvenile delinquency, and teen pregnancy (Coulton et al., n.d.).

Using substantiated and indicated cases reported to the Cuyahoga County Department of Human Services, my colleagues and I identified census tracts with differing rates of child maltreatment. Specifically, we have identified neighborhoods at high risk, medium risk, and low risk of child-maltreatment reports. Predominantly African-American and predominantly European-American neighborhoods of each type were included for ethnographic study. Ethnographers were blind to the risk status of each neighborhood. This model for studying neighborhood impact on child-maltreatment rates is based on earlier research by Garbarino and his colleagues (Garbarino & Crouter, 1978; Garbarino & Kostelny, 1992; Garbarino & Sherman, 1980).

Preliminary analysis of interviews of neighborhood residents (*N* = 121) indicates that residents from all three risk categories (low, medium, and high) report their neighborhoods to be high on positive attributes. Individuals in all neighborhood risk types report that neighbors generally know one another, help one another out, and look out for one another's children. However, reports of negative attributes of their neighborhoods varied across neighborhood risk types. Residents in low-risk neighborhoods are likely to report less crime, less danger, less drug use, and less dependence on public assistance in their neighborhoods. Residents of medium-risk neighborhoods and high-risk neighborhoods present the opposite profile (Korbin & Coulton, 1994). Medium-risk neighborhoods are interesting in that residents of these neighborhoods perceive their situation to be worse than it is by objective measures. A perceived downward slide is particularly disturbing to residents.

There are potential policy implications. Currently, programs are emphasized that use natural helping networks and attempt to focus on neighborhood strengths. Our preliminary findings suggest that it is important also to address the impact on families of negative conditions (e.g., crime, substance abuse, and deteriorating housing) that exist in many high-risk neighborhoods. The processes by which these negative social conditions affect neighbors' abilities to help one another and to provide a supportive and positive context for child rearing and family life are important to understand. As but one example from our current ethnographic work, an objective measure of a neighborhood might indicate the presence of a playground with excellent equipment. We might expect caregivers of young children to congregate at such a setting, which would afford an opportunity for an informal exchange of information and support. However, caregivers of young children might view this playground as dangerous because of crime, gangs, and rougher older children and therefore avoid the area. Conversely, a dead-end alleyway or a vacant lot within sight of a well-regarded adult might be viewed as an eyesore by an objective measure but as a neighborhood asset by caregivers of young children.

Networks also function within the larger context of cultural and social rules. Some rules are powerful and others open to exceptions, with rules about the exceptions (Edgerton, 1985). Laws and rules, in and of themselves, are not sufficient to prevent violence and maltreatment within the family. Spanking children in Sweden, for example, is prohibited by law. Rates of physical punishment of children are significantly lower in Sweden than in the United States (Gelles & Edfeldt, 1986). However, rates of severe violence against children are similar. Gelles (1991), arguing against a continuum-of-violence approach, suggests that this is because mild and severe violence are different entities, not merely two points on a continuum. Swedish professionals at the United States–Sweden conference in Satra Bruk in the early 1980s indicated that the point of the anti-spanking law was not to punish but to change cultural standards, to provide the moral high ground to those who opposed physical and verbal assaults in the context of child rearing.

DEMOGRAPHIC AND STRUCTURAL FEATURES

Social networks operate within the confines of structural features of the culture. One may argue that networks both contribute to and perpetuate these structural arrangements of society.

Child maltreatment. The cross-cultural record strongly suggests that children with diminished social networks are vulnerable to maltreatment. In the LeVines' work in East Africa, children from broken homes or out-of-wedlock births accounted for 2.5% of the population but 25% of malnourished children. Five of the eight deaths of children under five years of age during the two years of their study were born of illegitimate unions (LeVine & LeVine, 1981). Fraser and Kilbride (1980) similarly found that children from intertribal marriages among the Samia of East Africa were at increased risk of neglect. If the children were not well cared for, neither the kin of the mother nor those of the father felt that the children necessarily fell under their protection. In the United States and Europe, stepchildren are more vulnerable to abuse (Daly & Wilson, 1985) and sexual molestation (Finkelhor, 1985; Russell, 1984).

Sibling violence. Minturn and Lambert (1964) found that intracultural variability could exceed intercultural variability in child-rearing patterns. Among the most interesting of these findings concerns the impact of household composition on punishment for fighting among household children. Extended households are more likely to punish household children (siblings or cousins) severely for fighting among themselves. This pattern clearly has to do with the number of adults who are drawn into the fray. In nuclear households, one or two parents must negotiate the conflict. In extended households, the conflict expands to involve a greater number of adults. Consider this against the background of Straus et al.'s (1980) suggestion that sibling violence is the training ground for further violence within the family. Some types of family structure are more able to tolerate or accommodate child-on-child aggression.

Spousal violence. The cross-cultural record strongly suggests that the availability of supportive kin who will provide a place of safety for women decreases the likelihood of wife beating (Counts et al., 1992). Residence patterns that allow the husband or the wife to return to their family of origin, temporarily and without shame, can defuse a situation that might otherwise escalate to violence (Counts et al., 1992).

Cultural institutions that stabilize marital unions, however, do not necessarily work to the benefit of all individuals. In the practice of brideprice, for example, prevalent in East African cattle complex societies, the groom's family provides resources to the family of the bride. Brideprice received for a daughter is then used to secure brides for her brothers. The practice of brideprice thus serves to stabilize marriages. If a woman returns to her family of origin, not only is there shame and disgrace but the brideprice may also have to be returned to her husband and his family. Women's natal families, therefore, are under considerable pressure to cajole or force their daughter to stay in her new household. Her brideprice may have already been distributed to other households for her brothers' wives. The threat of brideprice return thus may serve society as stabilizer of marriages and so have a positive social function. It motivates individuals to make the best of their marriages and motivates their families to support them in remaining together. At the same time, it limits the options of individuals in bad marriages, including abusive marriages, and can act to the detriment of wives whose families either cannot or will not allow them to return home.

The cross-cultural literature lends support to the finding in the United States that spousal violence is more prevalent among younger couples (Straus et al., 1980). Wife beating is also more prevalent in young couples among the Kaliai of Papua New Guinea (Counts, 1992). The Navogisi (Nash, 1992) attribute the woman's greater vulnerability at younger ages to the fact that young and recently married couples are more violent with one another because they have not yet become accustomed to living together. The difficulty of adjusting to marriage is institutionally recognized in some societies. In a Highland Ecuador group, godparents are chosen by young couples to act as impartial arbitrators and help them through their early years of marriage (McKee, 1992). In addition to adjustment to marriage, structural factors may account for levels of spousal violence. In India, age brings relief from spousal violence as the subservient daughter-in-law increases her standing in the household with the birth of sons and then becomes a mother-in-law herself (Miller, 1992).

RESOURCES, POWER, AND RECOURSE

The ability of social networks to protect against intrafamilial violence is influenced by the relative resources (property and labor), power, and recourse strategies available to its members. The importance of economic contributions (property and labor) and control of resources has been suggested to contribute to multiple forms of intrafamilial maltreatment. Power is also an important factor in explaining family violence. In the United States, Finkelhor (1983) has suggested that a common feature of the different forms of family violence is that it may result from either an abuse of power or as a response to perceived powerlessness. Gelles further elaborates that those with power may feel the least need to impose it (Gelles, 1993). Related to power and resources, recourse involves the ability of an individual to retaliate against or to escape from violence and maltreatment. Retaliation may involve the intervention of living kin or of supernatural powers.

Child maltreatment. While children do not generally control resources, their treatment is likely to be enhanced if they are valued for their economic utility. Miller (1981, 1992) makes a compelling argument for differential treatment of female children in different geographic regions of India on the basis of the agricultural subsistence contributions of females. Logan (1979) argues that the change from an agrarian life-style in which children were producers to an industrialized one in which children are consumers has been suggested as putting children at risk for maltreatment when they strain household resources. In societies in which children make a major contribution to household subsistence, they may be protected from caloric deprivation at the expense of adults (see, e.g., Leonard, 1989).

Children in most societies cannot retaliate on their own and in general have little direct recourse to bad treatment. However, if kin and others in their social networks do not intervene on their behalf, ancestral spirits in some societies will. For example, in rural Hawaii, one mother acknowledged that she beat her 10-year-old daughter too often and too harshly. After one particularly harsh beating that left bruises, the child became ill. The mother viewed the illness as a sign from the ancestral spirits. In addition to being contrite and ashamed that she had hurt the child, the mother was fearful that the ancestors for whom the child was named would become angry at the child's mistreatment and take her away to be with them, where she would be treated more kindly (Korbin, 1990a).

Spousal violence. The cross-cultural literature strongly suggests that societies in which husbands and wives have an egalitarian relationship in resources and decision making are the least likely to involve intrafamilial violence (Draper, 1992; Levinson 1989). Where there is asymmetry in resources, power, or recourse, beating of wives is most likely (Counts et al., 1992; Draper, 1992). Cultures in which women make an important subsistence contribution and/or control a significant proportion of the resources afford some degree of protection from violence (Counts et al., 1992; Miller, 1992).

This decrease is not simply a matter of increasing resources to women. Among the changing circumstances in Taiwan, for example, is the fact that women now may have "private money" provided by their parents at marriage, which decreases women's total dependence on their husbands and should presumably lessen their vulnerability to maltreatment. In a case reported by Gallin (1992), however, the possession of resources led to a woman being beaten by her husband who wanted the money and by her father who wanted her to behave like a culturally appropriate good wife.

"Dowry deaths" are among the most egregious forms of intrafamilial violence tied to social networks and resources. Dowry deaths involve a pattern of spiraling demands for resources (dowry) from the bride's family. If resources are not forthcoming and particularly if the mother-in-law is dissatisfied with her new daughter-in-law, the young bride is set afire under the guise of a cooking fire accident. Dowry deaths occur predominantly in those areas of India in which women's contribution to subsistence is minimal. This geographical distribution is the same as that related to differential mortality for female children (Miller, 1981, 1992).

Elder maltreatment. The ability of elders to contribute to the economic needs of their household and community and to control resources has an impact on their treatment cross-culturally (Foner, 1984; Goldstein et al., 1983; Tout, 1989). The control of resources is important even in cultures with a strong value on filial piety and veneration for elders (Goldstein et al., 1983). In one poignant example from Nepal, an elder man who was poorly treated by his son's family was advised by an elderly friend to acquire a empty strongbox, to fit it with many locks, and to keep the keys securely tied on his person. If the son or son's wife inquired about the box, the man was advised to tell them that he had been keeping his valuables at his friend's house but now that he was older he wanted to keep the valuables closer at hand to ensure that the son and his family would get them upon his death. According to the elder man, once the strongbox appeared, his treatment improved. This is somewhat parallel to elders in Western countries threatening to write a nonattentive or troublesome offspring out of their wills.

INDIVIDUAL CHARACTERISTICS AND MOTIVATIONS

Individual characteristics or personality profiles associated with intrafamilial violence are difficult to assess cross-culturally. However, individual motivations cannot be left out of a discussion about family violence, even one that focuses on social networks. In my fieldwork in rural Hawaii, some people were simply regarded as more violent than others, as having a "hot temper" or "short guts." Some men beat their wives and children while others did not, and some women beat their children while others did not. One woman reported that, when her husband beat her, she had to be careful. Because she was substantially larger than her husband, she was worried that in raising an arm to shield herself from his blows, she might injure him and thus cause him to lose face. In the same community, a woman of approximately the same age and physically smaller than her husband asserted that he would never dare to raise a hand to her because he knew that, even if he was physically larger, she was strong and would give him a "dirty licking." Both women had children and kin in the community who could be called on for help. The Hawaiians with whom I worked were likely to attribute such differences to an individual's "ways." A number of individual characteristics thus could be attributed to a person without much speculation about etiology (Ito, 1987).

Cultural conceptions of self and the family also may motivate individuals to behave in given ways. Cultural conceptions of self and individuals' motivations to meet the standards of personhood in their culture affect family violence. Among the horticultural Bun of Papua New Guinea, for example, if a woman allows herself to be beaten, she accepts the status of a nonadult. She becomes a person of little worth, a "rubbish person" (McDowell, 1992). The right and responsibility to physically chastise another individual is restricted to the parent-child relationship. The marital relationship is one of equals, and physical violence against the wife defines her as less than a full person. To maintain a culturally accepted concept of self, wives are therefore motivated not to accept physical aggression from their husbands. Thus, Bun women assert their autonomy even in the face of beatings from husbands and male kin.

Conceptions of family are also important. Cross-culturally, intrafamilial child sexual misuse is likely to be identified in terms of a relationship violation rather than a specific sexual act (Korbin, 1990b). In traditional Samoan society, for example, brother-sister incest was regarded as the most serious potential incest violation and was surrounded by strict rules and prohibitions. However, father-daughter incest was considered the most serious actual transgression because of the presumed protective nature of the parent-child relationship: "Incest between father and daughter is worse than between brother and sister because it is less expected, or less comprehensible" (Shore, 1976, pp. 278–279).

Summary

The purpose of this chapter was twofold. First, the chapter put forward a brief cross-cultural perspective indicating that multiple types of intrafamilial violence occur cross-culturally. Second, the chapter placed social networks at the core of a complex etiology of intrafamilial violence. The purpose of giving centrality to social networks is not to suggest that social networks are the sole or primary agent contributing to family violence but to broaden the context in which family violence is viewed beyond that of the perpetrator, the victim/survivor, or the violent dyad.

NOTES

1. Descriptions of cultural practices are written in what is termed the "ethnographic present," or the time at which such practices were described in the literature. Use of the "ethnographic present" does not necessarily imply that such practices still occur.

2. Data presented by Levinson are based on the coding of ethnographer reports of behaviors in societies sampled from the Human Relations Area Files. Absence of a behavior does not necessarily imply that it never occurs in the society but that it was not reported or commented on by the ethnographer who may or may not have been attending to and/or interested in the subject of intrafamilial violence.

3. "Mutual combat" is the subject of substantial controversy (see, e.g., Dobash et al., 1992; Gelles, 1993; Gelles & Straus, 1988; Straus & Gelles, 1986, 1990).

REFERENCES

Adelson, L. (1961). Slaughter of the innocents. *New England Journal of Medicine, 264,* 1345–1349.

Baumeister, R. F., Chesner, S. P., Senders, P. S., & Tice, D. M. (1988). Who's in charge here? Group leaders do lend help in emergencies. *Personality and Social Psychology Bulletin, 14,* 17–22.

Briggs, J. (1975). The origins of non-violence. Aggression in two Canadian Eskimo communities. *Psychoanalytic Study of Society, 6*, 134–203.

Burbank, V. (1992). Fight! Fight! Men, women, and interpersonal aggression in an Australian aboriginal community. In D. Counts, J. Brown, & J. Campbell (Eds.), *Sanctions and sanctuary: Cultural perspectives on the beating of wives* (pp. 33–42). Boulder CO: Westview.

Coulton, C., Korbin, J., Chow, J., & Su, M. (in press), Community level factors and child maltreatment rates. *Child Development.*

Counts, D. (1992). "All men do it": Wife-beating in Kaliai, Papua New Guinea. In D. Counts, J. Brown, & J. Campbell (Eds.), *Sanctions and sanctuary: Cultural perspectives on the beating of wives* (pp. 63–76). Boulder CO: Westview.

Counts, D., Brown, J., & Campbell, J. (Eds.). (1992). *Sanctions and sanctuary: Cultural perspectives on the beating of wives.* Boulder CO: Westview.

Daly, M., & Wilson, M. (1985). Child abuse and other risks of not living with both parents. *Ethnology and Sociobiology, 6*, 197–210.

Das Gupta, M. (1987). Selective discrimination against female children in rural Punjab, India. *Population and Development Review, 13*, 77–97.

Davis, P. W. (1991). Stranger intervention into child punishment in public places. *Social Problems, 38*(2), 227–246.

Dobash, R., Dobash, R., Wilson, M., & Daly, M. (1992). The myth of sexual symmetry in marital violence. *Social Problems, 39*, 71–91.

Dovido, J. (1984). Helping behavior and altruism: An empirical and conceptual overview. In L. Berkowitz (Ed.), *Advances in experimental social psychology* (Vol. 17, pp. 361–427). New York: Academic Press.

Draper, P. (1992). Room to maneuver: !Kung women cope with men. In D. Counts, J. Brown, & J. Campbell (Eds.), *Sanctions and sanctuary: Cross-cultural perspectives on the beating of wives* (pp. 43–61). Boulder CO: Westview.

Edgerton, R. B. (1985). *Rules, exceptions, and social order.* Berkeley and Los Angeles: University of California Press.

Edgerton, R. B. (1992). *Sick societies. Challenging the myth of primitive harmony.* New York: Free Press.

Elmer, E. (1960). Abused young children seen in hospitals. *Social Work, 5*(4), 98–102.

Erchak, G. (1984). Cultural anthropology and spouse abuse. *Current Anthropology, 25*, 331–332.

Feldman, K. W., Monastersky, C., & Feldman, G. K. (1993). When is childhood drowning neglect? *Child Abuse and Neglect, 17*, 329–336.

Fergusson, D., Flemming, J., & O'Neill, D. (1972). *Child abuse in New Zealand.* Wellington: Government Press.

Fernea, E.20 (1965). *Guests of the shiek: An ethnography of an Iraqi village.* New York: Doubleday.

Finkelhor, D. (1983). Common features of family abuse. In D. Finkelhor, R. Gelles, G. Hotaling, & M. Straus (Eds.), *The dark side of families: Current family violence research* (pp. 17–28). Beverly Hills CA: Sage.

Finkelhor, D. (1985). *A sourcebook on child sexual abuse.* Beverly Hills CA: Sage.

Finkelhor, D., & Korbin, J. (1988). Child abuse as an international issue. *Child Abuse and Neglect, 11*, 397–407.

Foner, N. (1984). *Ages in conflict: A cross-cultural perspective on inequality between old and young.* New York: Columbia University Press.

Fraser, G., & Kilbride, P. (1980). Child abuse and neglect—rare, but perhaps increasing, phenomenon among the Samia of Kenya. *Child Abuse and Neglect, 4*, 227–232.

Gallimore, R., Boggs, J., & Jordan, C. (1974). *Culture, behavior, and education: A study of Hawaiian-Americans.* Beverly Hills CA: Sage.

Gallin, R. (1992). Wife abuse in the context of development and change: A Chinese (Taiwanese) case. In D. Counts, J. Brown, & J. Campbell (Eds.), *Sanctions and sanctuary. Cultural perspectives on the beating of wives* (pp. 219–227). Boulder CO: Westview.

Garbarino, J. (1977). The price of privacy in the social dynamics of child abuse. *Child Welfare, 56*, 565–575.

Garbarino, J., & Crouter, A. (1978). Defining the community context for parent-child relations: The correlates of child maltreatment. *Child Development, 49*, 604–616.

Garbarino, J., & Ebata, A. (1983). The significance of cultural and ethnic factors in child maltreatment. *Journal of Marriage and the Family, 45*, 773–783.

Garbarino, J., & Kostelny, K. (1992). Child maltreatment as community problem. *Child Abuse and Neglect, 16*, 455–464.

Garbarino, J., & Sherman, D. (1980). High risk neighborhoods and high risk families: The human ecology of child maltreatment. *Child Development, 51*, 188–198.

Gelles, R. (1983). An exchange/social control theory. In D. Finkelhor, R. Gelles, G. Hotaling, & M. Straus (Eds.), *The dark side of families: Current family violence research* (pp. 151–165). Beverly Hills CA: Sage.

Gelles, R. (1993). Through a sociological lens: Social structure and family violence. In R. Gelles & D. Loseke (Eds.), *Current controversies on family violence* (pp. 31–46). Newbury Park CA: Sage.

Gelles, R. J. (1987). What to learn from cross-cultural and historical research on child abuse and neglect: An overview. In R. Gelles & J. Lancaster (Eds.), *Child abuse and neglect: Biosocial dimensions* (pp. 15–30). New York: Gruyter.

Gelles, R. J. (1991). Physical violence, child abuse, and child homicide: A continuum of violence or distinct behaviors? *Human Nature 2*, 59–72.

Gelles, R., & Edfeldt, A. (1986). Violence towards children in the United States and Sweden. *Child Abuse and Neglect, 10*, 501–510.

Gelles, R. J., & Straus, M. A. (1988). *Intimate violence.* New York: Simon & Schuster.

Glascock, A., & Feinman, S. (1981). Social asset or social burden: An analysis of the treatment of the aged in non-industrial societies. In C. L. Fry (Ed.), *Dimensions: Aging, culture, and health.* New York: Praeger.

Goldstein, M., Schuler, S., & Ross, J. (1983). Social and economic forces affecting intergenerational relations in extended families in a third world country: A cautionary tale from South Asia. *Journal of Gerontology, 38,* 716–724.

Gordon, L. (1988). *Heroes of their own lives. The politics and history of family violence: Boston 1880–1960.* New York: Viking.

Graburn, N. (1987). Severe child abuse among the Canadian Inuit. In N. Scheper-Hughes (Ed.), *Child survival: Anthropological perspectives on the treatment and maltreatment of children* (pp. 211–226). Dordrecht, Netherlands: Reidel.

Gray, E., & Cosgrove, J. (1985). Ethnocentric perception of childrearing practices in protective services. *Child Abuse and Neglect, 9,* 389–396.

Green, J. W. (1982). *Cultural awareness in the human services.* Englewood Cliffs NJ: Prentice-Hall.

Hampton, R., & Newberger, E. (1985). Child abuse incidence and reporting by hospitals: Significance of severity, class, and race. *American Journal of Public Health, 75,* 45–58.

Hong, G., & Hong, L. (1991). Comparative perspectives on child abuse and neglect: Chinese versus Hispanics and Whites. *Child Welfare, 70,* 463–475.

Ima, K., & Hohm, C. (1991). Child maltreatment among Asian and Pacific Islander refugees and immigrants: The San Diego case. *Journal of Interpersonal Violence, 6,* 267–285.

Ito, K. (1987). Emotions, proper behavior (*hana pono*), and Hawaiian concepts of self, person, and individual. In A. Robillard, & A. Marsella (Eds.), *Contemporary issues in mental health research in the Pacific islands* (pp. 45–71). Honolulu: University of Hawaii, Social Science Research Institute.

Ito, K. (n.d.) *The ties that define: Metaphor, morality and aloha among urban Hawaiians.* Unpublished manuscript.

Keesing, R. (1982). Introduction. In G. Herdt (Ed.), *Rituals of manhood: Male initiation in Papua New Guinea* (pp. 1–43). Berkeley and Los Angeles: University of California Press.

Kempe, C. H., Silverman, F. N., Droegmueller, W., & Silver, H. K. (1962). The battered child syndrome. *Journal of the American Medical Association, 181,* 17–24.

Korbin, J. (Ed.). (1981). *Child abuse and neglect: Cross-cultural perspectives.* Berkeley and Los Angeles: University of California Press.

Korbin, J. (1987). Child maltreatment in cross-cultural perspective: Vulnerable children and circumstances. In R. Gelles & J. Lancaster (Eds.), *Child abuse and neglect: Biosocial dimensions* (pp. 31–55). Chicago: Aldine.

Korbin, J. (1989). Fatal maltreatment by mothers: A proposed framework. *Child Abuse and Neglect, 13,* 481–489.

Korbin, J. (1990a). *Hana'ino*: Child maltreatment in a Hawai'ian-American community. *Pacific Studies, 13*(3), 6–22.

Korbin, J. (1990b). Child sexual abuse: A cross-cultural view. In R. K. Oates (Ed.), *Understanding and managing child sexual abuse* (pp. 42–58). Sydney: Harcourt, Brace, Jovanovich.

Korbin, J., & Coulton, C. (1994). *Final report: Neighborhood impact on child abuse and neglect* (Grant 90-CA1494, National Center on Child Abuse). Washington DC: Department of Health and Human Services.

Kotch, J. B., Chalmers, D. J., Fanslow, J. L., Marshall, S., & Langley, J. D. (1993). Morbidity and death due to child abuse in New Zealand. *Child Abuse and Neglect, 17*, 233–247.

Leonard, W. R. (1989). Protection of children from seasonal nutritional stress in an Andean agricultural community. *European Journal of Clinical Nutrition, 43*, 597–602.

LeVine, S., & LeVine, R. (1981). Child abuse and neglect in SubSaharan Africa. In J. Korbin (Ed.), *Child abuse and neglect: Cross-cultural perspectives* (pp. 35–55). Berkeley and Los Angeles: University of California Press.

Levinson, D. (1988). Family violence in cross-cultural perspective. In V. Van-Hasselt, R. Morrison, A. Bellack, & M. Hersen (Eds.), *Handbook of family violence* (pp. 435–455). New York: Plenum.

Levinson, D. (1989). *Family violence in cross-cultural perspective.* Newbury Park CA: Sage.

Levy, J. (1964). The fate of Navajo twins. *American Anthropologist, 66*, 883–887.

Logan, R. (1979). Socio-cultural change and the perception of children as burdens. *Child Abuse and Neglect, 3*, 657–662.

Lynch, M. (1985). Child abuse before Kempe: An historical literature review. *Child Abuse and Neglect, 9*, 7–15.

McDowell, N. (1992). Household violence in a Yuat River village. In D. Counts, J. Brown, & J. Campbell (Eds.), *Sanctions and sanctuary: Cultural perspectives on the beating of wives* (pp. 77–88). Boulder CO: Westview.

McKee, L. (1992). Men's rights/women's wrongs: Domestic violence in Ecuador. In D. Counts, J. Brown, & J. Campbell (Eds.), *Sanctions and sanctuary: Cultural perspectives on the beating of wives* (pp. 139–156). Boulder CO: Westview.

Miller, B. (1981). *The endangered sex: Neglect of female children in rural North India.* Ithaca NY: Cornell University Press.

Miller, B. (1992). Wife-beating in India: Variations on a theme. In D. Counts, J. Brown, & J. Campbell (Eds.), *Sanctions and sanctuary: Cultural perspectives on the beating of wives* (pp. 173–184). Boulder CO: Westview.

Minturn, L., & Lambert, W. (1964). *Mothers of six cultures. Antecedents of childrearing.* New York: Wiley.

Myerhoff, B. (1978). Aging and the aged in other cultures: An anthropological perspective. In E. Bauwens (Ed.) *The anthropology of health* (pp. 151–166). Saint Louis: Mosby.

Nash, J. (1992). Factors relating to infrequent domestic violence among the Navogisi. In D. Counts, J. Brown, & J. Campbell (Eds.), *Sanctions and sanctuary: Cultural perspectives on the beating of wives* (pp. 99–100). Boulder CO: Westview.

National Center on Child Abuse and Neglect. (1981). *Study findings: National study of the incidence and severity of child abuse and neglect.* Washington DC: Department of Health, Education, and Welfare.

Nations, M., & Rebhun, L. (1988) Angels with wet wings won't fly: Maternal sentiment in Brazil and the image of neglect. *Culture, Medicine, and Psychiatry, 12*, 141–200.

Nelson, B. (1984). *Making an issue of child abuse: Political agenda setting for social problems.* Chicago: University of Chicago Press.

Newberger, E., Reed, R., Daniel, J., Hyde, J., & Kotelchuck, M. (1977). Pediatric social illness: Towards an etiologic classification. *Pediatrics, 60*, 178–185.

Nuitini, H., & Roberts, J. (1993). *Bloodsucking witchcraft: An epistemiological study of anthropomorphic supernaturalism in rural Tlazcala.* Tucson: University of Arizona Press.

O'Toole, R., Turbett, P., & Nalepka, C. (1983). Theories, professional knowledge, and diagnosis of child abuse. In D. Finkelhor, R. Gelles, G. Hotaling, & M. Straus (Eds.), *The dark side of families: Current family violence research.* Beverly Hills CA: Sage.

Pinholster, G. (1994). SIDS paper triggers a murder charge. *Science, 264*, 197–198.

Pleck, E. (1987). *Domestic tyranny: The making of American social policy against family violence from colonial times to the present.* Oxford: Oxford University Press.

Ritchie, J., & Ritchie, J. (1981). Child rearing and child abuse: The Polynesian context. In J. Korbin (Ed.), *Child abuse and neglect: Cross-cultural perspectives* (pp. 186–294). Berkeley and Los Angeles: University of California Press.

Rohner, R. (1986). *The warmth dimension: Foundations of parental acceptance-rejection theory.* Beverly Hills CA: Sage.

Russell, D. (1984). The prevalence and seriousness of incestuous abuse: Step-fathers versus biological fathers. *Child Abuse and Neglect, 7*, 133–146.

Scheper-Hughes, N. (Ed.) (1987). *Child survival: Anthropological perspectives on the treatment and maltreatment of children.* Dordrecht, Netherlands: Reidel.

Scheper-Hughes, N. (1992). *Death without weeping: The violence of everyday life in Brazil.* Berkeley and Los Angeles: University of California Press.

Schmidt, W. E. (1993, November 2). Two British boys, 11, on trial in killing. *New York Times*, p. A6.

Scrimshaw, S. (1978). Infant mortality and behavior in the regulation of family size. *Population and Development Review, 4*, 383–403.

Shore, B. (1976). Incest probibitions and the logic of power in Samoa. *Journal of the Polynesian Society, 85*, 275–296.

Stack, C. (1974). *All our kin: Strategies for survival in a Black community.* New York: Harper & Row.

Straus, M., & Gelles, R. (1986). Societal change and change in family violence from 1975–1985 as revealed by two national surveys. *Journal of Marriage and the Family, 48*, 465–479.

Straus, M., & Gelles, R. (Eds.). (1990). *Physical violence in American families.* New Brunswick NJ: Transaction.

Straus, M., Gelles, R., & Steinmetz, S. (1980). *Behind closed doors: Violence in the American family*. New York: Anchor.

Thompson, R. A. (1992). *Social support and the prevention of child maltreatment*. Paper prepared for the U.S. Advisory Board on Child Abuse and Neglect.

Tice, D. M., & Baumeister, R. F. (1985). Masculinity inhibits helping in emergencies: Personality does predict the bystander effect. *Journal of Personality and Social Psychology, 49,* 420–428.

Tout, K. (1989). *Ageing in developing countries*. Oxford: Oxford University Press.

Turnbull, C. (1961). *The forest people: A study of the pygmies of the Congo*. New York: Simon & Schuster.

Divorce and Custody: The Rights, Needs, and Obligations of Mothers, Fathers, and Children

Eleanor E. Maccoby
Stanford University

The Legal Rights and Obligations of Parents and Children

The law, as it concerns families, emphasizes primarily the needs or rights of children and the obligations of parents. In this sense, it is completely different from, say, contract law, which is built on concepts of social exchange and strives to sustain equity between contracting parties. Although the law does recognize a limited obligation of children to support indigent parents in their old age, this requirement can in no way be seen as an equivalent return for the investment parents make in giving birth to children and rearing them to adulthood, and the parent-child relationship is essentially an asymmetrical one, with parents giving and children receiving.

In earlier times, children were to some extent an economic asset: they could help with farm work or could work in mines or factories, and parents were legally entitled to their earnings. Indeed, Thomas Hobbes (cited in Mnookin & Weisberg, 1989) wrote: "There is not reason why any man should desire to have children or to take care to nourish them if afterwards to have no other benefit from them than from other men" (p. 190). In modern times, parents still retain a legal right to the children's earnings, but this "right" seldom has any significance. The movement of populations away from the farm, the enactment of child labor laws, and the mandatory attendance of children at school through adolescence have meant that children's economic contributions to the family have become negligible. Although many high school students do have part-time jobs, in Western industrialized countries they are usually considered to have the right to keep their earnings for their own present or future needs. However, Hobbes to the contrary, parents do still desire to have children and nourish them. Hobbesian doctrine would suggest that modern parents must be subject to greater temptations to neglect or abandon their children, now that there is so little economic payback from rearing them. We have no way of knowing whether such temptations have increased, but the fact remains that the vast majority of parents neither abandon nor neglect their children. Evidently, there are other motivational foundations for parental nurturance of the young than the potential payback Hobbes pointed to.

A powerful alternative view is that, in human beings and other species in which the young are not able to survive independently, parental behavior is instinctive. According to evolutionary theory, the propensity to reproduce ourselves—or more specifically, to see that our own individual genes are carried over into succeeding generations—is a necessary outcome of natural selection. All or most adults, then, will carry with them a predisposition to respond to the needs of their offspring—to feed and protect them and to do whatever else is necessary to help them to survive to reproductive age.

English common law sees the obligations of parents as based on natural law, and hence reflects more a Darwinian than a Hobbesian perspective. Sir William Blackstone, in his *Commentaries on the Laws of England* in 1762, said:

> The duty of parents to provide for the maintenance of their children, is a principle of natural law: an obligation, says Puffendorf, laid on them not only by nature herself, but by their own proper act, in bringing them into the world: for they would be in the highest manner injurious to their issue if they only gave their children life, that they might afterwards see them perish. By begetting them, therefore, they have entered into a voluntary obligation, to endeavor, as far as in them lies, that .

the life which they have bestowed shall be supported and preserved. And thus children will have a perfect *right* of receiving maintenance from their parents. (Blackstone, cited in Mnookin & Weisberg, 1989, p. 178).[1]

While in the eyes of the law the parental role has mainly entailed obligations toward children, parenthood has carried certain rights as well. A number of Supreme Court decisions have affirmed a right to "family integrity" protected under the 14th Amendment to the Constitution, such that parents have the right to determine the conditions of their children's upbringing without interference by the state. This means that parents are the ones empowered to decide where the child shall live, how it shall be fed and clothed, what discipline is appropriate, what school the child will attend, and what kind of moral and religious training it will receive. Reciprocally, children are enjoined to "respect and obey" their parents and accept whatever provisions their parents choose to make for them. The parental right to determine all aspects of their children's lives does have limits, however. The state is allowed to intervene and terminate these parental rights, placing the child for adoption or in foster care, on a showing of abuse or neglect. In Puritan New England, church elders sometimes exercised a power to take children from their families and place them with God-fearing foster parents if the elders deemed that the children's natural father was not fulfilling his duty to give the children adequate religious instruction. And seventeenth-century laws of Massachusetts, Connecticut, and Virginia authorized judicial authorities to indenture children away from home over the objections of their parents.[2] Since that time, however, greater protections have been erected in the law against arbitrary removal of children from parental care.

Who is it that has parental rights and obligations toward a given child? Is it always and only the biological parents? In evolutionary theory, the obligations of the parental generation toward the young apply to their own offspring—the ones carrying their own genes. Insofar as legal doctrine is based on "natural law," we would expect the law to give priority to the claims and obligations of natural parents. In fact, however, the law recognizes parental obligations and rights that are based on social, as well as biological, ties. When a legal adoption has occurred, the adoptive parents have the same obligations to provide support, and the adopted children the same rights to receive support, as is the case for "natural" children. There are a few cases in which the rights and obligations of biological parents have come into conflict with those of adoptive, or "social," parents, and no generally agreed-upon legal standard for such cases has yet emerged.

As far as the rights and obligations of children are concerned, their right to be supported implies the right not to be neglected or abused, and legal standards have been erected concerning the minimum standards of care that parents may be expected to maintain.

In recent years, "children's rights" issues have dealt less with what parents are obliged to do for them than with children's right to "emancipation"—their right to be free of parental control and supervision. Laws concerning "runaways" have been changing, and while runaway minors were formerly either returned home or put into detention as delinquents, many are now legally allowed to live independently of their parents (Handler & Zatz, 1982). Rights to education have also been at issue. In the famous case of *Wisconsin* v *Yoder*, the question was whether children have the right to go to school beyond the eighth grade even though their parents believe, as some Amish parents do, that an eighth-grade education is all they need.[3] A further question concerning emancipation is, Do children have the right to information their parents do not want them to have? This question has found its way into the courts in the form of disputes over what books may be in school libraries, but the most intensely debated current issue concerns whether adolescents should have the right of access to contraceptive information and devices without parental consent.

Are the Rights and Obligations of Fathers and Mothers Different?

Clearly, there are murky borders between the rights of parents, children, and the state, and these boundaries continue to be under active negotiation through the courts. Despite the borderline cases, however, the boundaries are fairly well understood and maintained in general. Much less clear is the borderline between the parental rights and responsibilities of mothers as compared with fathers. Until now we have been discussing parental rights and duties as though the parents were a unit and jointly held these rights and responsibilities. In fact, even in intact families, the law has assigned more responsibility for financial support to fathers. In the case of parental separation or divorce, the issue of whether the two parents should have different roles and responsibilities in the care of children after divorce comes into bold relief.

The history of divorce law, as it relates to custody and care of children, has been well reviewed elsewhere (Depner & Bray, 1993; Emery, 1988, chap. 7; Kay, 1990). For the present, we need merely to note three major recent trends. The first is the shift from fault-based to no-fault divorce adjudication. Custody decisions were once part of a systematic effort to punish the parent who was responsible for breaking up a marriage, so that custody was denied to the parent "at fault." Currently, mediators and judges involved in custody decisions are explicitly enjoined from taking "fault" into account, except as it directly affects the child's best interests. A second major trend has been toward deregulation of custody decisions. Courts now routinely rubber-stamp custody decisions arrived at privately by a divorcing couple and indeed put pressure on couples to work out their own custody agreement rather than rely on judicial intervention. Third, divorce laws have incorporated gender-neutral language. Before the 1980s, a body of case law had grown up favoring maternal custody, except when the mother could be shown to be unfit. Revisions of custody statutes in the late 1970s and early 1980s explicitly provided that neither parent should have preference in custody decisions on the basis of the parent's gender. Rather, the two parents should stand equally before the law, and their claims for custody of the children should be evaluated solely on the basis of the children's best interests. Many statutes embodied the presumption that it was in children's best interests to continue having access to *both* parents following divorce, and in the interests of maintaining bonds between children and both their parents, many statutes embodied liberal visitation rights for noncustodial parents or explicitly empowered judges to grant joint custody.

The efforts to make divorce law gender-neutral emerged mainly as a result of the upsurge of feminist values in the 1960s and 1970s. In 1970, the National Organization for Women issued a press release including the manifesto: "The care and welfare of children is incumbent on society and parents. We reject the idea that mothers have a special child-care role that is not to be shared equally by fathers." Feminist thinking was paralleled by a growing ideology surrounding "new fatherhood": men were urged to break away from the straightjacket imposed by old concepts of male roles and to share more fully with their wives the joys and responsibilities of parenthood. By so doing, it was thought, men would discover in themselves previously unrealized capacities for nurturance and intimacy (for a fuller exposition of these ideological trends, see Griswold, 1993, chap. 11).

Feminist language was picked up and utilized by fathers' rights groups, who challenged what they saw as the bias of courts in favor of granting custody to mothers when parents divorced. Advocates for fathers' rights were especially active in pressing for joint custody (Cook, 1984), and even when mothers were granted primary physical custody, fathers increasingly demanded joint *legal* custody, which would give them continuing rights to be involved in decisions affecting their children. As these rights for fathers became established in law, there was a growing backlash from feminist writers (e.g., Chesler, 1986) who began to argue that what looked like equality under the law in fact worked out to the disadvantage of women. Pointing to the realities of the sex-based division of labor in child rearing, Polikoff (1983) notes that mothers have almost always invested much more time in child rearing before divorce and indeed have often made career sacrifices in order to do so. Men, it is true, have usually made considerably greater contributions to the financial support of the predivorce family. But to treat mothers and fathers as though they had equivalent claims for custody, Polikoff argues, is to undervalue the maternal investment in child rearing and/or to consider the male financial contribution to be of equal value in determining with whom children should live. The implication of Polikoff's argument is that, when divorcing parents both want primary custody of children, day-to-day experience in the care of the children should be given priority over a history of having provided financial support. Presumably this argument rests in part on the idea that, if the two divorcing parents are to continue doing what they are most equipped to do in terms of their accustomed roles, mothers should generally receive custody, since they cannot continue day-to-day caregiving unless the children live with them while fathers *can* continue giving financial support whether the children live with them or not. To make custody laws gender-neutral, according to this position, the courts should give preference to whichever parent has been the primary caretaker. Fathers' rights groups, of course, regard this solution as merely a disguised form of maternal preference.

What about awards of joint legal custody in cases in which mothers are given primary physical custody? While this might seem a reasonable step toward recognition of the parental rights and responsibilities of both parents after divorce, there has been a backlash against this practice as well. Carol Smart (1989) argues that, while it leaves the day-to-day child-rearing responsibilities to mothers, joint legal custody allows fathers the right to interfere and enhances their continuing exercise of power over their children and former spouses.

The ideology of gender equality seems to be confronting deeply rooted differences in the actual parental roles of mothers and fathers. Legislators, family-court judges, lawyers, and divorcing parents continue to struggle to reconcile the two. A number of questions are relevant to the issue: Are the courts and court-appointed mediators in fact biased toward either parent? Do legal procedures place either parent at an unfair advantage? These questions lead immediately to a deeper one: What does fairness mean in the context of the de facto differences in the parental roles of mothers and fathers? If these roles only change very slowly, should the law attempt to be "out in front" of the change, attempting to contribute both symbolically and substantively to greater gender equality in the rearing of children? Or should the law instead reflect what *is*, rather than what many are urging ought to be?

We now briefly consider gender bias in existing legal procedures and then turn to the more difficult questions concerning the differential roles of mothers and fathers both before and after divorce. We may then be in a better position to consider what these differences imply in terms of the rights and responsibilities of the two parents.

Are Legal Processes Biased in Favor of Either Mothers or Fathers?

Most divorce decrees award physical custody of children to the mother. In most venues, this situation does not appear to have changed greatly in recent years, despite judicial reforms aimed at giving fathers greater access to custody. In states in which the law gives some preference to joint physical custody, this form of custody has indeed increased, but awards of either joint or father custody remain few compared with those vesting primary physical custody in the mother.

Does this imbalance imply judicial bias? We can argue plausibly that it does not. In most cases, the divorcing parents reach their own agreement concerning child custody. The initial petition for divorce—filed by either or both parents—specifies the form of custody desired. If one parent files the initial petition, the other parent usually does not contest the petitioner's request. And when a petition is uncontested, physical custody by the mother is requested in the very large majority of cases. In other words, when parents reach their own agreement concerning custody, they have usually agreed that the children will live with the mother (Maccoby & Mnookin, 1992; Mnookin et al., 1989; Poliakoff, 1983). These decisions have been reached without the intervention of formal legal agents, so any biases in the legal system have not been brought to bear. Instead, we see here the operation of a maternal custody norm that is understood and accepted by most divorcing parents.

Of course, it could be argued that these informal decisions are based on what parents *believe* to be biases in the judicial system (Mnookin & Kornhauser, 1979). We know that many fathers who say they would like to have physical custody or at least joint physical custody do not petition for what they want and allow custody to go to the mother by default. It has been argued that this happens, at least in some cases, because fathers believe that they would fail if they demanded custody, so that there is no point in putting the family through a custody battle to no avail. In interviews with divorcing parents, this factor is occasionally mentioned by fathers, but more commonly, parents seem to assume that the mother should be the primary caretaker because she is the one who has fulfilled this function before parental separation. In view of this social norm, what distribution of custody awards in contested cases would be "fair"? Fairness would certainly not require that fathers get physical custody 50% of the time, even in contested cases. All we can reasonably demand of the judicial system would be that in contested cases fathers' and mothers' claims should be evaluated with the same impartially applied criteria.

Disputed cases often involve a father's demand for joint physical custody while the mother wants sole (primary) custody. Only a few disputes involve each parent wanting sole physical custody. These are cases, however, that command the most media attention and around which case law has evolved through decisions of appellate courts. It is notable that, although mothers still win custody more often than do fathers in disputed cases, the father's chances are greater with court intervention than they are in agreements arrived at privately by the couple without court involvement.[4] And, in a study of more than 1,000 divorces in two counties in California, the more intensely the legal conflict was carried forward by a couple disputing over custody, the closer to an even chance of "winning" did the final custodial decrees approach (Maccoby & Mnookin, 1992). From one perspective, these findings might suggest greater gender-neutrality in the legal system than is found in the prevailing norms of the larger society. In fact, however, it is difficult to decide whether the legal system is biased.[5] And whether we interpret the high rates of maternal custody awards as a sign of bias must depend on whether we believe the greater involvement of women in the care of the children before divorce gives them greater legitimate claims to custody when divorce occurs (see Maccoby & Mnookin, 1992, pp. 153–154, for fuller discussion of these issues).

We have seen, then, that the incorporation of gender-neutral language in divorce law does not appear to have had a great effect on the distribution of physical custody awards between mothers and fathers. There may have been a greater effect of modern liberal ideology on awards of *legal* custody, however. In California, where the wording of the law clearly distinguishes between legal and physical custody, a large majority of divorcing families are now awarded joint legal custody, presumably giving both parents a voice in major decisions regarding the children's lives. Here is a case, then, in which the law has been out ahead of the social norms and may have functioned to counteract the gender biases inherent in these norms. It is important to note, however, that there is some doubt as to whether an award of joint legal custody has done much to change the way divorced parents make decisions. The current evidence suggests that, when parents have joint legal custody (but not joint physical custody), the noncustodial parent is no more involved in decisions regarding the children than he or she would be in the absence of a joint legal custody award (Albiston et al., 1990). Once again, then, we see the limitations of the law in bringing about social change.

Clearly, if we are to reason cogently about the rights and obligations of mothers as compared with fathers, we need to consider as deeply as possible the nature of the parenting functions carried out by the two different parents, and the nature of the relationships they form with children, in both the predivorce and postdivorce family.

Parental Roles of Mothers and Fathers in "Intact" Families

In most families, the parental roles of mothers and fathers are fairly distinct.[6] The distinction in parental roles is linked to the economic roles of the two sexes. In preliterate societies, women have usually done most of the work involved in producing and processing food but their work has been carried on at times and in places that permit them to breast-feed and supervise children; men's work has commonly taken them farther from the home base (e.g., for hunting, herding large animals). In the families of Western societies in the midtwentieth century or in Muslim societies up to the present time, wage earning has been carried on away from the home base and men have been the primary or sole wage earners, with married women being largely confined to the domestic arena. In this arrangement, the daily tasks of child care have fallen almost exclusively to mothers. Feminists have long recognized that the consignment of women to unpaid domestic work, including child care, constitutes an almost insuperable barrier to gender equality. There has been a twofold feminist agenda, therefore: to gain equal access to out-of-home paid employment for women and to get men to share fairly in domestic labor, including child care.

The achievement of the first part of this agenda has proceeded at a brisk pace. Since the 1960s, women have entered the labor force in ever-increasing numbers, with the fastest rates found among those who are the mothers of young children. Indeed, data from the United States indicate that by 1989 more than half the mothers with children under age three are in the paid labor force (U.S. House of Representatives, 1989, p. 87). When children are young, a responsible older person must be with them at all times. The out-of-home employment of mothers obviously makes child care an issue: Who is to care for the children during the hours when the mother is away? Specifically, will fathers cut back on their work hours to fill the child-care gap?

Harriett Presser (1989) has noted that work hours do not coincide for a third of dual-earner couples: that is, they work different shifts.[7] Here we see a major potential source of child-care coverage. In a substantial minority of families in which both parents work, the fathers can presumably take care of the children while the mother is at work, and vice versa. And obviously, another means of equalizing the child-care burdens between mothers and fathers would be to reverse traditional roles so that increasing numbers of fathers would stay home while the children were young and their wives would be the major breadwinners. Or mothers and fathers could take turns being the at-home parent until the children were old enough not to require constant adult attention. In these ways, the male-female ratio in taking on the home-bound portion of child-care duties could move toward equality.

Is there a powerful social trend in these directions? It would seem not, although the question is difficult to answer. A widespread ideology advocating "new fatherhood," at least among the better-educated segments of modern societies, enjoins fathers to participate more actively in rearing their children. Furstenberg (1988) has summarized evidence that increasing numbers of fathers are indeed participating more fully in household tasks, including child care, but there are also increasing numbers who are entirely uninvolved in their children's lives. Young couples expecting their first child may believe that they will share child-care duties equally, but the reality does not usually turn out that way (Cowan & Cowan, 1992), and new mothers can experience considerable resentment, and new fathers considerable guilt, over how traditional their division of labor quickly becomes. Many young fathers say they spend considerably more time caring for their children than their own fathers did, and consider themselves substantially involved. Yet time-use studies of large samples of parents have yielded ambiguous results as to whether there is an overall increase in the participation of fathers in child care. Time-use studies have attempted to find out exactly how much time each day or each week mothers and fathers spend in child care, but it is uncertain which activities constitute child care. Is child care to include only the directly interactive care-taking functions such as feeding children, reading to them, dressing them, bathing them, and putting them to bed? Or does it also include talking to them (or at least, answering their questions) while doing household tasks, sitting together to watch television or a home video, or simply being present and available in case of need, as when parent or child—or both—are asleep? (Parents who work night shifts sometimes sleep during portions of the day, with instructions to the child: "Wake me up if you need me.") Some time-use studies have distinguished direct interaction from being merely present and available from being the person responsible (see Lamb et al., 1987, for a summary of studies). Lamb et al. report that, in two-parent families, mothers are directly involved in interaction with the children about three times as often as are fathers; they are present and "available" (though not interacting) for about twice as much time; but it is in being responsible for the care of the children that the gender discrepancy is most apparent. Mothers are nine times as likely as fathers to be the parent who stays home with the child when the child is ill, who arranges for baby-sitters and medical appointments, and who is the only parent at home with the child at a given time. When fathers are at home, their wives are usually present as well and doing more of the child care. Mothers, on the other hand, are frequently at home when the father is not present. While the gender ratios are less extreme in dual-earner than single-earner families, they do not approach equality even when both parents work full time.

What appears to be the case is that mothers perform considerably less child care when they go to work, while fathers do not do a great deal more. Presser (1989) reports that, in families in which the mother works, the care giving for children during her working hours is provided by fathers about 14% to 15% of the time and that this figure has changed little over the past two decades. In a surprising report of time use based on a large national sample (Nock & Kingston, 1988), it was found that mothers were spending only about half as much time in carrying out a specified set of child-care functions when they were working as when they were not working. Fathers also spent less time in child care when a wife worked than when she stayed at home. *Both* parents, then, spent less time in child care when the mothers were working. Obviously, the gap in child care created when increasing numbers of mothers have gone to work is not being filled by fathers, at least not in most families; it is being filled by female relatives or by hired child-care providers—nannies, au pairs, baby-sitters, neighbors who run formal or informal family day-care homes, or professional child-care centers. And who are the people who fill in as nonparental caregivers? They are, of course, women. The basic reality that it is women who take care of children has hardly changed.

What has changed is that work that used to be done by unpaid mothers is now being made monetary: more and more, it is being done by paid female replacements. Large armies of women are earning some kind of living—albeit, a poor one—taking care of other women's children. In contemporary American society, the phenomenon is clearly class based: it is mainly poor and minority women who are doing the paid child-care work. In the famous case of Zoë Baird what everyone knew privately became public knowledge: paid child care frequently occurs as part of an underground economy in which taxes are evaded and workers do not receive the protection of social-security coverage.

Let me reiterate that there *has* been increased participation in child care by a new generation of fathers who are intensely committed to their families. But this trend appears to have been counterbalanced by an opposing trend, what Griswold (1993) has called a "flight from fatherhood." In the increasing numbers of single-parent families headed by women—women who are divorced or who have never married but are raising children—the fathers seldom join the women in the day-to-day tasks of child rearing. Added to these trends are some basic demographic changes: people are marrying at a later age and having fewer children. Taken together, these various trends mean that men, on the average, are spending increasingly smaller portions of their lives in the same household with children.

Women, too, with their smaller families and longer life spans, are spending smaller portions of their adult years in child rearing. But the fact remains that, when children *are* present in a household, it is still overwhelmingly women who take care of them. So, the second part of the feminist agenda—to achieve greater equality in the roles of the two sexes in child rearing—has proved to be difficult to accomplish and slow in coming. We now consider a set of possible explanations for this asymmetry.

Why the Gender Asymmetry in Child Care?

We cannot expect to identify any single factor that can be pointed to as *the* cause of gender asymmetry in child care. Many factors undoubtedly work together. Indeed, it is a phenomenon that is surely heavily overdetermined. We consider now a set of factors that appear to be good candidates for a causal role.

REPRODUCTIVE BIOLOGY

The fact that women gestate fetuses for nine months, give birth, and lactate, while men do not, is probably the most profound biological difference between the sexes. What does this mean for the roles of the two sexes in child care? In earlier times, when women breast-fed each child for more than a year and had a new child every two or three years, it seems obvious that they would be constrained to remain close to home and be involved in the daily care of young children for a substantial portion of their adult years. In modern times, when women breast-feed—if at all—for only 2–4 months on the average and many return to work fairly soon after an infant is born, there would seem to be no obvious reason why lactation in and of itself should tilt the gender balance in the care of children after the first few months. Of course, the division of labor between fathers and mothers with respect to the care of a new child may get established in the first few months when there are biological reasons for the mother to be at home, and once established this may acquire an inertia or momentum of its own. This could happen if the process of breast-feeding created a closer bond, a greater intimacy, a more sensitive responsiveness to the infant and/or a greater sense of caretaking competency on the part of a lactating mother than a father.

Lactation may not be the only biological factor at work in the postpartum period. Until recently, animal studies of the role of the hormones of pregnancy and parturition give inconsistent results, but there was no clear evidence that they played an important role in triggering nurturant behavior toward newborns. Recent work with lower mammals has indicated that, when virgin females are given combinations of hormones that mimic quite closely the hormonal events of late pregnancy and parturition in both amounts and timing, the females display increased responsiveness to infants (Stern, 1989). However, this work needs replication with species closer to human beings, and at present the issue of the effects of female hormones on parental behavior remains unresolved.

Perhaps the most reliable stimulus for the appearance of nurturant behavior in both male and female adult animals is the close presence of young animals—especially newborns—of their own species. But although males do have a variety of parenting behaviors in their repertoire, parenting behavior has a longer latency to appear in them than in virgin females, and males are more likely to injure the young. The possibility exists that it is not so much female hormones that activate responsiveness to the young as it is male hormones that suppress it (Money et al., 1968). If these suppressing or antagonistic effects of male hormones exist, the scanty evidence suggests that they reflect prenatal hormonal sensitization rather than concurrent activating effects.

One of the most pervasive sex differences in nonhuman primates, found across a number of species, is that juvenile females are much more interested in the newborn young of the troupe than are juvenile males (Lovejoy & Wallen, 1988; Meany et al., 1985). They seek opportunities to hold and groom the young and are much less likely than male juveniles to display aggressive behavior toward them (Chamove et al., 1965). We do not know whether these differential behaviors originate in prenatal hormonal sensitization, but they do point to a greater female readiness to display nurturant behavior in response to the young of their species.

SOCIAL LEARNING

Children growing up in every human culture become aware that it is women who are rearing the children. Children of both sexes come to take for granted that girls are the ones who will assume the major child-care role when they are grown. Cultures vary with respect to how much direct training girls are given for the nurturant role: in some societies, most girls between 6 and 13 are assigned responsibilities for the care of younger siblings or cousins (see Whiting & Edwards, 1988). Boys are assigned such tasks only when no girl of the right age is available to do them. It has been reported that boys who *do* participate in child care are less aggressive in their male play groups than are boys who have not had child-care experience (Ember, 1973), an indication of the effects of nurturing experience in moderating children's aggressive tendencies.

In our own society, most girls have relative few active child-care experiences in their middle childhood or adolescent years. But of course in their earliest years many are given dolls to play with, while most little boys are not. Recent research has pointed to an additional sex difference in the socialization of young children: girls are more often talked to about emotions—their own feelings and those of others—than are boys. This trend has emerged quite consistently in several different research programs (Dunn et al., 1987; Fivush, 1993; Radke-Yarrow et al., 1990). We do not yet know all the implications of this kind of emphasis in the rearing of girls but must assume it has something to do with supporting a young child's empathy and sympathy toward others. These will presumably be important attributes when the child becomes an adult charged with the nurturance of young children.

ECONOMIC CONSIDERATIONS

For many reasons, fathers earn considerably more than mothers do. In our study of approximately 1,100 divorcing families in California, employed fathers' earnings were twice as high as employed mothers', on the average, at the time the couple separated. If one parent needs to reduce working hours (or forgo any work outside the home for a period of time), the family can maximize its income by having the stay-at-home parent be the one who earns less. A couple interviewed by Cowan and Cowan (1992) in their study of first-time parents put the issues succinctly:

> JOSIE: Last week we had our hundredth talk about my going back to work. But, as Doug says, there's no way I can possibly earn anything close to his salary so that he could consider cutting back on his time.

DOUG: I'd say our discussion was academic. If Josie could go out and make sufficient money to support our lifestyle, I'd be perfectly willing to discuss taking a year off or six months off and staying home with Zack once he's weaned. Perhaps it's just as well that she doesn't, though. I wouldn't want to trade jobs with Josie. On my worst day I wouldn't want to trade jobs with her.

Although this couple, like many others in the Cowan and Cowan sample, expected to share child care as equally as possible, the reality was, according to the father's estimate, that 95% of the work of caring for their infant son had fallen to his wife. Doug says: "But I thoroughly enjoy him and don't feel deprived." His wife, on the other hand, feels resentful over how the division of labor has worked out.

While women may resent the unequal division of child-care responsibilities, men sometimes feel that their economic contributions are undervalued. As one of the fathers interviewed by Cowan and Cowan put it: "Most of my responsibility for the family is providing the bread. You know, . . . Daddy makes the money and Mommy makes the house and takes care of Faith. I get really pissed off at Celie's (wife's) friends. They're always asking her, 'How come Ray doesn't look after Faith more?' Man, I'm looking after Faith six days a week, ten hours a day, busting my ass at the plant" (Cowan & Cowan, 1992; p. 104).

The question of whether these two different—and highly gendered—kinds of contributions to the care of children should be given equal weight is a central one to which we will return.

THE POWER TO SAY "NO" TO CHILD-REARING CHORES

The young father quoted above as saying he wouldn't dream of exchanging jobs with his wife introduces a new element into the debate about the division of child-care work: the question of who is more willing to do it. Despite the many joys and rewards inherent in raising children, much of the day-to-day work is drudgery, and one of the most onerous aspects of the task is being "on call"—being available to put aside one's own adult activities at any moment to respond to the needs or demands of a child. While most parents think of themselves as being in charge of children, the fact is that, especially during the first few years, children could be said to be in charge of parents. At least, it is usually the infant or toddler who sets the pace of the parent-child interaction. There is evidence that, in cases in which the activities of mother and infant are well synchronized, it is the mother who has adapted herself to the rhythms of the child rather than vice versa. I do not wish to paint young children as being inevitably little tyrants, but the capacity of children to adapt themselves to adult demands develops only slowly, and in the first few years children are impulsive, unreasonable, and often noncompliant. As every parent knows, it take enormous patience and persistence on the part of parents to weather this period of child rearing with equanimity and gradually induct the child into a more civilized pattern of reciprocity in the social life of the family.

Presser (in press) cites some tangential evidence that men are more likely than women to find being at the beck and call of a young child especially onerous. Men enjoy playing with their young children, partly because they can have a measure of control over what activities the play will involve and when it will start and stop. But when it comes to allowing their adult activities to be constantly interrupted to serve an infant or toddler's moment-to-moment needs—this they avoid doing if possible. Of course, mothers too want uninterrupted time for their adult activities, and it is in their long-term economic interests to keep their out-of-home work on track with as little interruption as possible, especially if their work involves an incremental "career" rather than low-level hourly wage work. Why then should fathers be able to guard their adult autonomy from the inroads of young children more successfully than mothers? Presser's answer is simple: because men have more power to negotiate their preferences. This power, she believes, rests largely on societal beliefs—Presser regards them as myths—that parenting *should* be the primary province of women, especially for very young children. Women are believed to be more suited to child-care tasks by reason of temperament, or interactive styles, or learned skills. Or, they are thought to be more powerfully drawn to infants and toddlers. The assumption is that they enjoy intimacy with infants and young children more than men do—that the maternal instinct is somehow more powerful than the paternal one. Whatever the precise content of the beliefs, they add up to the idea that taking care of young children is and should be primarily women's job.

If there is any empirical basis for these beliefs we will have to consider whether there are policy implications with regard to the custody of children after divorce.

THE PARENTING STYLES OF MEN AND WOMEN

There is now an extensive literature on how mothers and fathers interact with their children. Some of our information comes from observations of family interactions at home or in laboratory observation rooms. Some comes from self-reports by parents or from the reports of children who are old enough to describe their interactions with each of their parents. Two major caveats emerge from this literature that we need to keep in mind as we compare mothers and fathers: any individual parent varies considerably from time to time in the mode of dealing with children. This is not just a matter of changing moods: parenting styles vary by family activity and the nature of the disciplinary issue, if any, that has arisen (Grusec & Goodnow, 1994). Yet certain individual consistencies over time can be detected. Perhaps more important than the variation in a given parent is the variation within a given sex of parent: fathers differ greatly among themselves with respect to how they deal with children; so do mothers. On every parenting measure researchers have employed, the distributions of mothers and fathers overlap greatly. Still, when mothers and fathers are compared, average differences emerge consistently with respect to certain aspects of parent-child interaction. I will give a few illustrations.

In the day-to-day life of families, when both parents are home, a higher proportion of fathers' interactive time with their children is spent in play, and fathers play more roughly with the children than mothers do. Mothers do more of the directing: telling the children when it is time to come to the table, do their homework, go to bed, turn off the TV. But fathers, of course, give some directives as well, and in doing so they use a somewhat different style. Specifically, they use simple power assertion with children more often than mothers do. Several sociolinguists have noted a consistently greater use of the imperative mode in father-to-child speech; mothers more often use questions or suggestions to indicate to the child what they want done (see Gleason, 1987, for a summary of studies).

Mothers are more reciprocal in their interactions with children. In infancy, this takes the form of responding in kind to infant vocalizations or facial expressions and being tuned in to the infant's momentary state, so that parental inputs are more closely geared to these states. Some observational research by Thomas Power illustrates this point. Power built on earlier work by Shaffer and Crook (1980), in which it was shown that mothers were more successful in getting an infant to follow a direction if they carefully monitored the infant's attentional state and adapted their intervention to this state. Power (1985) compared groups of mothers and fathers interacting with infants of ages 7, 10, or 13 months to see whether they differed with respect to this kind of sensitivity. His conclusion was as follows: "When attempting to influence their infants' behavior, mothers were more likely to follow up on their infant's natural curiosity . . . while fathers . . . often disregarded the infant's cues of interest and attention and often directly interfered with ongoing infant behavior" (p. 1522).

With toddlers and older children, mothers' greater reciprocity takes the form of a greater quality of give and take. They are more successful in understanding what children are trying to say and more likely to express their own instructions in terminology adapted to the child's level of understanding. More than fathers, they tend to avoid confrontations with the children and are more likely to listen to their children's point of view before settling on a directive. An illustration of this process comes from a report of a dinner-table exchange between parents and a preschool-age child (reported in a paper by the linguist Jean Berko Gleason, 1987):

MOTHER: Now I'm going to cut your roast beef, honey.
BOY: I don't want to eat it.
MOTHER: Well, I thought you liked roast beef!
BOY: I'm not going to eat it!
MOTHER: Why not?
BOY: I'm too full.
MOTHER: Okay, if you don't eat this roast beef you have no more twinkies. You understand that?
BOY: I'll eat one.
MOTHER: No, you'll eat half of it. I'll cut this much off.
FATHER: You just take it.

Mothers' greater willingness to negotiate their demands appears to lead children to assume they have a greater right to argue with their mothers. Children treat their fathers as having more authority and are more deferential toward them (Anderson, 1978; Cowan et al., 1984), and in dysfunctional families, aggressive children direct their coercive behavior far more often toward mothers than fathers (Patterson, 1980). On a more positive note, the fact that mothers chat and listen to their children more means that they know the children better—are more in touch with the details of their daily lives and more aware of their children's interests and problems.[8] This kind of intimacy facilitates monitoring of children's activities, and successful parental monitoring has repeatedly been shown to be important for keeping children out of trouble as they reach the preteen and teenage years (Buchanan et al., 1992).

An important difference between fathers and mothers is the degree to which they are concerned with what they deem to be appropriate sex typing in their children (Siegal, 1987), with mothers being fairly unconcerned and fathers more so. In particular, fathers are concerned with fostering masculine qualities in their sons. Fathers tend to react strongly to signs of effeminacy in a boy—more strongly than mothers do. These paternal reactions can start when a boy is quite young, as illustrated by an observation of at-home interaction between parents and a toddler boy (Gable et al., 1993): "The child has hurt himself, and cries. Mother says: 'Come here, honey, I'll kiss it better.' Father to child: 'Oh, toughen up. Quit your belly-aching.'"

The mother-father differences in parenting style parallel closely the differences in interactive style that are seen in the gender-segregated play groups of childhood. In these groups, girls more often than boys avoid confrontation with other girls, and they take a reciprocal style of verbal exchange in which they are more likely to listen to and respond to one another. They do try to achieve their own individual goals in the group but at the same time are concerned to maintain good relations within the group and focus on group as well as individual goals. Boys' play is rougher, and they use more power assertion toward one another, focusing more exclusively on protecting their own turf and achieving egoistic goals. Furthermore, girls are fairly tolerant of behavior in another child—either a boy or girl—that doesn't conform to gender stereotypes, while boys are notably intolerant of effeminate behavior in their male peers. I suggest that the distinctive styles of men and women in their parental roles stem to an important degree from the styles they developed in the segregated peer groups of childhood.

Let us go back to the question raised earlier: Are women in some way more suited to the day-to-day job of taking care of children and socializing them? As noted above, intimate knowledge of a child's activities, moods, and interest facilitates successful monitoring and supervision, and in this respect mothers generally have an advantage. The research on the outcomes of different parental styles indicates clearly what many would claim good parents know simply through common sense: that children need responsive, supportive, nurturant parenting but that they also need firm control and consistent discipline. A man and woman can make a good child-rearing team, then, in that although each parent usually can display either nurturant or controlling parental behavior, depending on the situation, the balance is tipped toward imperative control by fathers and responsive nurturance by mothers. While children need parental support, love, and responsiveness throughout childhood, the importance of discipline and control changes with the child's age. At least in the first two years, it is a less important element in the parental mix than the nurturant side, and for this reason, I would argue that the typical maternal style is more adapted to the needs of children during these tender years, while children benefit during most of childhood from the mix of styles provided by typical mothers and fathers and from the reinforcement the two parents give to one another. This line of argument suggests that two parents are better than one, *if* the two parents are able to function as a cooperative parental team.

Coparenting

In intact two-parent families, where a mother and father are trying to function as a child-rearing team, the process of raising the child involves not only the interactions of each parent with the child but the interactions of the two parents with each other. We noted earlier the widespread assumption that the day-to-day routine care of young children is more the mother's than the father's job, on the basis of a cluster of cultural beliefs about women being better suited for it or on men's greater power to avoid doing it. In many families, the two parents agree on the mother's being the person in charge where the children are concerned, with the father being cast in role of her helper. In some cases, the parents may agree on the father's having equal or even greater behind-the-scenes authority but may see the mother as his executive. In such cases, the father will try not to interfere or undercut the execution of her duties and may indeed provide reinforcement for her authority if the child is not cooperating with her. An illustration comes from the study of toddlers and their parents (Gable et al., 1993), in an incident in which a toddler has opened a cupboard and started to pull out a heavy, breakable object:

MOTHER TO CHILD: Get out of there!

FATHER TO CHILD: Listen to your mother! You're gonna get hurt, come over here!

Gable et al. (1993) reported that fathers offered this sort of support to their wives twice as often as wives offered it to husbands, no doubt a reflection of the fact that mothers were more often the ones to give directions to the child so that the occasion to offer support arose more often for fathers. Even when cast in the role of helper, however, fathers may expect to play a strong role in establishing the policies for running the household. Of course, husband and wife may not agree about the way in which their parental roles properly intersect. The way in which their different points of view can lead to conflict between them is illustrated by an observation of a moment in the life of two parents with a toddler son (Gable et al., 1993):

Child leaves the kitchen, walks down the hall toward the bedroom, carrying a frying pan. He accidentally bangs the pan against the wall. Father calls impatiently to the mother from the bedroom: "Hey, he's knocking holes in the wall!" Mother leaves the kitchen, goes down the hall and stops the child. She goes to the bedroom door and says quietly but firmly: "Then you can entertain him." Father says "I don't want to." Child remains in the bedroom with the father while the mother returns to the kitchen.

Here the father tries to use the mother as his executive. However, she does not acknowledge his right to do so, and they fail to negotiate their difference successfully. In some intact two-parent families, the parents have worked out a fairly clear understanding about who is responsible for doing what with the child at what times, but

THE INDIVIDUAL, THE FAMILY, AND SOCIAL GOOD

even in such cases, circumstances arise in which negotiation and accommodation are needed.

Coparents must negotiate not only the question of which one of them should respond to the child at a given moment but also any differences they have concerning the meaning of a child's behavior or the proper way to react to it. Is the child crying because he or she is hungry, scared, or just uncooperative? Should a crying infant be picked up immediately, or will this spoil the child and make him or her too demanding and dependent? Is it good for children to be exposed to cold fresh air while sleeping? Should they be allowed to pick and choose what they want to eat, or should they be required to eat whatever is on their plate? At what age, and in what places, is it safe for a child to ride a bike or use a skateboard? Should television watching be limited or regulated? Parents often find that they have different reactions when such questions arise. They have viewpoints they may not have previously realized they had, with roots in experiences of their own childhood. New issues constantly crop up as children grow older, and if the parents want to present a united front to the children, they recognize that they need to discuss what strategy to adopt, even though such discussions take time, effort, and willingness to compromise. Couples vary greatly in how many differences in child-rearing strategies they encounter and in how successful they are in resolving their differences and reaching a smoothly functioning parental teamship.

The Postdivorce Parental Roles of Men and Women

THE INCREASING GENDER DISCREPANCY IN RESPONSIBILITY FOR CHILD CARE

I have taken a long detour from the rights and duties of the two parents after divorce, but are ready to return to these issues now. I noted earlier the great asymmetry in favor of mothers awards of physical custody. This discrepancy appears to reflect two major factors. First, mothers much more frequently than fathers say they *want* sole physical custody of the children; furthermore, they act on their desires, petitioning the court for maternal custody in a large majority of cases. Most fathers cede the children to the mother by default: they make no claim for custody. We see here powerful evidence that having physical custody is more important to most mothers than to most fathers. Women are much less willing to give up, or even share, the parenting role. Second, divorce decrees by and large merely validate the residential arrangement already in place at the time a divorce settlement occurs. When parents separate, the father is usually the one to move out, leaving the mother and children together in the family residence. In other cases, the mother moves out, taking the children with her. It is rare for the mother to move out and leave the children with the father.

Sometimes, of course, a divorce decree does call for a different residential arrangement than the de facto one that is in place after the separation. The limited available evidence (Maccoby & Mnookin, 1992) indicates that, if the decree awards custody of the children to the mother when they are not initially living with her, they usually move in with her. If the children are living with the mother and the decree says they should be in joint or father custody, however, they seldom move into the residential arrangement called for. As Maccoby and Mnookin (1992) say: "It appears that the legal decree can function to confirm residence with the mother if it exists initially, and to bring it about if it does not exist initially. The decree is much less powerful in moving children out of maternal residence once it has been established" (p. 167). Two additional findings from this study are of interest: maternal residence proved to be a much more stable arrangement over time than did either dual or father residence and, when a change in the children's residence was triggered by a residential move on the part of either the mother or the father, the move was more often in the direction of children moving into sole residence with the mother than into sole residence with the father. All this evidence suggests a powerful gyroscopic pull toward mothers as the continuing primary parent.

After divorce, the disparity between mothers and fathers in the amount of time they spend with children is of course even greater than it was before the parental separation. In the usual case, fathers who used to be available to children on a daily basis during their nonworking hours are now available only on some weekends and holidays. It is possible that the time these noncustodial fathers do spend with their children is of a higher quality than their at-home time used to be, in that divorced fathers are likely to set aside the times when their children visit for special child-centered activities. Noncustodial fathers often complain, however, that visitation time seems unnatural and strained and that they quickly lose touch with the details of their children's lives (Braver et al., 1993).

When children live with their mothers after divorce, most do visit their fathers at least over several years, but visitation tends to diminish over time and a substantial minority of fathers "drop out" of their children's lives. Among the much smaller group of families in which the children live with their fathers, however, a loss of contact between children and nonresidential mothers is much less common, and visitation with nonresidential mothers is sustained or even increased (Furstenberg et al., 1983; Greif & Pabst, 1988; Maccoby & Mnookin, 1992; see also review by Depner, 1993, p. 43, of studies indicating greater continuing involvement of noncustodial mothers with their children). In cases of joint physical custody, mothers continue to carry more of the managerial responsibilities (e.g., arranging medical care) than do fathers.

SHIFT OF ECONOMIC RESPONSIBILITIES TO MOTHERS

Much has been written concerning the great economic disadvantages that divorce brings to women and children. It has been thoroughly documented that mothers have much more to lose economically than do fathers through divorce, even after accounting for the amount that fathers pay in child and spousal support. Perhaps the most striking change in the roles of the two parents after divorce is that mothers take on primary responsibility for the economic support of the children—a responsibility formerly carried mainly by fathers (Maccoby & Mnookin, 1992, chap. 10; Weitzman, 1985).

From a purely economic point of view, then, it remains something of a mystery why women are so much more often the ones who most want to leave a marriage and why they strive so fiercely to keep custody of the children, despite the economic burdens they know it will entail. It may be that the prospect of receiving some support money from their husbands makes it somewhat easier to contemplate divorce, and perhaps many women underestimate the economic hardship they will face. But the question remains as to why women whose husbands are willing or eager to assume custody of the children do not more often cheerfully relinquish it, knowing as they do that the men can better afford to raise the children.

It seems obvious that women's strong ties to their children override economic considerations. It has been suggested that the main thing many women want from marriage is children, and as long as they believe they can keep the children, they are satisfied to leave a marriage and live without the company of an adult male (see, e.g., DuPlessix-Gray, 1989). But this analysis ignores the fact that the large majority of divorced women remarry. We are left with the simple fact that, regardless of the circumstances of the divorce, women almost universally want to keep the children and usually succeed, even thought they will have to assume the main burden of economic support.

PRIMARY CUSTODIAL PARENTS: DO THEY BECOME "BOTH FATHER AND MOTHER"?

After divorce, whichever parent becomes the primary custodial parent must take on some functions previously performed by the other parent. In the typical case, transitional adjustments are especially great for custodial fathers, in that they must adjust to the pressures of primary parenting—a role to which mothers are usually already accustomed. Primary fathers report, too, that their new responsibilities make inroads on their jobs and their career prospects, just as they have done all along for primary-caretaking mothers (see Depner & Bray, 1993, pp. 48–49, for a review of studies of the difficulties faced during the transition to single parenting by men who have received custody of their children at divorce). Mothers, for their part, must learn to handle the household chores formerly done by their husbands.

More important for our present purposes, we must ask whether custodial parents take on the psychological qualities of the other parent to any extent. Are custodial fathers able to be "both mother and father" to their children, in the sense of becoming more "tuned in" to their children's interests and states of mind? Do custodial mothers become more effective disciplinarians? What meager information we have suggests that, while divorced single parents do adapt, there is some carryover of the parental characteristics each displayed during the marriage: custodial mothers report somewhat more difficulty in maintaining discipline and being firm and patient than do custodial fathers—just as they did before the divorce—while difficulty in keeping track of their children's activities and interests is reported somewhat more often by custodial fathers than custodial mothers (Maccoby & Mnookin, 1992). Adolescents whose parents have divorced and who live with their mothers report feeling somewhat closer to their mothers than father-resident adolescents feel toward their fathers (Buchanan et al., 1992), a further indication that mothers typically maintain a greater degree of intimacy with the children who live with them after divorce than do custodial fathers. These differences are small, however, and in most cases the relationships between children and their custodial parents appear to be quite close regardless of which parent the child lives with primarily.

THE COSTS AND BENEFITS OF CONTINUED CONTACT WITH BOTH PARENTS

It is a sad fact that we have very little information concerning the long-term outcomes for children of spending varying amounts of time with their fathers, whether in intact or separated families (Furstenberg & Harris, 1993; Griswold, 1993). We have noted that children typically keep some degree of contact with the nonresidential parent after their parents have divorced, at least over a period of several years, and that the contact with their mothers for children who live with their fathers is likely to be more frequent and more enduring than contact with fathers for mother-resident children. It becomes important to know what difference such contact makes. Do children benefit from maintaining a relationship with an "outside" parent? It seems obvious that a child's pain and fear over being abandoned when a parent moves out of the household should be softened if the child can continue to see the missing parent. However, there may be counterbalancing risks in continued contact. For one thing, when children continue to visit the nonresidential parent, the two parents themselves must remain in contact to arrange the visitation, possibly sustaining or exacerbating their conflict. And continued conflict between divorced parents is harmful to children. Furthermore, if children spend time in both parental households they are more likely to be exposed to different sets of standards and different expectations about their conduct and responsibilities, with resulting confusion over values on the part of the child. Also, in some families children are exposed to undermining and derogation of their primary parent when visiting the nonresident parent, triggering both loyalty conflicts and some loss of trust in or respect toward the primary parent.

In view of the possibility that the risks and benefits from continued contact with "outside" parents could cancel each other out, it is perhaps not surprising that, among children living with their mothers, the amount of contact with their fathers has not been found to be systematically related either positively or negatively to the children's adjustment if one considers the average adjustment of groups of mother-resident children who have different amounts of contact with their fathers (see Maccoby et al., 1993, for a summary of studies). We may suspect that, while some children clearly do benefit from continued contact with their nonresidential fathers, visitation thrusts others into conflicts that are difficult to cope with. Furstenberg and Harris (1993) have reported, in a 20-year follow-up study of the children of teenage mothers (most of whom were black and poor), that there was no overall effect of simply maintaining contact with their fathers over time. However, in the relatively rare cases in which the father and child had formed and maintained a close bond, the children did indeed benefit in terms of their achievements, lowered rates of antisocial behavior, and emotional well-being.

In several studies of children living with their fathers, more general benefits have been found from maintaining contact with their nonresidential mothers (Camera & Resnick, 1988; Maccoby et al., 1993; Zill, 1988). It would seem that, for father-resident children, the benefits of visiting their mothers more often outweigh the costs. Zill (1988), comparing children living with a remarried mother and those living with a remarried father, says that "contact with an outside mother seemed to be more critical for a stepchild's well-being than contact with an outside father," (p. 363), and his conclusion is borne out by studies of other children in divorced families, whether their parents have remarried or not.

Implications for Divorce Policy

I come now to the most difficult issues: What is the relevance of the material summarized so far for social and legal policy? These issues are intensely politicized. It is not possible to talk about them without walking into a mine field sown with potential explosive reactions to any position one might take. But let us make an attempt at objectivity.

The evidence reviewed above points quite clearly to the primacy of the mother-child bond. The fact that mothers receive custody of children in the great majority of cases, then, is something that reflects social realities—realities that have proved to be very difficult to change. We must recognize at once that these realities reflect what *is*, not what inevitably must be. From the standpoint of those of us who are concerned that fathers are becoming progressively more marginalized in their children's lives and who believe that this trend poses dangers to our society, the review has been sobering but not hopeless. Although the number of fathers who live separately from their children may be increasing and although these nonresident fathers of course spend less time with their children than do fathers in two-parent families, there is some compensating increase in the involvement of live-in fathers with children, and probably an increase in many families in children's contact with fathers who live apart from the family. While it is not certain, it appears likely that changes in divorce law, especially those that specifically assume that both parents should continue to be involved in their children's lives despite parental separation, have had at least a modest effect in shifting families toward sustained visitation with nonresidential parents or even toward attempting to maintain joint custody (Mnookin et al., 1989). While existing legal processes do seem to be operating in consonance with traditional maternal and paternal roles, statutory reform can be said to have had some liberalizing effect.

In view of the evidence we have reviewed, what can we say about what kind of custodial arrangements are fair to divorcing mothers and fathers? It seems that both the parents themselves and the courts have been giving enormous weight to continuity in caregiving. That is, children generally live with mothers after divorce mainly because mothers are almost always the ones who have been doing most day-to-day child care all along. The fact that fathers join or help the mothers in many child-rearing functions while providing most of the economic support does not appear to carry with it an equal claim to physical custody; it only implies an obligation to continue providing money for child support after parental separation. When a father in an intact family sticks to a job he does not like or works overtime to earn income for his family, this kind of sacrifice does not feed directly into improved relationships with his children; indeed, it may work the other way. A mother's day-to-day nurturance and care giving *does* have a direct impact on the mother-child relationship and thereby on the child's sense of security and growing competence. As a society we seem to have implicitly assumed that it is more important for a child's well-being to maintain the relationship with the parent who has had the most frequent and continuous direct interactive role in the child's life than it is to keep in daily contact with the parent who has had the more indirect economic support role, especially since fathers can be made to pay even if they are not present.

Is it fair to fathers that their economic contribution and supportive parenting should be valued less when it comes to custody awards than the mother's history of investment in primary child rearing? From the standpoint of many noncustodial fathers, it clearly is not. After his day's work, he can no longer come home to his children, or to a home with food, amenities, and comforts that a wife formerly provided through his income. Of course, single people living alone without children can and do create comfortable homes for themselves, but in the immediate postdivorce period, a nonresidential father is likely to have to go "home" after work to a small, barren, lonely hotel room or apartment or trailer. Still, he is required by law to continue providing financial support to the household of which he is no longer a part. It is no wonder that this seems like involuntary servitude to many divorced men, even though their former household makes much less demand on their income than it formerly did.

Is the traditional award of custody and child support to mothers fair to mothers? They have been able to keep certain central elements of their homes relatively intact: the presence of the children most of the time and their homemaking routines. On the other hand, they usually find that the economic support they receive from their former husbands is inadequate for their needs and does not come close to replacing the husband's lost income. In many cases, they must increase their out-of-home working hours and struggle to find adequate child care for these hours. On the other hand, most divorced single mothers report that it is easier for them to raise the children than it was before the divorce. Presumably, the loss of the father's backup in child rearing is outweighed by the fact that the mother no longer has to negotiate with an incompatible spouse over child-rearing issues and no longer has to mediate between the spouse and the children. It is difficult to compare the gains and losses of the two parents, but overall it would appear that a mother-custody arrangement is not as "fair" to fathers as to mothers, in that mothers get more, and lose less, of what has been central to their lives.

Let us consider what would happen to the balance of fairness between the two parents if we systematically awarded physical custody more often to fathers, perhaps by tossing a coin when custody is contested or by awarding fathers custody whenever they were in a better financial position to raise the children. From the standpoint of most women, such decisions would be grossly and doubly unfair. A major reason that fathers are generally in a stronger financial position, they would say, is that the mothers have made career sacrifices to give priority to child rearing and homemaking. The law deals with these complexities by attempting to adhere closely to the principle that custodial decisions should not rest on the relative financial status of the two parents, because postdivorce deficits in a custodial parent's financial resources can be at least partially rectified through payments of child and spousal support.

From the women's standpoint, their heavier investment in the children—both biologically and in terms of child-care commitment—is what gives them a greater right to custody. It means that they have a closer two-way bond with the children, so that it would be more agonizing for them to give up the children than it would be for most fathers. Indeed, David Chambers (1984) has argued for a primary-caretaker preference in custodial awards, not mainly on the grounds that it is necessarily better for the children—although it may be—but because of the likelihood that a parent who has served as primary caretaker will usually be more distressed over the loss of custody than a parent who has not. Without denying that fathers suffer greatly over separation from their children, Chambers's argument is that mothers would suffer even more if denied custody.

In making custodial decisions, it would appear that it is almost impossible to be equally fair to all parties concerned. While the children's welfare must surely be the first consideration, the interests of mothers and fathers must also be served as far as possible, not least because to do so will ultimately redound to the benefit of the children. The fathers' sense of unfairness over being separated from their children while nevertheless being required to pay support for them has been eased by providing liberal visitation and by denying mothers the right to veto visitation unless it is clear that such visits endanger the children. While liberal visitation might appear to create for the children a fractionated, unstable life, the evidence so far is that it does no harm in the typical case and that it is something that most children and most nonresidential parents continue to want.

In the long run, the terms of discourse between divorcing parents need to be changed. While custody disputes have often revolved around questions of who "owns" or "gets" the children or has greater "rights" to them, a more productive negotiation would proceed from a focus on how the two parents can best continue jointly to provide what the children need. As we saw earlier, parenting is much more a matter of making sacrifices for children than it is of exercising rights, although parents do derive many long-term satisfactions from having raised children successfully. Some legal jurisdictions are trying to move away entirely from the concept of custody (e.g., the 1987 Washington State Parenting Act; see Ellis, 1990) and instead require divorcing parents to develop a feasible parenting plan that will ensure the welfare of the children while at the same time optimizing the satisfactions of both parents as far as possible. These approaches are intended to modify the adversarial nature of divorce proceedings and reduce interparental conflict over the children. It remains to be seen whether they will succeed.

NOTES

1. Mnookin and Weisberg (1989) noted the weakness of the Blackstone doctrine, in that the law did not initially provide for enforcement of parents' "natural" obligations if they failed to support their children.

2. It is notable that magistrates were authorized to "bind out" children *of the poor* (see Mnookin, 1973, p. 599).

3. Although the Supreme Court ruled in favor of the rights of Amish

parents to keep their children out of school, Justice Douglas, in his dissent, made a strong plea for the rights of children to be heard as interested parties when their wishes did not coincide with those of their parents.

4. See Polikoff (1983) for a summary of studies available to that date, showing that in contested cases fathers received custody in 40 to 50% of the cases. See Maccoby and Mnookin (1992) for more recent data.

5. The fact that fathers have greater success in getting custody the farther the dispute is carried through the steps of legal conflict may reflect a selective bias, in that it may be only in cases where the fathers have the best claims for custody (or mothers the weakest claims) that the legal dispute is sustained through the full sequence of court procedures. On the other hand, the legal dispute may be sustained by fathers who have enough money to pay continuing legal fees, forcing mothers to give up the fight for lack of money.

6. There are some pitfalls in the choice of terminology to describe families made up of a mother, father, and the children of their union. *Nondivorced* is a possibility, though it emphasizes what they are not rather than what they are. *Two-parent families* is another possibility, although this term might apply to stepparent families as well as to those with two natural parents. There have been objections to the term *intact* on the grounds that single-parent families can be considered intact, expecially in cases where the single parent has never married and where there has therefore never been a breakup. For the purposes of this chapter, I want to contrast the situation of families with two natural parents living together with that of families in which the natural parents have divorced and live separately. The terms *intact* vs. *divorced* seem to convey this distinction reasonably well.

7. Presser (1989) noted that wives appear to have adapted their working schedules to those of their husbands more often than vice versa. That is, for wives, the factors predicting the choice of shift include the husband's working hours, while the husband's shift depends entirely on extra-marital factors such as the nature of his job skills and the available jobs.

8. In a set of studies in which adolescents were interviewed about their relationships with their two parents, Youniss and Smollar (1985) report that adolescents feel their mothers know them better than their fathers do; however, they regard their two parents as equally important when it comes to setting and maintaining standards.

REFERENCES

Albiston, C. R., Maccoby, E. E., & Mnookin, R. H. (1990). Does joint legal custody matter? *Stanford Law and Policy Review, 2*, 167–179.

Anderson, E. S. (1978). Will you don't snore, please? Directives in young children's role-play speech. *Papers and Reports on Child Language Development, 15*, 140–150.

Braver, S. L., Wolchik, S. A., Sandler, I. N., & Sheets, V. L. (1993). A social exchange model of nonresidential parent involvement. In C. E. Depner

& J. H. Bray (Eds.), *Nonresidential parenting: New vistas in family living* (pp. 87–108). Newbury Park CA: Sage.

Buchanan, C. M., Maccoby, E. E., & Dornbusch, S. M. (1992). Adolescents and their families after divorce: Three residential arrangements compared. *Journal of Research on Adolescence, 2,* 261–291.

Camera, K., & Resnick. G. (1988). Interparental conflict and cooperation: Factors moderating children's post-divorce adjustment. In E. M. Hetherington & J. Arasteh (Eds.), *Impact of divorce, single parenting, and stepparenting on children* (pp. 169–195). Hillsdale NJ: Erlbaum.

Chambers, D. (1984). Rethinking the substantive rules for child-custody disputes. *Michigan Law Review, 83,* 477–569.

Chamove, A., Harlow, H. F., & Mitchell, G. (1965). Sex differences in the infant-directed behavior of preadolescent rhesus monkeys. *Child Development, 38,* 329–336.

Chesler, P. (1986). *Mothers on trial.* New York: McGraw-Hill.

Cook, J. A. (1984). California's joint custody statute. In J. Folberg (Ed.), *Joint custody and shared parenting* (pp. 168–183). Washington DC: Association of Family and Concilliation Courts.

Cowan, C. P., & Cowan, P. A. (1992). *When partners become parents: The big life change for couples.* New York: Basic.

Cowan, G., Drinkard, J., & MacGavin, L. (1984). The effects of target, age and gender on use of power strategies. *Journal of Personality and Social Psychology, 47,* 1391–1398.

Depner, C. E. (1993). Parental role reversal: Mothers as non-residential parents. In C. E. Depner & J. H. Bray (Eds.), *Nonresidential parenting: New vistas in family living* (pp. 37–57). Newbury Park CA: Sage.

Depner, C. E., & Bray, J. H. (Eds.). (1993). *Nonresidential parenting.* Newbury Park CA: Sage.

Dunn, J., Bretherton, I., & Munn, P. (1987). Conversations about feeling states between mothers and their young children. *Developmental Psychology, 23,* 132–139.

DuPlessix-Gray, F. (1989). *Soviet women: Walking the tightrope.* New York: Doubleday.

Ellis, J. (1990). Plans, protections and professional interventions in divorce custody reform and the role of legal professionals. *University of Michigan Journal of Law Reform, 24,* 67–188.

Ember, C. (1973). Feminine task assignment and the social behavior of boys. *Ethos, 1,* 424–439.

Emery, R. E. (1988). *Marriage, divorce and children's adjustment.* Newbury Park CA: Sage.

Fivush, R. (1993). Emotional content of parent-child conversations about the past. In C. A. Nelson (Ed.), *Minnesota Symposium on Child Psychology: Memory and affect in development* (Vol. 26, pp. 39–77). Hillsdale NJ: Erlbaum.

Furstenberg, F. F., Jr. (1988). Good dads—bad dads: Two faces of fatherhood. In A. Cherlin (Ed.), *The changing American family and public policy.* Washington DC: Urban Institute.

Furstenberg, F. F., Jr., & Harris, K. M. (1993). When fathers matter/why fathers matter: The impact of paternal involvement on the offspring of adolescent mothers. In A. Lawson & D. L. Rhode (Eds.), *The politics of pregnancy: Adolescent sexuality and public policy*. New Haven CT: Yale University Press.

Furstenberg, F. F., Jr., Nord, C. W., Peterson, J. L., & Zill, N. (1983). The life course of children of divorce. *American Sociological Review, 48*, 656–668.

Gable, S., Belsky, J., & Crnic, K. (1993, March). *Coparenting in the child's second year: Stability and change from 15 to 21 months*. Paper presented at the meeting of the Society for Research in Child Development, New Orleans.

Gleason, J. B. (April, 1987). *Language and psychological development*. Keynote address at the Stanford Child Language Forum, Stanford CA.

Greif, G. L., & Pabst, M. S. (1988). *Mothers without custody*. Lexington MA: Lexington.

Griswold, R. L. (1993). *Fatherhood in America: A history*. New York: Basic.

Grusec, J. E., & Goodnow, J. J. (1994). Impact of parental discipline methods on the child's internalization of values: A reconceptualization of current points of view. *Developmental Psychology, 30*, 4–19.

Handler, J. F., & Zatz, J. (1982). The implementation system: Characteristics and change. In J. F. Handler & J. Zatz (Eds.), *Neither angels nor thieves: Studies in deinstitutionalization of status offenders*. Washington DC: National Academy Press.

Kay, H. H. (1990). Beyond no-fault: New directions in divorce reform. In S. D. Sugarman & H. H. Kay (Eds.), *Divorce reform at the crossroads* (pp. 6–36). New Haven CT: Yale University Press.

Lamb, M. E., Pleck, J. H., Charnov, E. L., & Levine, J. A. (1987). A biosocial perspective on paternal behavior and involvement. In J. B. Lancaster, J. Altmann, A. S. Rossi, & L. R. Sherrod (Eds.), *Parenting across the lifespan: Biosocial dimensions*. New York: Gruyter.

Lovejoy, J., & Wallen, K. (1988). Sexually dimorphic behavior in group-housed rhesus monkeys (macaca mulatta) at 1 year of age. *Psychobiology, 16*, 348–356.

Maccoby, E. E., Buchanan, C. M., Mnookin, R. H., & Dornbusch, S. M. (1993). Postdivorce roles of mothers and fathers in the lives of their children. *Journal of Family Psychology, 7*, 24–38.

Maccoby, E. E., & Mnookin, R. H. (1992). *Dividing the child: The social and legal dilemmas of custody*. Cambridge MA: Harvard University Press.

Meany, M. J., Stewart, J., & Beatty, W. W. (1985). Sex differences in social play: The socialization of sex roles. In J. S. Rosenblatt, C. Beer, C. M. Busnell, & P. Stater (Eds.), *Advances in the study of behavior* (Vol. 15, pp. 1–58). New York: Academic Press.

Mnookin, R. H. (1973). Foster care: In whose best interest? *Harvard Educational Review, 43*, 599–638.

Mnookin, R. H., & Kornhauser, L. (1979). Bargaining in the shadow of the law: The case of divorce. *Yale Law Journal, 88*, 950–997.

Mnookin, R. H., Maccoby, E. E., Albiston, C. R., & Depner, C. E. (1989). Private ordering revisited: What custodial arrangements are parents negotiating? In S. D. Sugarman & H. H. Kay (Eds.), *Divorce reform at the crossroads* (pp. 37–74). New Haven CT: Yale University Press.

Mnookin, R. H., & Weisberg, D. K. (1989). *Child, family and state: Problems and materials on children and the law* (2nd ed.). Boston: Little, Brown.

Money, J., Ehrhardt, A. A., & Masica, D. N. (1968). Fetal feminization induced by androgen insensitivity in the testicular feminizing syndrome: Effect on marriage and maternalism. *Johns Hopkins Medical Journal, 123,* 105–114.

Nock, S. L., & Kingston, P. W. (1988). Time with children: The impact of couples' work-time commitments. *Social Forces, 67,* 59–85.

Patterson, G. R. (1980). Mothers: The unacknowledged victims. *Monographs of the Society for Research in Child Development, 45*(5).

Polikoff, N. D. (1983). Gender and child-custody determinations: Exploding the myths. In I. Diamond (Ed.), *Families, politics and public policy: A feminist dialogue on women and the state.* New York: Longman.

Power, T. G. (1985). Mother- and father-infant play: A developmental analysis. *Child Development, 56,* 1514–1524.

Presser, H. B. (1989). Can we make time for children? The economy, work schedules, and child care. *Demography, 26,* 523–543.

Presser, H. B. (in press). Are the interests of women inherently at odds with the interests of children or the family? A viewpoint. In K. O. Mason & A. M. Jensen (Eds.), *Gender and family change in industrialized countries.* Oxford: Oxford University Press.

Radke-Yarrow, M., Belmont, B., Nottelman, E., & Bottomly, L. (1990). Young children's self-conceptions: Origins in the natural discourse of depressed and normal mothers and their children. In D. Cicchetti & M. Beeghly (Eds.), *The self in transition: Infancy to childhood.* Chicago: University of Chicago Press.

Shaffer, H. R., & Crook, C. K. (1980). Child compliance and maternal control techniques. *Developmental Psychology, 16,* 54–61.

Siegal, M. (1987). Are sons and daughters treated more differently by fathers than mothers? *Developmental Review, 7,* 183–209.

Smart, C. (1989). Power and the politics of child custody. In C. Smart & S. Sevenhuijsen (Eds.), *Child custody and the politics of gender* (pp. 1–26). London: Routledge.

Stern, J. M. (1989). Maternal behavior: Sensory, hormonal, and neural determinants. In F. R. Brush & S. Levine (Eds.), *Psychoendocrinology.* New York: Academic Press.

U. S. House of Representatives. (1989). *U. S. children and their families: Current conditions and recent trends.* Report of the Select Committee on Children, Youth and Families. Washington DC: U.S. Government Printing Office.

Weitzman, L. J. (1985). *The divorce revolution: The unexpected social and economic consequences for women and children in America.* New York: Free Press.

Whiting, B. B., & Edwards, C. P (1988). *Children of different worlds: The formation of social behavior*. Cambridge MA: Harvard University Press.

Youniss, J., & Smollar, J. (1985). *Adolescent relations with mothers, fathers, and friends*. Chicago: University of Chicago Press.

Zill, N. (1988). Behavior, achievement and health problems among children in stepfamilies: Findings from a national survey of child health. In E. M. Hetherington & J. Arasteh (Eds.), *The impact of divorce, single-parenting, and stepparenting on children* (pp. 325–368). Hillsdale NJ: Erlbaum.

Epilogue: Psychology, Law, and the Family

Ronald Roesch
Simon Fraser University

I appreciated the invitation to participate in the 42nd Annual Symposium on Motivation and to prepare some comments on the symposium presentations and the subsequent chapters that this book comprises. It was especially an honor because the symposium also marked the 20th anniversary of the Law/Psychology Program at the University of Nebraska–Lincoln. This program, under the initial leadership of Bruce Sales and then of Gary Melton, has had remarkable success training psychology-and-law scholars and practitioners (see Melton, 1990; Ross & Sales, 1985).

I must confess to having been a little hesitant to accept the invitation to participate in this symposium as initially I wondered what I could contribute to the discussion since families have not been a direct focus of my own research. As I thought more about it, however, I felt that some of my research and other interests do indeed relate to family matters. In fact, this symposium became a learning experience that has helped me to begin to view my research and other psychology-and-law research differently. While this may simply be cognitive dissonance at work, I think the effects of the decline of communities and changes in family structure can be seen in several areas of interest to me in my own research, and, in the broader context, to psychology-and-law researchers. For example, in a recent study, my collegues and I collected data on the prevalence of spousal assaulters among offenders on probation. We found that nearly 20% of all offenders currently on probation in one jurisdiction in British Columbia had a history of spousal assault in their files (Hart et al., in press), yet almost no services dealing with family violence were offered to these offenders or their families. The impact of this form of violence on families is substantial. For children, simply observing spousal assault might have serious long-term effects, and there is without a doubt a strong need for intervention with both the adults and child victims of domestic violence.

Some other examples of psychology-and-law research related to family issues are sexual abuse, which is often committed by live-in boyfriends or stepfathers (another sign of changing family life), divorce and custody (with the associated issues of the impact of joint custody and the allegations of sexual abuse that arise during custody disputes), adolescent depression, violence among youth, and other delinquent behavior. While I do not believe that the family should be seen as the cause of all these or other adolescent problems, I do believe that the family can have negative effects as well as be a source of strength and stability that can help youths through difficult times (see Wolchik et al., 1989).

I also came to be interested in this topic from the perspective provided by my background in community psychology. Consider how we deal with the problem of juvenile delinquency as an example. From a prevention standpoint, we typically wait too long to try to mount interventions to minimize or prevent the problems that we see in young people. Indeed, in juvenile justice, much of our efforts can be described as tertiary prevention at best, as we are simply seeing youths too late to even consider what we do as secondary prevention. Furthermore, and most important from the perspective of this symposium, as I will comment on later, many of the interventions do not involve the family, focusing instead on juveniles in isolation from the family and other social systems of which they are a part. This ignores the vast literature demonstrating the relationship between family risk factors and child maladjustment (e.g., Garbarino et al., 1991; Kessler & Neighbors, 1986; Myers et al., 1992; Seidman, 1991). As I read the chapters in this volume, which provide many insights into family life, I was often led to think of the implications for change. The approach I am taking to this chapter follows from this, in that I will try to identify the strategies for prevention and intervention that may help ameliorate the negative consequences of changing family life that were discussed in the symposium.

Changing Family Life

The chapters in this volume, based on the papers presented at the symposium, provide a rich analysis of the problems facing families today. One theme of the symposium was that family life has changed considerably in the past few decades. Allen Parkman, an economist-lawyer, reviews some of the statistics, showing the decline in the number of marriages, the increase in divorces, and the decline of two-parent families. Parkman's thesis is that marriage has become a less attractive alternative for couples. Further, using measures such as the reported cases of child abuse as an indicator of the quality of life in families, he argues that family life has deteriorated. His analysis focuses on the impact that changes in divorce laws, particularly the establishment of no-fault divorce laws, have had on family life. He comments that, while protection for long-term commitments is the most important incentive for the formation of a family, the practice of no-fault divorce provides little protection for this commitment. What are the alternatives? Parkman suggests that divorce could be limited to situations in which there is mutual agreement by the spouses. Under this system, a divorce would only occur when "the collective benefits exceeded the costs."

Parkman makes some assumptions that I think are worth discussing. Approaching this issue with an economist's perspective of the costs and benefits of decisions, he notes that if people considering marriage knew that the only way to dissolve the marriage was through mutual consent, then possibly incentives would increase to negotiate premarital agreements that specify grounds for divorce. The mutual-consent alternative would, in his view, increase the attractiveness of marriage and encourage couples to approach marriage with more care. The marriage rate would, in Parkman's view, increase as marriage would be more attractive to people looking for long-term commitment, which should in turn improve the quality of family life and marriage. Divorce, in his view, would be an option only when the net benefits are positive. This is an interesting hypothesis, one that could only be tested if we made a major shift in divorce-law policy and statutes.

Parkman's analysis of marriage and divorce is thoughtful and intriguing. His call for a shift from a no-fault divorce policy to one requiring mutual consent would result in substantial changes in the law and practice of divorce. He does recognize, of course, that there may be situations in which consent is impossible, such as when one spouse is the victim of cruelty or adultery and the guilty spouse does not want a divorce. In these cases, Parkman suggests that there would be a role for *fault* divorce, in which clear and convincing evidence of such fault grounds as cruelty or desertion could be the basis for divorce. I cannot judge how realistic Parkman's proposals are, in large part because they would require some major changes in marriage and divorce law, but I do know that such a shift would certainly send a message about the importance of the family over individual needs.

Eleanor Maccoby's analysis of divorce and divorce policy has implications for research and policy and for the future of families. She identifies the reasons children more often go to the mother than to the father after divorce and notes that fathers are becoming increasingly marginalized. Maccoby addresses a number of issues related to custody practices as well as the costs and benefits of continued contact with the noncustodial parent. We have some data on custody arrangements but, as with most areas of research, more research is needed. How fair are decisions about custody (Maccoby notes that it is probably impossible to be equally fair to mothers, fathers, and children), and what effect does the type of custody have on children and their parents? How do we move toward her call for a more productive negotiation focusing on how the parents can best continue jointly to provide what the children need? As Maccoby concludes, many changes being discussed would serve to minimize the adversarial nature of divorce and reduce conflict between parents over their children. I liked her thoughtful approach to the issue of custody, and I hope that the changes she discusses will indeed lead to less harmful divorce and custody proceedings.

In considering policies about divorce and custody, we also need to be aware of special circumstances. Shared parenting implicitly assumes that the parents are rational and will act in the best interests of the children. Of course, this is not always true. Consider, for example, the case of battered women. Should these women be put in a situation involving shared custody and continued contact with the batterer? One conclusion that might be made from the literature is that perhaps the major critical factor in divorce is parental conflict. Joint custody, for example, may at times exacerbate tension and stress for both children and parents. Regardless of the type of custody, parental conflict is associated with greater numbers of negative outcomes for children, higher levels of stress, and lower levels of well-being for parents, particularly mothers (Felner & Terre, 1987).

Socially Toxic Environments

James Garbarino presented a lucid analysis of the effect that socially toxic environments can have on children. He identifies a number of risk factors that have a cumulative effect on children, including many parent variables that may impair the ability to be an effective parent: single parenthood, low income, drug and alcohol addiction, being a victim of racism, and emotional problems. I think he is correct in his identification of the need to focus on preventing the long-term effects of the accumulation of risk, particularly since repeated exposure will eventually overcome the natural resilience and coping mechanisms that youths can draw on.

Garbarino concludes his chapter with some helpful general suggestions. I agree with him that we, as citizens of this country, need to come together to fight social toxicity, to work toward a refocus of television content, and help place the family first among political priorities. So much of our resources go into the dealing with the effects of socially toxic environments that I wonder how we can shift these resources to areas that in the long run will do so much to prevent the social problems that are the fallout of socially toxic environments. Research on risk factors does provide us some direction for preventive interventions. For example, Myers et al. (1992) found that high stress levels in the family, particularly among mothers, predicted child behavior problems in inner-city black children. Sampson and Laub (1994) presented data showing the strong effects of poverty, low supervision, weak parent-child relations, and erratic and harsh discipline are linked to juvenile delinquency. In the Cambridge Study of Delinquent Development, Farrington (1990) conducted a longitudinal study of London males from ages 8 to 32. He identified a number of risk factors for antisocial behavior, the most important of which seem to be socioeconomic deprivation, poor parenting, family deviance, school problems, hyperactivity-impulsivity-attention deficits, and antisocial child behavior. Clearly, the home life of children is important, and Farrington calls for behavioral parent training as well as preschool enrichment programs as the most hopeful areas for intervention. I believe this type of research is important because it identifies possible areas for intervention. Myers et al. (1992), for instance, found that a variety of coping strategies, particularly directed at helping families seek help and acquire social supports, were effective moderators of risk.

A recent review of the literature on early risk factors associated with later delinquency by Yoshikawa (1994) reinforces Garbarino's analysis of risk factors. Yoshikawa identified a number of family factors that contribute to an increased risk of delinquency. On the basis of a large number of studies, Yoshikawa concluded that longitudinal evidence converges on the findings that hostile or rejecting parenting and lack of supervision have direct effects on antisocial behavior and delinquency and that the effects of family-structure variables, such as broken homes, separation from parents, and number of parents in the family, are indirect and mediated by parenting variables (p. 33). He adds that individual variables, such as insecure attachment and child maltreatment, are also associated with negative outcomes on measures such as delinquency and violence. The most important implication of his review, in my opinion, is that early intervention can have powerful long-term preventive effects by mitigating the effects of social toxicity. Yoshikawa found that family support and parent and child educational programs could have an impact on delinquent behavior. Most of these programs also attempt to strengthen family ties and community support networks. We need a social and public policy that places value and resources on these interventions, which may not have immediate effects perhaps but in the long run offer better value. Yoshikawa found that, while these programs are initially costly, they are cost-effective in the long term because of their preventive effects.

These ideas about the preventive benefits of family and child interventions are not new, of course, but they seem to be increasingly recognized in the psychology community. Zigler et al. (1992) reviewed the literature on the relationship between early-childhood intervention and later juvenile delinquency. They noted that few programs directed at reducing delinquency have shown lasting effects, largely because, by the time of the intervention, the problems are of long standing and not easily reversed. But perhaps of most interest is their finding that some early-childhood intervention programs, which did not aim specifically at reducing delinquency but rather at preventing school failure, may well be having a preventive effect on antisocial behavior. This is consistent, of course, with Farrington's (1990) recommendation. Zigler et al. (1992) comment that these programs embrace an ecological view of child development by treating the children through their broad environment rather than through an isolated intervention (p. 997). These programs, such as the Perry Preschool Project and the Yale Child Welfare Research Program, do not treat the child in isolation but work with families and the schools in order to strengthen the social competency of both the families and the children. Suggestions by several of the authors in this volume call for this to begin even prenatally.

Garbarino's analysis shows that the problems facing youths today in terms of accumulated risk in a socially toxic environment are multifaceted. Solutions to these problems will require a broad approach focusing not just on families but on neighborhoods, schools, and society at large. School-based interventions offer considerable promise (see, e.g., Pedro-Carroll et al., 1986; Seidman, 1991; Seidman et al., 1994). One of my graduate students, for example, helped develop a program in which high school students worked one-on-one with elementary school children who were identified as having social, family, and academic problems (Inouye, 1992). We must be careful with these kinds of interventions to avoid making the problem worse by identifying certain children as problem children. In this particular study, we minimized this effect by including a random sample of other children in the intervention so that it would not appear that we were only offering the program to certain children.

Viewing the problem as a multifaceted one requiring solutions that integrate interventions at multiple levels will not be an easy task. Mark Jacobs (1990), in his provocatively titled *Screwing the System and Making it Work*, presents a simple yet profound thesis. In his examination of the way in which the juvenile justice system deals with young offenders, he concludes that our institutions evade by their nature responsibility for their actions. He claims, "It is altogether too easy for Americans—public officials and delinquents alike—to evade responsibility for their actions. . . . The United States lacks not only the authoritative capacity for achieving valued social goals, but even a civic philosophy capable of appointing individual or institutional responsibility" (Jacobs, 1990, p. 265).

Jacobs refers to this as the "no-fault society." He goes on to argue that the problems of delinquency, as an example, cannot be solved until we as a society recognize that problems cannot be dealt with in isolation. Jacobs's analysis of juvenile probation suggests that the way in which probation officers are forced to identify and treat young offenders is doomed to fail, as it already has. He identifies a complex system for shifting the focus of blame. Using a number of case illustrations, Jacobs argues that the problems experienced by most youth in trouble stem from a complex interaction of problems centering in the family, the schools, and the workplace. He refers to this as the ecological dimension of the problem, but notes that the parties involved are not able to recognize or define the problem in this way, and as a consequence, each party isolates one or more of the other parties as a target of blame. In one example, a girl named Rose, Jacobs notes that the girl's "mother blamed her 'uncontrollable' nature, the court psychologist blamed Rose's neurological deficiency . . . ; the neurologist blamed Rose's 'emotional disturbance' (something the schools were responsible for and presumably competent to overcome); while the schools blamed Rose's 'social maladjustment' (the 'fault' of Rose and her mother, something outside their responsibility and competence)" (Jacobs, 1990, p. 270).

In Garbarino's term, the problem lies within the socially toxic environment. This perspective is also similar to William Ryan's (1971) analysis in his book *Blaming the Victim*. I am reminded of a statement from one educator, who claimed that inferior schools were not the problem but rather that the schools have been getting an inferior type of student. We, as a society, need to adopt a broader approach to change. This kind of change is difficult but not impossible to achieve. It requires substantial alterations in the way in which we think about the cause of a given problem. This might lead to attempts to facilitate solutions that do not "blame the victim" but rather address social and family conditions that may retard individual growth and achievement.

A Psychological Sense of Community

Tom Tyler and Peter Degoey extend their analysis of procedural justice to families. Procedural justice refers to the notion that fairness is
a key concept in determining the extent to which people are willing
to obey laws or decisions made by others. Procedural justice in families has not been a focus of much research, but Tyler and Degoey
make a convincing case for its value in understanding parent-child
relations. For me, this chapter demonstrates the importance of a
psychological sense of community, a concept Seymour Sarason
(1974) elaborated many years ago in his book of the same title. How
are emotional bonds created in families that lead members to feel a
sense of community and identification with the family? I think Tyler
and Degoey's work provides some valuable insights into these matters. As in the issue of water conservation discussed in their chapter,
individuals sometimes have to set aside personal needs for the good
of the larger community, and Tyler and Degoey's research focuses
on the circumstances under which individuals are motivated to do
so. Their respondents were more willing to conserve resources if
they defined themselves as belonging to a community and identified themselves with other community members. They were also
more likely to do so if they expected other community members to
reciprocate. Tyler and Degoey note that the enhancement of an individual's identification with the community may be important in conserving a scarce resource. They also comment that people's self-interested motivations may be supplemented by social motivations.
The two mechanisms of individual and collective restraint can be ap
plied to families, as family members are often expected to set aside
individual needs for the good of the family or to defer to the judgment of other family members. But Tyler and Degoey identify some
important differences between communities and families. Their research suggests that, in families, the existence of emotional bonds
may be the essential factor, particularly as contrasted with the greater
importance of the actions of authorities and perceptions of procedural justice in their community sample. Several of the chapters in
this volume and numerous studies suggest, however, that many
families are not effective in establishing these bonds. It is likely that
emotional bonds and the sense of long-term connections with family may be weakened by the changes in family life identified by Park-

man, Maccoby, and Garbarino. The process of divorce, with protracted and often bitter custody battles, also weakens these emotional bonds, as parents are perceived to value more highly their own interests than those of the children. In his presentation at the Nebraska symposium, Tyler responded to a question from the audience, in which he clarified that his data showed central tendencies of groups. Data showing a tendency that people will behave in certain ways do not mean, of course, that all individuals will behave in a given way, as Tyler properly noted. I think this has profound implications for psychologists interested in change. What accounts for these individual differences? Why do some victims of sexual abuse, for example, later become offenders, while others do not? Why do some adolescents who have strong emotional bonds with their families nevertheless choose to break the law, while others with weak bonds conform their behavior to the law? Understanding the reasons for these different responses to similar experiences might help us understand individual motivation and also lead to preventive programs that will minimize the long-term negative effects of early harmful experiences. Tyler's research on procedural justice and social identification may provide a useful approach to studying these individual differences.

A Perspective from the East

Mati Heidmets, a scholar from Tallinn Pedagogical University in Estonia, provides a comparison of the emphasis in the former Soviet Union on social good and communal living with the focus in Western society on individual freedom. This is a time, of course, of great change in his part of the world, and he notes that many are looking to the West for ideas as they begin to create new political and economic models. Heidmets and others are appropriately skeptical of shifting to an individualist model. Indeed, many of the chapters in this volume point to the problems that result from the increased emphasis on individual satisfaction, often to the detriment of family, community, and the society at large. He comments that the unfettered pursuit of self-interest inevitably brings alienation and the loss of motivation. The psychological sense of community and identification of social good as a priority over individual needs that were so much a part of the Communist ideology may now give way to the focus on materialism and individual needs. Heidmets is clear that the Soviet experience with Communism came at a high cost. Not just individuals, but families, neighborhoods, and communities were considered less important than the good of the state. He recognizes that the current social transformation will result in a blending of Eastern and Western approaches, but he hopes that the new system will still place more emphasis on the social good than has been typical in the West while also being more sensitive to individual needs than was the case under the Communist system. I think Heidmets is correct in his reservations about the Western system, and I agree with him that a continued emphasis on the social good might help to prevent some of the problems identified by the authors of the chapters in this volume. Indeed, some have suggested that communal parenting and increased community responsibility for its members will help alleviate the problems of today's youths (see, e.g., Bowser, 1991). Heidmets also comments that there has been a drastic decrease in the number of researchers in his country, which I find to be an unfortunate situation since it seems that the changing social and political climate provides an ideal opportunity to assess the impact of these changes on individuals, the family, and the community.

Family Violence

Jill Korbin, an anthropologist, contributes a review of family violence from a cross-cultural perspective. Her work provides valuable insight into the variability between and within cultures and also helps us appreciate and understand the ways in which violence is expressed in families throughout the world. I thought her analysis of neighborhoods by risk type and her epidemiological and ethnographic research on neighborhood factors associated with child maltreatment were especially useful in providing some guidance and directions for possible interventions. One important implication of her work is that we should not be too quick to embrace certain theories or interventions as a panacea for the problems centering around family violence. She points out, for example, that while social-support systems can provide needed help to families experiencing family violence, they are not always a positive or helpful resource. She cites examples of networks that actually support and reinforce violent attitudes and behaviors, so we must be careful to look more closely at the nature of a specific individual's or family's social-support systems.

Concluding Comments

When analyzing family life I think we need to be careful not to overstate or overemphasize the relation between changes in family life and social problems. With respect to delinquency, for example, Wells and Rankin (1991) conducted a metanalysis of 50 studies examining the relation between broken homes and delinquency. They found that the relation was not as strong as some have suggested; the prevalence of delinquency in broken homes was about 10 to 15% higher than in intact homes. Family status probably does affect delinquent behavior, but countless other areas, such as those suggested by Tyler and Degoey's chapter, must also be identified in order to account for more of the variance.

I believe we must first recognize this reality, and then we can begin to try and evaluate possible solutions and early interventions at several levels, including the individual, the family, the schools, and the community. I do not profess to know what those solutions are, but I am glad to see a symposium of this stature begin to grapple with this. Certainly, as Garbarino urged, we must insist on economic policies that make families a political priority. Obviously, this strategy necessitates efforts to influence the legislative process by sharing our research findings through testimony and amicus briefs (Maccoby et al., 1983; Roesch et al., 1991). This has not been the case to date, but the need to focus on public and federal policy is reinforced by Hartman (1992), who stated, "The dismantling of social and maternal and child health programs, the lack of action around a national health care plan; and the reduction of Title XX funds, which provide monies to the states for most family support programs, point to a disinterest in the welfare of families" (p. 388). The presenters at the Nebraska Symposium on Motivation leave one with the undisputed conclusion that we cannot allow this lack of interest to continue.

REFERENCES

Bowser, B. P. (Ed.). (1991). *Black male adolescents: Parenting and education in community context*. Lanham MD: University Press of America.

Farrington, D. (1990). Implications of criminal career research for the prevention of offending. *Journal of Adolescence, 13*, 93–113.

Felner, R. D., & Terre, L. (1987). Child custody dispositions and children's adaptation following divorce. In L. A. Weithorn (Ed.), *Psychology and child custody determinations: Knowledge, roles, and expertise* (pp. 106–153). Lincoln: University of Nebraska Press.

Garbarino, J., Kostelny, K., & Dubrow, N. (1991). What children can tell us about living in danger. *American Psychologist, 46*, 376–383.

Hart, S. D., Kropp, P. R., Roesch, R., Ogloff, J. R. P., & Whittemore, K. (in press). Wife assault in community-resident offenders. *Canadian Journal of Criminology*.

Hartman, A. (1992). Murphy Brown, Dan Quayle, and the American family. *Social Work, 37*, 387–388.

Jacobs, M. (1990). *Screwing the system and making it work: Juvenile justice in the no-fault society*. Chicago: University of Chicago Press.

Inouye, T. (1992). *An assessment of the effects of intervention in high risk elementary school children*. Unpublished masters thesis, Simon Fraser University, Burnaby BC.

Kessler, R., & Neighbors, H. (1986). A new perspective on the relationships among race, social class, and psychological distress. *Journal of Health and Social Behavior, 27*, 107–115.

Maccoby, E. E., Kahn, A. J., & Everett, B. A. (1983). The role of psychological research in the formation of policies affecting children. *American Psychologist, 38*, 80–84.

Melton, G. B. (1990). Realism in psychology and humanism in law: Psycholegal studies at Nebraska. *Nebraska Law Review, 69*, 251–277.

Myers, H. F., Taylor, S., Alvy, K. T., Arrington, A., & Richardson, M. A. (1992). Parental and family predictors of behavior problems in inner-city black children. *American Journal of Community Psychology, 20*, 557–576.

Pedro-Carroll, J. L., Cowen, E. L., Hightower, A. D., & Guare, J. C. (1986). Preventive intervention with latency-aged children of divorce: A replication study. *American Journal of Community Psychology, 14*, 277–290.

Roesch, R., Golding, S. L., Hans, V. P., & Reppucci, N. D. (1991). Social science and the courts: The role of amicus curiae briefs. *Law and Human Behavior, 15*, 1–11.

Ross, M. V., & Sales, B. D. (1985). Legal/forensic training in clinical psychology. In D. P. Farrington & J. Gunn (Eds.), *Reactions to crime: The public, the police, the courts, and prisons* (pp. 87–111). New York: Wiley.

Ryan, W. (1971). *Blaming the victim*. New York: Random House.

Sampson, R. J., & Laub, J. H. (1994). Urban poverty and the family context of delinquency: A new look at structure and process in a classic study. *Child Development, 65*, 523–540.

Sarason, S. (1974). *The psychological sense of community*. San Francisco: Jossey-Bass.

Seidman, E. (1991). Growing up the hard way: Pathways of urban adolescents. *American Journal of Community Psychology, 19,* 193–205.

Seidman, E., Allen, L., Aber, J. L., Mitchell, C., & Feinman, J. (1994). The impact of school transitions in early adolescence on the self-system and perceived social context of poor urban youth. *Child Development, 65,* 507–522.

Wells, L. E., & Rankin, J. H. (1991). Families and delinquency: A meta-analysis of the impact of broken homes. *Social Problems, 38,* 71–93.

Wolchik, S. A., Ruehlman, L. S., Braver, S. L., & Sandler, I. N. (1989). Social support of children of divorce: Direct and stress buffering effects. *American Journal of Community Psychology, 17,* 485–501.

Yoshikawa, H. (1994). Prevention as cumulative protection: Effects of early family support and education on chronic delinquency and its risk. *Psychological Bulletin, 115,* 28–54.

Zigler, E., Taussig, C., & Black, K. (1992). Early childhood intervention: A promising preventative for juvenile delinquency. *American Psychologist, 47,* 997–1006.

Subject Index

Author Index